COMIC FASCISM

STUDIES IN COMICS AND CARTOONS
Charles Hatfield and Rebecca Wanzo, Series Editors

COMIC FASCISM

IDEOLOGY, CATHOLICISM, AND AMERICANISM IN ITALIAN CHILDREN'S PERIODICALS

Zane Elward

THE OHIO STATE UNIVERSITY PRESS
COLUMBUS

Library of Congress Cataloging-in-Publication Data

Names: Elward, Zane, author

Title: Comic fascism : ideology, Catholicism, and Americanism in Italian children's periodicals / Zane Elward.

Description: Columbus : The Ohio State University Press, 2025. | Series: Studies in comics and cartoons | Includes bibliographical references and index. | Summary: "Analyzing comics from 1922 to 1948, as well as documents from state and publisher archives, shows how Italian comics reflected the entanglement of conservatives and Catholics with the Fascist project and offers insight into the role of American comics in shaping Italian youth"—Provided by publisher.

Identifiers: LCCN 2025010342 | ISBN 9780814215920 hardback | ISBN 9780814284230 ebook

Subjects: LCSH: Comic books, strips, etc.—Italy—History—20th century | Fascism and culture—Italy—History—20th century | Comic books, strips, etc.—Political aspects—Italy | LCGFT: Comics criticism

Classification: LCC PN6765 .E49 2025 | DDC 741.5/945—dc23/eng/20250321

LC record available at https://lccn.loc.gov/2025010342

Other identifiers: ISBN 9780814259528 (paperback)

Cover design by Laurence J. Nozik
Text design by Juliet Williams
Type set in Adobe Minion Pro

For my loving wife and partner, Lauren, without whom this project would not have been possible

CONTENTS

ILLUSTRATIONS

ABBREVIATIONS

AC	Azione Cattolica
AFS	Associazione Fascista della Scuola
AME	Arnoldo Mondadori Editore
AOI	Africa Orientale Italiana
API	Associazione Pionieri d'Italia
B.	Busta (case)
Corrierino	*Corriere dei Piccoli*
DC	Democrazia Cristiana
F.	Fascicolo (folder)
FAAM	Fondazione Arnoldo e Alberto Mondadori
GIAC	Gioventù Italiana di Azione Cattolica
ISACEM	Istituto per la Storia dell'Azione Cattolica e del Movimento Cattolico in Italia (Roma)
MCP	Ministero della Cultura Popolare

ONB	Opera Nazionale Balilla
PCI	Partito Comunista Italiano
PNF	Partito Nazionale Fascista
PPI	Partito Popolare Italiano
PSI	Partito Socialista Italiano
RSI	Repubblica Sociale Italiana
Sf.	Sottofascicolo (subfolder)
SPD	Segretaria Particolare del Duce
Vitt	*Vittorioso*

INTRODUCTION

Italy in the 1920s, '30s, and '40s navigated a contested political and ideological space as the nation underwent political and social transformations. Even under the Fascist regime, Fascists, Catholics, and conservatives contested what Fascist Italy should look like as a society. The ideological struggle was expanded to rival political positions by the transition to democracy following World War II. This contestation manifested itself in political debates, academic discussions, and cultural production. Questions abounded as to how best to represent and advocate visions for society to those who would one day lead it: children and adolescents.

As comics rose in popularity during this first half of the twentieth century, intellectuals and artists became involved in utilizing comics to tell the stories of the Italian nation and relay social norms and values to children. The debates, conferences, and policies surrounding comics in children's periodicals demonstrate the importance that political organizations placed on the youth in shaping the future, as did the involvement of numerous diverse sociopolitical circles. The comics industry of the 1930s and '40s comprised publishers from conservative, Catholic, and Fascist orientations, and figures on the Left began printing comics after the Second World War. Periodicals featured Italian originals as well as popular stories imported from the United States. The stories within these periodicals reflected particular interpretations of Italian history, perspectives on gender and race, and visions of what it meant to be

Italian, and the rivalry between periodicals to attract readers was a part of a wider effort to reach Italy's youth.

Readers thus encountered a variety of models for modern society, and comics were integrated into the broader political debates on modernity, religion, gender, empire, Americanization, Italian identity, and the meaning of Fascism. Because comics magazines were printed by a range of publishing houses associated with diverse sociopolitical positions, the stories offer insight into ideological entanglements and tensions between these positions. Ultimately, the many differences and tensions resulted in a superficial base for the Fascist regime that crumbled during the Second World War.

However, the comics from the 1920s to the mid-1940s examined in this study reveal significant points of commonality which smoothed the transition to the dictatorship and helped Fascism maintain power. Many studies of Italian comics during this era identify the fascistization of comics primarily from the late 1930s, but many comics periodicals printed Fascist stories or comics with themes that resonated with Fascist ideas much earlier.[1] Similarly, archival documents reveal that the inclusion of these themes was not solely due to Fascist censorship and pressure, contrary to the interpretation often offered by scholars studying comics not published directly by the Fascist Party.[2]

Indeed, it becomes clear that many nationalist and authoritarian-minded conservatives and Catholics were entangled in the Fascist cultural and political project, whatever hesitations and differences they maintained. Conservatives and Catholics tended to be less radical and violent than Fascists but desired to raise Italy to the status of a world power, feared parliamentary democracy had weakened Italy, and believed socialism needed to be resisted by any means. Mussolini attracted these more traditional fellow travelers by presenting Fascism as an alternative that could counter their common enemies, defend Italian traditions, and rejuvenate the nation. The commonalities between these positions, along with Fascist coercion, meant that differences were expressed as contestation *within* the Fascist parameters of discourse, rather than in opposition to the regime. In any case, the depiction of Fascist values within these comics depicted an image of compatibility between the Fascist state, on the one hand, and Catholics and conservatives, on the other.

The societal models portrayed in these comics magazines were not static but reflected the phases of the Fascist regime, the changing international

1. Bonsaver, *America in Italian Culture,* 291; Carabba, *Il fascismo a fumetti,* 7, 41; Meda, *Stelle e strips,* 9; and Gadducci et al., *Eccetto Topolino,* 119, 126.

2. Rumi, "Un'occasione di riconoscimento"; Preziosi, *Il Vittorioso,* 79, 156; Vecchio, *L'Italia del Vittorioso,* 13; Fava, "'Il *Vittorioso*,'" 652; Carabba, *Corrierino, Corrierona,* 73; and Fava, "Il progetto culturale," 70.

context, and the social transformations of the first half of the twentieth century. Analysis of the production of comics illustrates the strategies employed by Fascist cultural institutions as they sought to first appropriate and then tightly control cultural production; the evolving international context is at the center of these shifting policies. After the regime fell, comics continued to offer commentary on the meaning of the Fascist past, the ongoing social transformations, and aspirations for the future. As the political and civil sphere expanded in the postwar era, comics magazines reveal the growing divisions between the anti-Fascist coalition as forces on the political Right and Left divide with the emerging Cold War. This study demonstrates how various publishers responded to and navigated the complex web of formal and informal censorship in the struggle to bring their visions for Italian society to young readers. Both during and after the Fascist regime, reaching children remained a priority for those involved in political and civil life; publishers considered comics a means to do so.

Political and social organizations in the late nineteenth and early twentieth centuries increasingly turned their attention to the formation of youth organizations, partly in response to the various changes unfolding in Italian society.[3] The peninsula was consolidated into a single state in the years between 1861 and 1870. Public education initiatives, youth groups, and children's literature were all a part of the subsequent program to nationalize Italian youth. Youth groups of the Catholic Church date to this era as well, rooted in the effort to maintain the influence of the Church following the loss of its secular realm, the Papal States, in 1866.

In 1922 Mussolini rose to power by harnessing the nationalism unleashed after World War I, channeling fears of communism, and exploiting discontent with the established "liberal" political system. King Victor Emmanuel III appointed Mussolini prime minister following the March on Rome in October, ushering in twenty years of Fascist rule. After a few years sharing power with other nationalist parties on the political Center and Right, Mussolini established his dictatorship in 1925. The dictatorship was consolidated throughout the 1920s by a mixture of coercion and incentivized collaboration, and the regime underwent a phase of radicalization in the late 1930s.

Throughout its reign, the Partito Nazionale Fascista (the Fascist Party, or PNF) poured great effort into indoctrinating Italian youth to ensure a foundation for the future. The PNF intervened in education and monopolized youth

---

3. Cavazza, "Formazione dei giovani e fascismo," 88–89; Dogliani, *Storia dei giovani*, 7–8; and E. Harvey, "Cult of Youth," 67.

groups (though, Catholic youth groups were allowed to continue operating).[4] Children's leisure activities were scrutinized by the regime, including the movies they watched and stories they read; the latter increasingly included comics. The regime's concern about youth continued until its ultimate collapse in the Second World War.

Following World War II, another era of transformation hit as Italians worked to establish a new constitution, rebuild Italy, and voted to become a republic. Political debate expanded during the postwar years, as positions forcibly oppressed by the regime now organized out in the open. Rival youth groups were again allowed to operate, and those of the Catholic Church and the Communist Party competed to influence youth in these transformative years.

In each of these eras, publishers, editors, and artists participated in the debates over Italian society. From the outset, comics in Italy—popularized by *Corriere dei Piccoli,* launched in 1908—served an educational agenda to spread bourgeois values.[5] *Corriere dei Piccoli* provided a model for the creation in 1923 of the Fascist Party's own periodical, *Il Giornale dei Balilla,* named for the party's youth groups. The conservative and nationalist values depicted in *Corriere dei Piccoli* smoothed the transition to Fascism by advocating ideas aligned with those of the regime, while *Balilla* actively promoted Fascist ideology. The market expanded in the 1930s as publishers began printing periodicals devoted exclusively to comics, including many from the US. The popularity of comics—*fumetti* in Italian—exploded at this point, with hundreds of thousands of issues circulating each week by the end of the decade, reaching as many as three million readers weekly.[6]

Most significant among the publishers of foreign comics were the Società Anonima Editrice Vecchi, the Casa Nerbini Editrice, and Arnoldo Mondadori Editore. Vecchi was the first to issue a periodical devoted to comics, *Jumbo,* launched in 1932. Nerbini quickly printed a rival with *Topolino,* as Mickey Mouse was known in Italy. Nerbini followed up with *L'Avventuroso,* a magazine devoted to action comics such as "Flash Gordon." Soon after, Mondadori purchased the rights to *Topolino,* and Nerbini and Mondadori competed to attract young readers with their mixtures of Italian and American stories. The connections between the Fascist regime and Mondadori and

---

4. Cavazza, "Formazione dei giovani e fascismo," 89; Koon, *Believe, Obey, Fight,* xvi; Ponzio, *Shaping the New Man,* 7; and Griffin, "Sacred Synthesis," 10.

5. Carabba, *Corrierino, Corrierona,* 17; and Fava, "Il progetto culturale," 19.

6. Ferris, "Parents, Children and the Fascist State," 185. Domenico Lombrassa estimated the number of comics readers in 1938 based on the trend of sharing issues among reader. Forgacs and Gundle, *Mass Culture and Italian Society,* 36.

Nerbini—connections which predated Mussolini's rise to power—and the popularity of the comics from the US printed in *Topolino* and *L'Avventuroso* make these periodicals particularly significant.

The comics industry expanded again in 1937 with the creation of *Il Vittorioso* by the youth group of the lay Catholic association, Azione Cattolica, or Catholic Action. *Vitt,* as fans referred to it, was a response to the popularity of American comics, which many Catholics deemed corrupting in their depiction of the destabilizing American way of life. The periodical embodied the Vatican's uneasy alliance with the regime. The Catholic Church's collaboration with the regime made such a periodical possible, and yet it competed with the state for the hearts and minds of Italian youth.

The evolving priorities of the regime shaped the comics industry. The regime's relatively open cultural policies during the first half of the 1930s enabled the flourishing of American comics in Italy, and the toleration of American culture reflected the positive relations between the two countries. Yet this changed following the 1935 Italian invasion of Ethiopia, after which Italo-American relations deteriorated and the Fascist state embraced a policy of cultural autarky aimed at the *bonifica* or "reclamation" of Italian national culture. American comics were suppressed after this point, though exceptions were made, most notably for Mickey Mouse. The Second World War brought more changes, including a more rigid enforcement of the ban on comics from the US. Fascist propaganda in comics created by Italian artists became increasingly overt but nonetheless continued to represent trends in Italian society.

All comics magazines—indeed, virtually all publications—ceased printing after Mussolini's removal from power in 1943 and Italy's descent into a phase of occupation and civil war. Children's periodicals gradually began to resurface in 1945. Although the Fascist regime was gone, many of those who had once produced comics retained their positions. As private firms, publishing houses were typically family owned and were thus likely to maintain the same culture, structure, and even personnel after the war. These producers—former collaborators entangled in the Fascist cultural policies—set out to integrate themselves into the new political landscape, sometimes falling silent on the past or else attempting to emphasize their anti-Fascist credentials. Their comics reflected the transformations in Italian society alongside the persistence of many of the themes and messages that had once facilitated their entanglement with the regime.

To further contest the postwar cultural climate, Leftist groups began to publish their own comics; the contestation of social values within comics expanded into an ideological struggle that spanned the political spectrum. The anti-Americanism of intellectuals on the Left translated into critiques of comics, perceived as vehicles of American cultural imperialism.[7] The Italian Communist and Socialist parties nevertheless experimented with comics, adopting the medium popular with children to reach them with their vision for society.

The magazines referenced above, selected as the main periodicals of this study, represent a range of sociopolitical circles. *Balilla* embodied the most radical, depicting the model for society presented by Fascism to Italian youth. Nationalist conservatives dominated the industry through *Corriere dei Piccoli*, Mondadori's *Topolino*, and Nerbini's *L'Avventuroso*. The Church had *Il Vittorioso*, and, in the postwar years, the Left issued a string of periodicals before establishing its most important contribution with *Il Pioniere* in 1950.

The involvement in the comics industry of many sociopolitical circles resulted in the depiction of a variety of visions for society. Under the Fascist regime, formal state mechanisms of censorship and the practice of self-censorship ensured publishers adhered to Fascist principles. Nonetheless, the regime first maintained a policy of relative cultural openness, preferring to appropriate and modify rather than ban outright, thereby attracting more supporters; Fascism represented a form of big tent politics in which many cultural and sociopolitical currents were welcome.[8] This policy helped align conservatives and authoritarian Catholics with the regime, fellow travelers who represented political positions which were not as radical or violent as those of the first-hour Fascists but shared enough of the big ideas of Fascism to justify collaboration.[9]

These entangled political positions at times contested elements of Fascist ideology, and real tensions existed between them. Debate persisted regarding the nature of Fascist society and modern Italian life. The stories printed in periodicals reflected this entanglement and contestation, as the vague nature of Fascist cultural policies left creators of comics to interpret Fascist principles through their own philosophies and agendas. *Il Vittorioso*, for instance, often depicted a "Catholicized" Fascism. However, these distinctions did not prevent their models from aligning with the society envisioned by Fascists, nor did they lead to a consistent opposition or subversion of Fascist values in the stories printed for youthful readers. Rather, the incorporation of Fascist stories into conservative and Catholic periodicals signified *legitimation* for

---

7. Meda, *Stelle e strips*, 237–38; and Franchini, *Diventare grandi con il Pioniere*, 8.

8. Ben-Ghiat, *Fascist Modernities*, 17; and Stone, *Patron State*, 4.

9. Lutz, "Pluralities of National Socialist Ideology," 75, 77–78. On the popularity of the "big ideas" of Fascism, even when the Fascist Party itself was less popular, see Duggan, *Fascist Voices*, xxi, 203.

the regime by depicting Fascist values to readers and presenting an image of compatibility.

This entanglement and the state's preference for appropriation extended to American comics, though not without limitations. American comics and American culture in general proposed a rival model of modernity and, more troublingly, a particular understanding of leisure. The American notion of leisure privileged entertainment, a distinction from the Italian tendency to explicitly fuse ideology and leisure. Even as many Fascist, conservative, and Catholic intellectuals denounced American culture as decadent in its obsession with wealth, sexualized women, and a cult of technology, positive Italo-American relations kept this network of exchange open. Moreover, not *all* Fascists denounced American culture, and there was enough overlap in the values presented in American comics to suggest that the evolving American model of modernity might align with that advocated by Fascist Italy. Indeed, the often-generic nature of narratives in comics from the United States lent themselves to Fascist appropriation. It was only with the shifting geopolitical context, as Italo-American relations deteriorated after the 1935 Italian invasion of Ethiopia and Italy drew closer to Nazi Germany, that American comics *became* marked as anti-Fascist.

This book is primarily a cultural history, utilizing comics to engage with the intersection of political ideology and popular culture and evaluating the place of comics in the Italian sociopolitical process. As comics were produced by publishers and artists spanning the ideological spectrum, analysis of the values and themes within comics printed in Italy during these years illustrates how producers of comics depicted divergent yet overlapping visions for society. Through examining these models, I identify competing frameworks for society depicted in comics and demonstrate how they interreacted. In doing so, this book expands beyond Fascist ideology by examining the interactions between countries (namely, Italy and the United States), as well as between Fascism and other sociopolitical movements to examine the Fascist "universe."[10]

Extending this study into the postwar years additionally allows for a deeper understanding of the overlap between these sociopolitical positions and Fascism. Many such ideological entanglements persisted after the fall of the regime, challenging the notion of a sharp break between Fascism and the Republic. While there were cultural and political ruptures with the fall of Fascism, many cultural and social trends transcended the regime change and

10. David D. Roberts emphasizes the need to expand beyond a strict study of Fascist ideology: see Roberts, *Fascist Interactions.*

Fascist values did not vanish from political discourse.[11] Some sources of continuity were rooted in the persistence of Fascist thought in cultural production and political discourse, albeit in transformed ways. Other continuities included Italian traditions and values that predated the regime, as well as the continuation of cultural trends which emerged *despite* the regime, including the early development of consumer culture.[12]

Comics and children's periodicals at large reflect many of the major transformations in Italian society during these tumultuous years. Tracing the evolution of the rival depictions of society present within them and extending this study beyond the periodization of the Fascist era illuminates both the legacy of Fascism and the ways in which the Republic represented a rupture with the past.

Studying Comics as Historical Sources

The Italian comics industry—the various publishers who printed and distributed comics—is approached in this study as participating in a cultural struggle aimed at the construction or reinforcement of hegemony. Hegemony, as defined by Antonio Gramsci, refers to political leadership or control and is comprised of cultural, economic, and political elements. Cultural production in this sense is understood at least in part as attempting to foster specific mentalities and consent to augment support for the regime alongside the coercive mechanisms of the state.[13] Publishers can either stand adjacent to the state as a part of its cultural apparatus (even if tensions flared at times), or against it. The expression of genuine opposition was only possible after Fascism's defeat, and so those operating under Mussolini's dictatorship were forced to align themselves with the political demands and parameters for publication of the time.

The production of comics under the Fascist regime in Italy was subjected to mechanisms of censorship, and ties between publishers and state cultural institutions further compromised producers of comics as collaborators. Comics of this era thus share many of the characteristics of the mass culture denounced by Walter Benjamin and members of the Frankfurt School as a

---

11. Forgacs and Gundle, *Mass Culture and Italian Society*, 4, 45, 268.

12. Bonsaver, *America in Italian Culture*, 12, 501–2; Cavazza, "La politica di fronte al consumo di massa," 15; De Grazia, *Irresistible Empire*, 54, 318; and Forgacs and Gundle, *Mass Culture and Italian Society*, 1.

13. Gramsci, *Gramsci Reader*, 194–95; and Bates "Gramsci and the Theory of Hegemony," 352, 354.

medium utilized by Fascists to organize the masses while simultaneously suppressing them.[14] According to this understanding, comics under the Fascist regime did not genuinely reflect Italian society, but rather a constructed and censored version. However, there is never only one culture or set of cultural patterns, but rather a plurality, and Fascism never truly established itself as the hegemonic culture and defining reference point for society, as is clear from its continued reliance on violence and coercion. It is for this reason that the Fascist state permitted a degree of plurality, allowing entangled positions to coexist within its worldview, as it sought to broaden its appeal.[15] Although Fascists set the parameters of discourse, their Catholic and more conservative allies promoted their own norms, values, and definitions, leading to the appearance in comics of diverse understandings of Fascism and distinctive models of society.

In addition to publishers navigating Fascist cultural policies according to their own principles, they had to attract readers to be profitable and spread their own agendas. Firms had different motivating drives. The more commercially oriented ventures of Nerbini, Mondadori, and *Corriere dei Piccoli* were likely more concerned with their profits but had to ensure that they toed the regime's line in order to remain in operation. Other magazines, such as state's *Il Balilla* and *Il Vittorioso* of the Catholic Church, were concerned primarily with their cultural and political missions. Yet even those periodicals aimed to remain profitable or at least break even.

Publishers therefore had to be sensitive to what readers found appealing and aimed to print stories with themes and topics familiar to readers, reflecting their interests and experiences. Comics are situated toward an ideal reader and form a sort of contract with their readers, who learn what they can expect each week in the strips or serialized stories because of common themes, formulas, and recurring characters.[16] The formulas and recurring themes reflect the experiences and expectations of producers and consumers alike, offering insight into popular perspectives, assumptions, and concerns of the era in which they were produced.[17] They additionally convey socially approved behaviors by drawing on recognizable conventions of everyday life, social relations, and identities.[18] The competing demands on publishers to follow the dictates of the regime, pursue their own agendas, and remain profitable

14. Benjamin, *Work of Art*, 33, 41; and Hall, *Cultural Studies 1983*, 16–17.

15. Ben-Ghiat, *Fascist Modernities*, 11–12; Cannistraro, *La fabbrica del consenso*, 57, 69–70; and Lutz, "Pluralities of National Socialist Ideology."

16. Barker, *Comics*, 133, 256.

17. Wright, *Comic Book Nation*, xv–xvi.

18. Barker, *Comics*, 251; and Bramlett, "Role of Culture."

resulted in stories that reflected Italian society in a more genuine way than Benjamin theorized.

My methodology for engaging with the comics draws on tools from comics studies as well as more sociological and historical approaches to those who created the comics. In examining the stories told through comics, I identify recurring tropes and themes and draw on Thierry Groensteen's approach to comics, in which he analyzes the panels and their components to identify the system of meaning-making they form through the ways in which they relate, emphasizing the "primacy of image."[19] However, while many youthful readers may have privileged images in their reading of comics, I approach comics as a form of mixed media and therefore place importance on the interplay between text and images. Words and visuals can work together to provide a deeper meaning than either could achieve independently. Conversely, at times one can undermine the meaning provided in the other.[20] This potential for one or the other to subvert or alter the meaning provided by the other allows for the possibility of the incorporation of themes that nominally align with the cultural agenda of the state and yet nonetheless challenge or contest the official ideology in some way.

This study is more concerned with the stories and values depicted in comics than with the people creating them, embracing a sociological and historical approach grounded in the production of culture. Broadening beyond the individual creators, I focus more on the social and political parameters in which these comics were produced.[21] In particular, state policies regarding censorship were crucial in determining what publishers could and could not produce. The dominance of imported material from the United States made copyright and licensing important as well. Additionally, the market shaped what was printed based on what publishers could reasonably expect to be profitable. Finally, each publishing firm had its own organizational structures and cultural agenda, which editors pursued within this context of censorship, copyright, and the market. Understanding the social and historical context is essential, as this context provides the parameters within which producers could publish stories and deeply impacted the potential interpretations for readers. How we interpret stories is shaped by our experiences and social settings, meaning that readers in 1938 would likely identify meanings different from those reading the same story in 1946 or 2024.

---

19. Groensteen, *System of Comics*, 11–14. For more on narratology, semiotics, and other approaches to studying comics, see Kukkonen, *Studying Comics and Graphic Novels*.

20. Mitchell, *Picture Theory*, 89; and Hall and Whannel, *Popular Arts*, 44.

21. Peterson, "Five Constraints," 143, 146–48.

Combining these approaches provides a clearer understanding of the interaction between politics and comics during the Fascist era and the early Republic. Through analyzing stories, I identify the values, ideas, and models of social interaction depicted within them, engaging with where ideas literally *appear.* This is significant because I aim to avoid labeling producers of comics as Fascist or anti-Fascist (unless they identify themselves as such) and focus instead on the themes readers encountered. The parameters set around publication make it difficult to determine the reasons or sincerity of belief behind the publication of certain stories and values, and many authors, artists, and publishers likely had reservations about Fascism. And yet this does not change the fact that their young readers consistently encountered Fascist values in their stories. Although I am often more focused on the stories, in an effort to understand why these themes are present, I incorporate documents concerning cultural policies to convey the parameters of production as well as documents from the publishers to illustrate how they navigated these conditions.

Censorship, Cultural Policies, and Comics

Our understandings of censorship and the relationship between politics and culture is key here, as it influences our understanding of cultural products. Studies from recent decades have greatly enhanced our understanding of this relationship by expanding beyond the legal framework, which had remained relatively underdeveloped until the mid-1930s.[22] The inconsistent application of *formal* censorship measures by ill-formed cultural institutions was buttressed by the use of enticements to influence intellectual and cultural work. Contracts, academic positions, appointments in cultural institutions, and subsidies were awarded to those whose activities aligned with the agenda of the regime. While cooperation was incentivized, active dissent was repressed.[23] Fascist authorities likewise exploited the market, the circulation of schoolbooks, and fear of lost profits to foster the collaboration of publishers and a high degree of self-censorship.[24]

This intricate system thus offered benefits and profits for those who operated within its established parameters, while violence and reprisals—ever present in Fascist Italy—discouraged opposition and fostered passivity and resignation. Questions of collaboration are rendered difficult to resolve by

22. Cannistraro, *La fabbrica del consenso,* x, 8, 108, 287, 322.

23. Stone, *Patron State,* 9, 15, 65.

24. Galfré, *Il regime degli editori,* xv, 78.

the fact that consent and cooperation was always structured by the threat of coercion.[25]

Studies of literature and film in Fascist Italy have demonstrated how this more complicated relationship between politics and culture operated in this context of rewards and punishments. The ad-hoc system regulating cultural production allowed space for negotiations and fostered relationships that were "self-adjusting, complicit ones," rather than oppositional. Guido Bonsaver's argument that literature under Fascism operated within the "grey zone" between opposition and collaboration applies to cultural production as a whole.[26] Steven Ricci similarly reveals a middle ground in the Fascist treatment of American culture; cultural authorities did not reject all aspects of American culture and relied on a range of mechanisms to mediate those qualities which were condemned.[27]

These studies inform the approach to comics in this book by providing a more nuanced understanding of the entanglement between politics and cultural production. The period predating the 1938 state decrees regulating the production of comics was still characterized by a mixture of state incentives and repression as informal mechanisms of censorship fostered collaboration. The fear of reprisal engendered a culture of self-censorship, while the myriad ways in which Fascism was understood and the popularity of its core ideas ensured that Fascist values appeared in comics during both the 1920s and the "comics craze" that occurred between 1932 and 1938. Comics were a part of the Fascist cultural project from the rise of the regime.

The regime's interaction with American comics likewise appears more nuanced in light of studies on American films in Italy. Although many criticized American comics and lambasted aspects of the American way of life, it must be remembered that Italo-American relations were positive until the invasion of Ethiopia, that Mussolini held a largely positive view of the US, and that the vast majority of comics imported from the US were provided by King Features Syndicate (owned by William Randolph Hearst) and Walt Disney, two figures known to be sympathetic to Fascism.[28] The targeting of American comics after 1938 should not be read backward to mean that American comics published before 1938 were innately anti-Fascist and that the state would inevitably repress them.

---

25. Pergher, "Ethics of Consent," 314.

26. Bonsaver, *Censorship and Literature,* 3, 5, 265.

27. Ricci, *Cinema and Fascism,* 66, 71, 130, 142.

28. Bonsaver, *America in Italian Culture,* 206, 209–12; Dunnett, "Anti-Fascism and Literary Criticism," 112–14; Diggins, *Mussolini and Fascism,* 48, 145–47; and Ricci, *Cinema and Fascism,* 128.

This study sheds light on the formal and informal mechanisms of censorship used to shape the production of comics and identifies the values represented in comics that aligned with Fascism, including in American comics. My intention is to illuminate the ways in which the producers of comics interacted with Fascist rhetoric and ideas—how they represented them in their stories—at times shaping Fascist principles and propaganda according to their own values. I consider the production of comics a manifestation of Bonsaver's "grey zone" that represents a contestation over the shape Italian society should take. I therefore approach the creation of comics as an engagement with Fascism's ideas, sometimes corroborating the regime's cultural project, while at other times offering alternative definitions, interpretations, and priorities.

In tracing the evolving policies of the Fascist state, I demonstrate how the regime at first sought fellow travelers and allies whose visions for Italian society were compatible with or similar to their own, thereby helping to generate support for the regime. The state appeared successful in attracting intellectuals, publishers, and artists to its agenda, and the comics reveal much overlap between conservative, Catholic, and even American values with those of Fascism. In the mid-to-late 1930s, though, a hegemony crisis emerged as Fascist Italy became internationally isolated and Fascist penetration into Italian society appeared insufficient for an allegedly encircled country, suggesting that the success of the earlier policy of cooptation and mediation was superficial. As the regime radicalized, cultural institutions imposed greater control over publishers. But even then, Fascist hegemony proved to only ever be partial, as the challenge of the Second World War fractured the diverse cultural apparatus the state had built around it.

My focus in this section has primarily been on the relationship between culture and politics in the Fascist era, despite the scope of this study expanding into the postwar years. This is because the state's role in cultural production under Fascism was highly complex due to the regime's objective to shape culture while maintaining a façade of cultural freedom, obscuring its mechanisms of censorship and systems of rewards and punishments. The political influence on culture did not decrease in the Republican era; it merely changed in nature and degree and became more diffused. The interaction between cultural, political, and economic factors predated the Fascist regime and continued long after it.[29] The postwar era is different, though, in that freedom of expression returned and the state no longer had a monopoly in its exertion

29. Forgacs, *Italian Culture*, 32–33; and Forgacs and Gundle, *Mass Culture and Italian Society*, 3, 96, 197–98.

of influence. But public calls for governmental regulations of children's periodicals remained.

Political involvement in cultural production also continued, as political and social organizations continued to participate in the publication of comics. Catholic Action, which published *Il Vittorioso,* forged close ties with the Democrazia Cristiana, while the youth organization of the Partito Comunista Italiano launched *Il Pionere* in response to the popularity of *Vitt* and American comics. These comics reflect the rising tensions between the political Left and Right.[30] Together, these factors make the study of the intersection between politics and culture just as relevant in the decades following Fascism.

Structure

This book is primarily organized chronologically, progressing from the 1920s until 1948 according to developments in the history of Italian comics. The first three chapters discuss early developments in the field of Italian comics which coincided with distinct phases of the Fascist regime. The Fascist state first had to determine how to contend with existing comics periodicals and form its own, then how to respond to the challenge of American comics and that of the Catholic youth groups. Fascist cultural institutions and informal mechanisms of control operated to take hold of each. In the final three chapters, publishers are forced to respond to and navigate an ever-changing political situation as the state introduces more severe censorship policies, enters World War II, and then collapses, transforming the political landscape.

The book begins with a chapter discussing comics in Italy as the Fascist Party gained and consolidated power in the 1920s. During this period, the conservative and nationalist *Corriere dei Piccoli* aligned with the agenda of the regime enough to help smooth the transition to the dictatorship, explaining the stance of more gradual fascistization granted to the periodical and other fellow travelers. *Corriere dei Piccoli* was also significant in that it served as a model for Fascism's own periodical, *Il Giornale dei Balilla. Il Balilla,* as it was quickly renamed, overtly depicted Fascist values for Italian youths. These periodicals reveal that the state understood the role of comics in shaping children's worldview.

The second chapter focuses on the influx of American comics into Italy in the 1930s and the reaction they provoked. In examining the values expressed in American comics alongside the criticism of them, it becomes clear that

30. Meda, *Stelle e strips,* 266.

what was most threatening about the imported comics was their foreign nature and the privileging of entertainment over politically structured leisure time. Despite this criticism, American comics initially persisted. In this chapter, I emphasize that it was through the deterioration of Italo-American relations that American comics became branded anti-Fascist by the state.

The third chapter focuses specifically on the Catholic Church's response to the challenge of popular comics with the formation of *Il Vittorioso.* I argue that *Vitt* was a counter to American comics *and* to the influence of the Fascist state on youth organizations. It was a means to spread Catholic values to Italian children, values which contested but overlapped with those of the regime. The periodical represented a more traditional and less aggressive vision for society, and it placed the Catholic Church at the center of authority and identity in Italians' lives. Yet even as the periodical was itself a form of competition with the state, the content in *Il Vittorioso* reflected the Vatican's official position of collaboration with the regime.

The fourth chapter recenters the state, examining the shift in cultural policies from a stance of relative openness to cultural autarky. The chapter examines the impact of decrees from the Ministero della Cultura Popolare (Ministry of Popular Culture, MCP) on Italian comics, as publishers sought to incorporate Fascist themes and Italian settings more explicitly into their stories. However, the persistence of *some* American comics demonstrates that the realm of cultural production remained characterized by negotiation, so long as the Fascist state could claim the accomplishment of its goal of cultural reclamation.

Chapter 5 traces the trajectory of World War II as reflected in comics, which captured the atmosphere in Italy as it transitioned from uncertainty and fear to guarded enthusiasm, then to renewed uncertainty. Comics, like all of the press in Italy, were heavily shaped by the MCP during World War II. Nonetheless, comics reflected sources of support for the war that existed among conservative and Catholic circles. As the war effort deteriorated, though, this support collapsed.

The final chapter examines the values depicted in comics magazines during the postwar transition to democracy, during which conservative publishers sought to distance themselves from Fascism and publishers on the Left began to publish comics magazines of their own. I argue that many values associated with Fascism remained in the comics of the Right. While its more violent and militaristic elements disappeared, themes that had once enabled collaboration persisted; these postwar comics depict a continued concern for Italy's lost colonies, law and order, communism, and Catholic identity. Furthermore, when considered alongside the comics published by the Left, these periodicals reflect the increasing tensions between the political sides during the lead up to the Cold War.

The chronological structure adopted for this study traces the evolution of the regime's cultural policies regarding comics, as the state's relative openness changes into control and centralization. It further serves to highlight the progression of Italian perspectives on American culture, the development of a new form of consumerism in Italy, the change of social norms, and the transformation of the Vatican's attitude toward mass media and politics, even as it remained constant in other ways. These evolutions seen in Italian comics more broadly illuminate changes and continuities in Italian social and political discourse during this transformative era.

A Note on Citations

Where possible, I have provided full citations for comics. However, pages in comics periodicals were often unnumbered, and so many of these citations lack pages. Additionally, I did not include where these comics were accessed but instead will provide that information here.

I viewed copies of *Corriere dei Piccoli* in the volumes of *Il Meglio del Corriere dei Piccoli* published by Rizzoli in 1978 and 1980. Scans of *Il Balilla* are held on microfilm at the Biblioteca Comunale Centrale in Milan. The Istituto per la Storia dell'Azione Cattolica e del Movimento Cattolico in Italia (ISACEM) houses issues of *Il Vittorioso.* While I conducted research at the ISACEM, I was prevented by the pandemic from viewing these issues in person. Dr. Giorgio Vecchio was generous in sharing his own scans from the ISACEM. As for *Topolino,* Editrice Comics Art published collected volumes of full issues of the periodical. Volumes spanning from 1936 through 1947 are accessible at the Billy Ireland Cartoon Library & Museum at Ohio State, as are many issues of *L'Avventuroso* and its supplements. Finally, *Il Pioniere* and its predecessors are viewable online on a digital archive dedicated to the periodical.[31]

31. Il Pioniere, http://www.ilpioniere.org/.

CHAPTER 1

Fascism Infiltrates Comics

Il Corriere dei Piccoli and *Il Giornale dei Balilla*

The socialization and indoctrination of younger generations was a key objective of the regime from the start. When Mussolini became prime minister in 1922, the Fascist Party contended with competing youth organizations in its goal of regimenting childhood and fascistizing the youth.[1] As the Fascist Party began to organize its youth initiatives, it identified children's periodicals as one avenue to engage with and socialize Italy's youth.

Corriere dei Piccoli was illustrative here, as it had demonstrated the ability to reach adolescents with a mixture of comics and short stories. More importantly, the periodical had proven its potential to use comics and stories to promote political and nationalist agendas, as with its support for Italy's military campaigns in the Italo-Turkish War and World War I. As Fascism rose to power, the nationalist and conservative *Corriere dei Piccoli* helped to legitimize and normalize the regime, as well as offered a model for the Party's more radical and propagandistic youth periodical, *Il Giornale dei Balilla*.

The Milan-based *Corriere dei Piccoli* launched in 1908 as a supplement to *Corriere della Sera*. Aptly named "Courier of the Children," the periodical primarily targeted children with illustrated stories and comic strips.[2] The editors

1. Cavazza, "Formazione dei giovani e fascismo," 88–89; Dogliani, *Storia dei giovani*, 10, 106; and Ponzio, *Shaping the New Man*, 36–39.

2. For reference, British newspapers only began to adopt the multipanel form of comic strips around 1907, primarily led by William Keeridge Haselden at the *Daily Mirror*. Chapman et al., *Comics and the World Wars*, 36.

envisioned the publication as a means to both entertain and educate Italian youths, spreading bourgeois values.[3]

The popularity of the periodical helped to spread comics in Italy, which was an emerging medium at the time. Illustrated stories had a long history in Italy, with numerous precursors to comics appearing in the 1800s, but comics only took form in the United States in the 1890s. *Corriere dei Piccoli* printed Italian comics as well as comics from the United States with Italianized names: "Happy Hooligan" by Frederick Burr, for instance was retitled "Fortunello." *Corriere dei Piccoli* additionally replaced speech balloons with captions in rhyme. This was partially a production-based decision, as *Corriere dei Piccoli* was republishing these stories on smaller pages, reducing the dimensions of the panels and making the text in the balloons too small.[4] It was also culturally motivated, however, as one of the periodical's key authors, Antonio Rubino, disliked speech balloons as a distinctly American contribution to comic strips; Rubino and the director, Silvio Spaventa Filippi, believed the captions better stimulated the imagination.[5] The periodical therefore foreshadowed both the popularity of American comics, and the desire by many in Italy to Italianize these stories.

The periodical did more than adapt American comics, though. Italian artists Antonio Rubino, Attilio Mussino, and Sergio Tofano (Sto) created many beloved characters, the most renowned being Sto's "Bonaventura," and therefore exhibited the potential for popular Italian comics. More significantly for the purposes of the Fascist regime, *Corriere dei Piccoli* also demonstrated the propagandistic potential of the medium, first using stories to support the Italian war against the Ottoman Empire in Libya, and then its participation in the First World War.[6] As nationalists and supporters of Italian intervention in the war, Spaventa Filippi, Rubino, and others believed that comics must spread messages of sacrifice, duty, and patriotism. The periodical's agenda shifted from pedagogy more broadly to explaining the reasons for the war, the necessity of social cohesion, and the importance of supporting the war

---

3. Carabba, *Corrierino, Corrierona,* 18; and Carli, "Paola Marzòla Lombroso," 25, 35–38.

4. "Scoperta l'origine della copertina del primo numero del 'Corriere dei Piccoli,'" *Fumetto Logica,* updated 16 October 2018, https://www.fumettologica.it/2018/10/corriere-dei-piccoli-buster-brown/.

5. Pizzi, "'L'Intuizione del fantastico,'" 404; and Spaventa Filippi, *Silvio Spaventa Filippi,* 22.

6. Carabba, *Il fascismo a fumetti,* 265; and Loparco, *I bambini e la guerra,* 193–94. This development was not unique to Italy. Haselden and the *Daily Mirror* incorporated support for World War I into his comics as early as October 1914. Comic strips were also utilized in the US for propagandistic purposes during World War I. Chapman et al., *Comics and the World Wars,* 37, 84.

without complaint.[7] The use of *Corriere dei Piccoli* for propaganda purposes provided the inspiration for the periodical of the Fascist youth group, *Giornale dei Balilla*.[8]

This chapter begins with an evaluation of *Corriere dei Piccoli* in the years surrounding the Fascist seizure of power to demonstrate how its alignment with key Fascist values reflected and smoothed the transition from Liberal to Fascist Italy. This alignment continued and deepened throughout the 1920s, even if the periodical did not print overt Fascist propaganda. Its more gradual fascistization does not allude to anti-Fascism, as Claudio Carabba and Sabrina Fava have suggested. Rather, the slow appropriation of the periodical by the state reflects the regime's policies during its consolidation and suggests that values depicted in the weekly were considered aligned enough with those of the Fascist Party to reinforce their cultural objectives.[9] Allowing *Corriere dei Piccoli* to retain its conservative nationalist orientation and only gradually fascistize its content throughout the 1920s served a purpose by maintaining its readership and helping to normalizing the regime. *Il Giornale dei Balilla*, by contrast, depicted overt Fascist propaganda. The final section focuses on *Il Giornale to Balilla* to demonstrate how it adapted the style of *Corriere dei Piccoli* toward the conveyance of political ends and how it represented Fascism to its young readers.

Corriere dei Piccoli: From the Liberal State to the Fascist Dictatorship

At the time our story begins in the 1920s, *Corriere dei Piccoli* was *the* preeminent children's periodical in Italy. Beloved by many to this day, it is no surprise that *Corrierino* ("Little Courier," as *Corriere dei Piccoli* was nicknamed) is often praised as remaining resistant to Fascism throughout the 1920s, even by scholars, and has been credited as going so far as to print subtly anti-Fascist stories.[10] However, critiques of Fascism rarely graced its pages and were

7. Loparco, *I bambini e la guerra*, 25, 29, 194, 195. For comparison, see Spagnolli, "Bambini in guerra." Popular examples of strips during the Great War include "Italino" by Rubino and "Schizzo" by Mussino.

8. Meda, *Stelle e strips*, 23–24.

9. Carabba, *Corrierino, Corrierona*, 73; Fava, "Il progetto culturale," 70; and Spaventa Filippi, *Silvio Spaventa Filippi*, 27.

10. Spaventa Filippi, *Silvio Spaventa Filippi*, 27; and Fava, "Il progetto culturale," 70–71. Allegedly, the periodical's director, Silvio Spaventa Fillipi, rejected the push from Fascist cultural institutions to include more overt Fascist propaganda concerning the Balilla groups. No details or sources are provided, though, making it difficult to substantiate. Fava, "Il progetto culturale," 70.

ambiguous at best when present. The traditional and often nationalist stories it published often *aligned* with Fascist values, shedding light on why a more gradual fascistization was deemed appropriate in regard to *Corrierino.*

The conservative nationalist orientation of *Corriere dei Piccoli* was inherited from its parent periodical, *Corriere della Sera.* Financially backed by Milanese industrialists, *Corriere della Sera* was aligned with the "historic Right" in support of the constitutional monarchist state. This included Right-leaning liberals, who believed in limited state power and parliamentary politics, but remained skeptic of democracy. Liberals favored policies to promote economic development and the alleviation of social inequality but were adamantly anti-socialist. To the Right of liberals were the conservatives of the nineteenth century, who favored increased power for the monarch and were even more hostile to democracy and the extension of suffrage. "Conservative" in this study refers to both of these positions, which in the 1920s oriented *against* the expansion of democracy and mass politics and saw in Fascism a potential means to strengthen the state against socialist and democratic rivals. *Corriere della Sera* represented these positions.

Under the direction of Luigi Albertini, the periodical became a veritable national press and reached a daily circulation of 500,000 copies by the Great War, providing the paper a platform from which the interventionist cause was championed.[11] The pages of *Corriere dei Piccoli,* too, were employed in support of the war, as discussed in the introduction.

Following the First World War, *Corriere della Sera* reflected the Lombard industrial elite's stringent opposition to socialism. The periodical was also critical of the democratic liberalism of Giovanni Giolitti (Prime Minister for the fifth time in 1920 and 1921), who was viewed as powerless against the Bolshevik-style revolution perceived as imminent during the labor unrest that marked the "biennio rosso" of 1919 and 1920.[12] By this point, Luigi Albertini had delegated the position of director to his brother Alberto, due to Luigi's election to the Italian senate in 1915. The two brothers' hostility to both Giolitti and socialism initially fostered sympathies for Fascism, viewed as a potential means to crush the Left and strengthen the Liberal state.[13] The delusion that Fascism could be tamed and harnessed by liberals and conservatives led to support in the pages of *Corriere della Sera,* including backing the nationalist list in the 1921 election, which included Fascist candidates.[14]

11. Forgacs, *Italian Culture,* 35, 36; and Bricchetto, "Aldo Borelli," 546.

12. Musella, "Il fascismo dei moderati," 33, 44.

13. Cannistraro, *Historical Dictionary,* 11; Carabba, *Corrierino, Corrierina,* 59; and Forgacs, *Italian Culture,* 73–74.

14. Nasi, *Il peso della carta,* 174.

No overt endorsement of Fascism appeared in *Corriere dei Piccoli* in those years (which would have been an odd choice for a children's periodical), but the periodical did reflect the anxieties present in *Corriere della Sera.* The stories of *Corrierino* emphasized themes of patriarchy, the defense of the family, hierarchy, and a conservative orientation which at times conveyed a disdain for socialism.[15] For instance, "Legge di obbedienza" (Law of Obedience), a translation of an English story, tells of a worker bee who leads a revolution to overthrow the queen bee after overhearing a conversation between two children in which one tells the other that "kings and queens are useless. Indeed, they are beings against nature, because all creatures are created equal by nature." The worker bee is thus inspired to rally its fellows to create "a republic of workers without a queen," directly casting the uprising as socialist in nature, further demonstrated by the bees' embrace of the red flag of socialism.[16] In the end, the protagonist realizes that life without the queen is too chaotic, as the newly freed workers cannot agree on anything without her leadership. The necessity and indeed the benefits of a traditional monarchy are reaffirmed in the same instance that socialism is projected as misguided and doomed to fail.

Much of the content of *Corriere dei Piccoli* appears more neutral on the surface. The bulk of the comics, for instance, were either pure entertainment or moralizing stories, be they imports from the US or Italian classics such as "Bonaventura." Indeed, Sergio Tofano's classic provided a strip that could always be counted on for an uplifting ending, as Bonaventura's weekly stories invariably began with a misfortune that inevitably benefited others and then, following his good deed of the week, Bonaventura would be rewarded with a million lire. The goofy, uplifting stories were fun but also encouraged readers to stay positive and embrace virtues such as honesty. Although these themes were not Fascist in nature, Fascist leaders drew on traditional morals, exploiting them toward the end of deference to authority and national devotion. More importantly, stories such as "Bonaventura" did not *clash* with Fascist rhetoric, posing no opposition to the regime's emphasis on obedience and order, monarchal authority, and the woes of socialism. That these values were depicted in stories such as "Legge di obbedienza" highlights the ways in which *Corrierino* exemplified the liberal conservative alignment with Fascism in the years leading up to Mussolini's installment as Prime Minister, without which the Fascist seizure of power would have been much more difficult, if not impossible.

---

15. Becciu, *Il fumetto in Italia,* 176, 92; Carabba, *Il fascismo a fumetti,* 265; and Meda, *Stelle e strips,* 19.

16. "Legge di obbedienza," *Corriere dei Piccoli* (1921).

The sympathy afforded Fascism by the Albertini brothers waned with the March on Rome, although their disillusionment with Fascist violence did not stop them from crediting the new regime with restoring order and economic stability.[17] Yet their newfound hostility to Fascism did not appear much in the pages of *Corriere della Sera* throughout 1923 and 1924. The new state moved quickly to establish mechanisms of censorship to control the press, largely by strengthening legislation already in place.[18] This semilegal fascistization of the press was accompanied by extralegal violence organized by Fascist militants and aimed at political opponents.[19] If these pressures were not enough, *Corriere della Sera* was personally targeted by Fascist leader Roberto Farinacci.

Silence on the part of the Albertini brothers ended following the murder of socialist politician Giacomo Matteotti in June 1924, which provoked virulent opposition that nearly toppled the regime.[20] Luigi Albertini openly added his voice to this opposition, numbering among the signatories of Benedetto Croce's "Manifesto of Antifascist Intellectuals."[21] Later that year, Albertini stepped down under threat that his paper would be sequestered, and the Albertini ownership stake in *Corriere della Sera* was purchased by their erstwhile partners, the Crespi brothers.[22] Alberto Albertini was replaced briefly by Pietro Croci and then Ugo Ojetti, who had signed Giovanni Gentile's "Manifesto of *Fascist* Intellectuals."[23] The resulting change was less dramatic than might be expected; although the periodical shed some of its more liberal ideals and adopted a Fascist orientation, Mussolini instructed Aldo Valori, *Corriere della Sera*'s director in Rome, to avoid the same "propagandist exaggerations" endemic to official Party papers in order to retain a reliable image for its substantial foreign audience.[24]

---

17. Forgacs, *Italian Culture*, 73–74; Cannistraro, *Historical Dictionary*, 11, 438; and Carabba, *Corrierino, Corrierona*, 47, 59.

18. In particular, the Fascist regime exploited a circular on the press from September 1898 which granted prefects the ability to suspend a periodical for up to three months. Bonsaver, *Censorship and Literature*, 14.

19. Bonsaver, *Censorship and Literature*, 19, 20.

20. Bonsaver, *Censorship and Literature*, 20; and Talbot, *Censorship in Fascist Italy*, 30.

21. Carabba, *Corrierino, Corrierona*, 69. The "Manifesto degli intellettuali antifascisti," published 1 May 1925 in *Il Mondo*, was a response to the "Manifesto degli intellettuali fascisti" written by Giovanni Gentile.

22. Cannistraro, *Historical Dictionary*, 58; and Carabba, *Corrierino, Corrierona*, 70.

23. Forgacs, *Italian Culture*, 73–74. Ugo Ojetti only remained director until 1927, though, replaced by Maffio Maffii and then, in 1929, Aldo Borelli. Borelli remained the director of *Corriere della Sera* until Mussolini's dismissal from power in 1943.

24. Melograni, Introduction to *Corriere della Sera (1919–1943)*, lxxv; Forgacs, *Italian Culture*, 75; and Murialdi, *La stampa del regime fascista*, 13.

The dismissal of Albertini and the tightening of the regime's control over the press following the Matteotti crisis made the appearance of anti-Fascist sentiments in *Corriere dei Piccoli* virtually inconceivable after 1925. Presses not aligned with the regime were either silenced or taken over.[25] Nonetheless, so long as Silvio Spaventa Filippi remained the director of *Corrierino,* the periodical did not make references to the Fascist youth groups, despite pressure to do so, nor did it include comics or stories of an explicitly Fascist nature. Carabba and Fava (among other scholars) have thus approached Spaventa Fillipi as an anti-Fascist hero who resisted collaboration.[26] While this perspective likely holds truth, it begs the question of why *Corriere dei Piccoli* was permitted such a neutral or even anti-Fascist orientation, particularly after the fascistization of its parent periodical had begun.

It seems likely that in the years from 1925 until Spaventa Filippi's death in 1931, *Corriere dei Piccoli* benefited from the more neutral image Mussolini intended for *Corriere della Sera.* Wholesome stories such as "Bonaventura" offered no critique of Fascism and thus did not warrant suppression. This interpretation fits with the state's official reaction to comics from the United States in the 1930s and demonstrates the regime's skill at appropriating neutral or generic stories for the Fascist cultural project by positioning Fascist stories around them to coopt or transform their meanings.

Other stories in the children's periodical aligned more with Fascist rhetoric during these years than has been previously acknowledged. Stories such as "L'uovo di Colombo" (The Egg of Columbus) told of "the great Italian who gave Spain a vast amount of empire and glory" and served the same end as the biographies of national heroes featured in *Balilla,* discussed below.[27] Similarly, imperialistic tales told of Europeans' "burden" to bring civilization to the so-called *selvaggi* or "savages." In "Un giornalista tra i selvaggi" (A Journalist among the Savages), the hero makes his way to an unspecified location in Africa, and, perpetuating the stereotype of African cannibalism, he proclaims that, although "your laws and the traditions of your ancestors [. . .] order you to eat me immediately," he promises he will teach them all he knows if they refrain from eating him.[28] After sharing his knowledge of printing, the tribe nonetheless attempts to eat our poor journalist. The story, typical of European imperialism, extends the possibility of "uplift" and praises European intentions,

25. Cannistraro, *La fabbrica del consenso,* 174, 177.

26. Carabba, *Corrierino, Corrierona,* 73; Fava, "Il progetto culturale," 70; and Spaventa Filippi, *Silvio Spaventa Filippi,* 27.

27. "L'uovo di Colombo," *Corriere dei Piccoli,* n. 10 (1929).

28. "Un giornalista tra i selvaggi," *Corriere dei Piccoli,* n. 20 (1927). Throughout this book, bracketed ellipses are my own, while unbracketed ellipses are in the original text.

all the while affirming a limit to the potential of the supposedly inferior people of Africa. It would have been equally at home published in *Balilla.*

Overlap existed within the comic strips as well, including critiques of modernity with which Fascists would have agreed. One possible reading of the good-natured "Sor Pampurio" exemplifies this. In a string of stories, Sor Pampurio attempts in vain to find an apartment in the city. The first apartment is too noisy, transforming his beautiful home into a nightmare. Next, he is inconvenienced by the supposedly convenient elements of modern life, be it a malfunctioning elevator in his building or living above noisy offices. Modern society is full of pitfalls and drawbacks, making an unstable existence for Pampurio's family. Another strip portrays the woes of consumerism, as his daughter is so enthralled with the nearby cinema screening American films that his family again sets out to find another apartment.[29] As Giulio Cuccolini has argued, "Sor Pampurio" thus becomes an "allegory of the petite bourgeoisie with scarce virtues and many defects."[30]

"Sor Pampurio" was not unique in expressing concerns about modern life. "Dottor Piramidone" questions the continual progress promised by science, as the well-meaning inventions of the doctor continually go awry and create chaos for all involved.[31] Meanwhile, "Mortadella" tells of an obese bourgeois man who lacks the necessary discipline to diet as his doctor orders.[32] By critiquing bourgeois lifestyles and assumptions, these stories echoed the Strapaese (super-country) artistic and intellectual movement, which championed the virtues of rural life over life in corrupt cities.[33] The stories further aligned with Fascist calls for a new man, who would be fit, virile, and aggressive, an image far from the obese Mortadella and the leisure-filled bourgeois life.[34]

It is worth noting, though, that Carabba presents "Sor Pampurio" not as a critique of the bourgeois lifestyle, but rather as a search for a normalcy that is constantly interrupted. In this light, it has been read as a critique of Fascism.[35] Though plausible, the ambiguous nature of the strip, which focuses on the

29. "Sor Pampurio," *Corriere dei Piccoli,* n. 17 (1929); "Sor Pampurio," *Corriere dei Piccoli,* n. 24 (1929); "Sor Pampurio," *Corriere dei Piccoli,* n. 10 (1931); and "Sor Pampurio," *Corriere dei Piccoli,* n. 47 (1931).

30. Cuccolini, "Carlo Bisi, sociologo a quadretti," 51.

31. "Dottor Piramidone," *Corriere dei Piccoli,* n. 11 (1927); "Dottor Piramidone," *Corriere dei Piccoli,* n. 22 (1927); and "Dottor Piramidone," *Corriere dei Piccoli,* n. 31 (1927).

32. "Mortadella," *Corriere dei Piccoli,* n. 34 (1928); and "Mortadella," *Corriere dei Piccoli,* n. 35 (1928).

33. Adamson, "Culture of Italian Fascism," 560–71; Cavallo, *Soffici e Malaparte,* 67–70; and Seroni, "Fascismo e riviste letterarie italiane," 548–49.

34. On the importance of the new man to Fascism, see Gentile, *Sacralization of Politics,* 59; Berezin, *Making the Fascist Self,* 5; and Falasca-Zamponi, *Fascist Spectacle,* 8.

35. Carabba, *Corrierino, Corrierona,* 78.

E di nuovo Marmittone
è assegnato alla prigione.

FIGURE 1.1. A typical end for Marmittone. The accompanying rhyme reads, "And again Marmittone is consigned to prison." *Corriere dei Piccoli*, n. 43 (1928).

disruptive nature of neighbors, noises, and the features of modern life, makes the critique a subtle one open to interpretation.

This ambiguity extends to another comic considered a parody of Fascism: "Marmittone." The strip tells of the well-meaning but incompetent rooky (as the title indicates) who always messes up and ends up in prison, as seen in figure 1.1. For instance, when troops are mustered in the morning for roll call, Marmittone alone does not hear it. Running to catch up, he runs into the captain and lands himself in prison. In another, Marmittone is dutifully cleaning his room, and, swinging his broom to remove a spiderweb, he hits his captain in the face just as he enters the room. He is again imprisoned.[36]

36. *Corriere dei Piccoli*, n. 5 (1928); and *Corriere dei Piccoli*, n. 6 (1928).

According to one interpretation, Marmittone's exploits leave little room for the glorification of military life. As Carabba explains, the strip depicts "an Italian reality in stark contrast to the superman culture (*superomismo*) of Fascism that the omnipresent Duce sought to forge in those years" and so expresses skepticism that Fascism would ever create its new man.[37] Perhaps the critique was subtle enough to fly under the radar of the censors, allowing it to remain in print until World War II: Marmittone did have a loveable, well-meaning nature, and his uniform was neither the blackshirt of the Fascists nor the gray-green of the Italian army. Indeed, this interpretation is plausible in that it shares commonalities with *The Good Soldier Švejk* by Jaroslav Hašek, in which a Czech serving in the Austro-Hungarian army continuously thwarts military authority through apparent incompetency. Like Marmittone, it is unclear if Švejk is truly incompetent or if he is only pretending to be in an act of passive resistance.[38] Marmittone's lack of lines makes this interpretation less clear in his case, though, as he does not speak in "double talk" or claim his incompetency to be an act as Švejk does. Furthermore, Marmittone appears rather demoralized by his situation in figure 1.1, rather than relieved, as if he had gotten out of service.

Nevertheless, comics, like much of popular culture, may not point to a single interpretation shared by all but have meanings shaped instead by an individual's experiences and the discourses within which they are oriented. What is now perceived by anti-Fascists and fans of *Corriere dei Piccoli* may have been read differently by a Fascist official or young reader in the 1920s. From another perspective, "Marmittone" may have been a cautionary tale, informing readers of the need to take military training seriously, to discipline oneself, and to follow orders. The consequence of not doing so was evident: imprisonment. This interpretation aligns with comic strips printed in *Balilla*, in which children are reprimanded and even arrested for seemingly small infractions.

Corrierino may not have printed overtly Fascist propaganda during the 1920s. Yet it also did not typically present values overtly *at odds* with Fascism. Indeed, the messages it primarily conveyed, such as the defense of family, traditions, and hierarchy, often *aligned* with the regime's rhetoric, especially during the 1920s, when the dictatorship was still under construction and Mussolini sought to coopt and attract what he could of existing Italian cultural strains. *Corriere dei Piccoli*'s traditional and nationalist orientation fit this mold well. After Spaventa Filippi's death in 1931, *Corrierino* was more explicit in its alignment with the regime, as his successor Franco Bianchi proved more willing to collaborate.

---

37. Carabba, *Corrierino, Corrierona*, 83.

38. Parrott, introduction to *The Good Soldier Švejk*, xv.

Il Giornale dei Balilla and the Conditioning of Italian Youth

The first issue of *Giornale dei Balilla* was published on 18 February 1923, only four months after the March on Rome and King Victor Emmanuel III's subsequent decision to appoint Mussolini prime minister. Inspired by *Corriere dei Piccoli,* the weekly was the official periodical of the Balilla youth groups, organized in January 1923 for boys aged eight to thirteen.[39] The name "Balilla" referred to the nickname given to Giovanni Battista Perasso, credited with inspiring the revolt against Austrian control of Genoa in 1746 at the age of eleven. The title thus served to connect the Fascist youth to the struggle for an independent and unified Italy.[40]

The Fascist youth groups were tasked with organizing young Fascist supporters and advancing Fascist influence among the non-politically committed youth. Their leaders organized gyms, reading rooms, conferences, and recreation, with the goal of reaching the entire youth population outside of schools, as it was believed that teachers trained under Liberal Italy could not be entrusted to fascistize students. From the beginning, educating Italian youth according to Fascist principles was an essential goal of the regime to be pursued fervently.[41]

The efforts of the Partito Nazionale Fascista (PNF), though, were inhibited by more established youth groups in Italy. The development of children's organizations had expanded during the nineteenth century throughout Western societies, and Italy was no exception.[42] Azione Cattolica (Catholic Action, the lay Catholic social group) had numerous youth groups for both boys and girls, and there was also the Young Italian Explorers (Boy Scouts), the Republican Youth Federation, and the Socialist Youth Federation.[43] As the regime had not yet established its monopoly on political power and could therefore not ban outright rival youth groups, the leaders of the Fascist organizations had to rely on recreation and propaganda in order to expand membership, which, in turn, motivated undertakings such as *Giornale dei Balilla.*

Printed by Imperia, the publishing house of the PNF, the periodical was placed under Defendente de Amici as the managing director, although Dino

39. The Fascist preoccupation with Italian youth predated the rise of the regime. Ponzio, *Shaping the New Man,* 25–31.

40. Cavazza, "Formazione dei giovani e fascismo," 102.

41. Cavazza, "Formazione dei giovani e fascismo," 89; Koon, *Believe, Obey, Fight,* xvi; and Ponzio, *Shaping the New Man,* 34.

42. Cavazza, "Formazione dei giovani e fascismo," 88; and McLean, *Mussolini's Children,* 15.

43. Ponzio, *Shaping the New Man,* 39.

Grandi and Francesco Meriano might have been the true directors during these early years.[44] The cultural agenda to "educate" Italian youth was made evident from the start. As Grandi wrote in the first issue: "Our Balilla [. . .] will find nourishment for their intelligence and their hearts in these pages. The soul of the nation will never be conquered if the intellectual and moral education of children and youth is not cared for and the sacred bonds that unite one generation to another are not cultivated."[45]

The weekly initially sold for 35 lira-cents per issue (*Corriere dei Piccoli* cost only 20).[46] By the end of the year it dropped to 30 cents.[47] The format of *Giornale dei Balilla* changed several times during its first year, fluctuating from sixteen pages to twelve in July before returning to sixteen by the end of the year. The division of content also varied, with no established number of pages devoted to articles or to illustrations and comics: while issue n. 13 in May 1923 had ten pages with comics and illustrations, most issues had around seven. The content, though, consistently promoted Fascist and nationalist themes. Biographies of Italian heroes were regular features, as were descriptions of the diverse regions of Italy to foster a sense that the various provinces were united.

Whatever the format, the periodical was designed to reinforce Fascist values and encourage Italian boys to join Balilla groups. The use of "boys" here is intentional, as there was no Fascist youth group for girls until 1929. The language of the periodical made this targeting of male children evident, writing, for instance, that "*we* men are obliged to defend" Italian women, using "we" to identify the reader with the author and mark both as male.[48]

The educational and propagandistic purpose of *Giornale dei Balilla* was further demonstrated when it was incorporated in June 1925 as an official supplement for *Popolo d'Italia,* the official paper of the PNF directed by Mussolini's brother, Arnaldo.[49] The change was celebrated in *Giornale dei Balilla* by two letters printed under an image of the Duce. In the first letter, newly appointed *segretario* of the Fascist youth organizations, Renato Ricci, stressed that the new status of *Giornale dei Balilla* was "very opportune, especially in this moment in which one of our greatest concerns is the education of our youth." Ricci emphasized the role of periodicals and the Balilla groups

44. Carabba, *Il fascismo a fumetti,* 268.

45. Quoted in Meda, *Stelle e strips,* 26.

46. *Giornale dei Balilla,* n. 13 (13 May 1923).

47. By comparison, the price of bread per kg was 2.19 lire on average throughout the 1920s, and the average wage per day was 12–14 lire for agricultural work and 16 lire for industrial labor. Scarpellini, *Material Nation,* 110; and Helstosky, *Garlic and Oil,* 57, 58, 69, 73.

48. *Giornale dei Balilla,* n. 14 (20 May 1923). The emphasis is mine.

49. Carabba, *Il fascismo a fumetti,* 268; and Meda, *Stelle e strips,* 24.

because "public instruction is insufficient to form a complete man." Arnaldo Mussolini acknowledged the importance of the weekly in the second letter, insisting the periodical "must direct and prepare the spirit of our children toward the strongest, most strident, and most beautiful conception of renewing Fascism."[50]

Giornale dei Balilla was retitled simply *Il Balilla* in 1926, just as the Fascist youth organizations were reorganized under Ricci as the Opera Nazionale Balilla (ONB) and officially incorporated into the state under the Consiglio dei Ministri. The restructuring was intended to rationalize the various youth groups, create additional sections, and provide the groups with greater resources. The institutionalization of the ONB provoked concerns in competing youth organizations, and rightly so. Despite assurances from Mussolini to Pietro Tacchi Venturi (interlocutor for the Vatican) that he did not intend to grant the ONB a monopoly over youth organizations, the state *did* move to ban rival youth groups in January 1927.[51] Only the youth organizations of the Catholic Church were exempted, out of a desire to maintain negotiations toward the Concordat. Pope Pius XI acceded first to limits on the Catholic Boy Scouts and ultimately to their disbanding in order to avoid further state repression toward the more religiously oriented Italian Catholic Youth Society.[52] The prohibition of rival youth groups was celebrated in *Balilla* as key to the development of Italian youth; with Mussolini as their comrade, the young must study, learn, exercise, and, "prepare the soul for sacrifice."[53]

Fascism, the Sacred, and the Catholic Church

The editors and directors made clear the Fascist orientation and "educational" agenda of *Balilla* (I will hereafter refer to both *Giornale dei Balilla* and *Balilla* by its final name for simplicity). Politicians and intellectuals had fretted over the perceived lack of Italian national identity since unification in 1861, a process not entirely completed until 1871. Italian society was often criticized as divided along class as well regional lines, while the Italian people themselves were disparaged as undisciplined and narrowly self-interested. Fascist

50. *Giornale dei Balilla,* n. 112 (18 June 1925), 2.

51. Ponzio, *Shaping the New Man,* 35; Stellavato, "La nascità dell'Opera nazionale balilla," 27; and Zapponi, "Il partito della gioventù," 598.

52. Ponzio, *Shaping the New Man,* 39–40; and Stellavato, "La nascità dell'Opera nazionale balilla," 77.

53. *Il Balilla,* n. 196 (27 January 1927), 6.

FIGURE 1.2. Lio is shown here as emerging from what is described as "a grand tricolor flower." *Il Balilla*, n. 193 (6 January 1927), 1.

intellectuals drew on these notions and sought to create a new political culture, new Italians, and a new Italy.[54]

Nothing embodied this more than the recurring comic strip "Lio Balilla" by Antonio Rubino, hired in 1927.[55] The comic focused on Lio, a young Italian clad in a blackshirt and devoted wholeheartedly to the nation. Figure 1.2 depicts his "birth" in the first episode: as he bursts from a flower made up of the colors of the Italian flag (green, white, and red), Lio is told by a fairy "You are fortunate! You are born in Italy with the Black Shirt!"[56] Lio's birth provides a symbolic *rinascimento* (rebirth) for Italy. It thus embodies Fascism's rhetorical obsession with youth, not just in the literal sense of Italian children, but that *Fascism* was a youthful and even (as Roger Griffin argues) palingenetic movement, destined to lead the renewal of the Italian nation.[57]

54. Adamson, *Avant-Garde Florence*, 3, 11; and Patriarca, *Italian Vices*, 131–34.

55. Carabba, *Il fascismo a fumetti*, 268.

56. *Il Balilla*, n. 193 (6 January 1927), 1.

57. On Mussolini's rhetorical use of "youth" in reference to the Fascist movement, see Mussolini, "Il primo discorso presidenziale al Senato," 25; and Mussolini, "La forza e la saggezza governano l'Italia," 36. For comparison, see Falasca-Zamponi, *Fascist Spectacle*, 72; and Harvey, "Cult of Youth," 76–78. For Griffin's discussion of the "palingenetic myth" at the core of Fascism, see Griffin, *Nature of Fascism*, 26, 32–36.

The nation, then, was to be sacred and serve as the basis of renewal and provide a sense of belonging. As the realm of traditional religion shrank and society splintered into separate sectors with the separation of church and state, religion became less dominant in people's lives in the sense that the Catholic Church lost its all-encompassing hold on society (quite literally in the Papal States, where the pope had been both the Vicar of Christ and the head of state). Politics underwent a "process of sacralization" as the notion of the sacred became affixed to the state through the adoption of rituals, liturgy, and the appropriation of religious icons and language, thereby diffusing the sacred throughout society, making it no longer the purview of religion alone.[58]

According to Emilio Gentile, a new collective identity was to be forged as rituals, monuments, and symbols of the Patria (or homeland) mobilized people, tied them to the regime, and expressed its messianic agenda of national rebirth. Many scholars have employed the term "political religion" to argue that the Fascist regime essentially sought to create an alternative to religion that provided a new source of transcendence and faith.[59] The features on Italian heroes in *Balilla* were intended to provide a new array of national saints, ranging from Petrarch to Giuseppe Verdi and often including Catholic saints. Figures were included for their contribution to Italian history. Verdi, for instance, represented the sense of national awakening during the Risorgimento and the drive toward unification: "Verdi contributed as he could, with his melodies and with patriotic songs inserted into his work, rousing spirits and instilling in them vigor and courage."[60]

Comics, too, portrayed Fascism's claim on the sacred. "Fasciolino" (literally, "Little Fascio") was a recurring character and strip in the early years of *Balilla,* dressed in the uniform of the Balilla youth group: the blackshirt of the Fascists, the black fez of the Arditi soldiers, and grey-green trousers. Figure 1.3 shows one rather representative episode, in which Fasciolino reads a poster calling for citizens to donate in support of a memorial "to the glorious who have fallen for the homeland," and is distraught because he has nothing to give. When a notice is put up offering reward money for a missing dog, Fasciolino rounds up all the dogs in town until he finds the correct one, then races off to donate his reward of 100 lire.

58. Gentile, *Sacralization of Politics,* 301; and Adamson, "Fascism and Political Religion," 44.

59. Gentile, *Sacralization of Politics,* 306–9; and Griffin, "'Holy Storm,'" 217. The concept of "political religion" is contested, and Walter L. Adamson emphasizes the broader "historical process of secularisation" in which it needs to be contextualized. Adamson, "Fascism and Political Religion," 44, 49; and Roberts, "'Political Religion,'" 396–97.

60. *Giornale dei Balilla,* n. 87 (12 October 1924), 12.

FIGURE 1.3. Fasciolino leaps into action in order to earn money that he can donate toward the monument for the those who died for Italy in World War I. *Giornale dei Balilla*, n. 13 (13 May 1923).

This episode of Fasciolino draws on Fascist rhetoric and its "cult of the fallen." World War I inspired a new myth around the nation in many countries, instilling it with a sacredness and a register of martyrs. Fascist intellectuals asserted a claim on what was a universal postwar phenomenon, rapidly representing "themselves [as] the main authors of this return to a 'patriotic religion.'"[61] With the nation at the center, a new secular religion was offered to Italians and overseen by the state and the PNF, promising a unity that transcended class and even death, as those who died in service to the nation were immortalized in monuments such as that funded by Fasciolino. Through comics like this one, authors sent messages of devotion to the nation and further established Fascism's claim on the cult of the fallen by highlighting the role of the Balilla and Fascists in the construction of these monuments. Moreover, the strip provided a call to action: Italian youth were called to sacrifice their time and money for the Patria and to honor those in its service.

Fascism's claim on the sacred raised the question of its relation to the Catholic Church. Many Catholics rejected what they viewed as the Fascist worshipping of the state and, later on, the cult surrounding Mussolini.[62] Yet, despite Mussolini's early anticlericalism, his pragmatic approach to politics pushed him to woo the Catholic Church in a dominant Catholic country rather than attempt to fight it from the start.[63] Even before his rise to power, Mussolini

61. Gentile, *Sacralization of Politics*, 17, 18.

62. Gentile, "New Idols," 146; Kertzer, *Pope and Mussolini*, 176; and Adamson, "Fascism and Political Religion," 63.

63. Despite the widespread anticlericalism in Italy, Kertzer records that 99 percent of the forty million Italians identified as Catholic on the eve of Pius XI's coronation. While this number is likely high and unverifiable, it illustrates the dominant role of the religion in Italy. Kertzer, *Pope and Mussolini*, 17.

made it clear that Fascism could defend and even extend the authority of the Vatican, offering the Catholic Church respect and prerogatives not granted to it by the Liberal state. Pope Pius XI responded positively to these overtures, believing Fascism would reestablish a role for the Church in education and the state as well as be an ally against their common enemies of communism, liberalism, and democracy. In short, each side viewed the other as a means to further their own goals of the conquest of Italian society.[64] This is not to say, though, that no tension existed over the relationship of the state and religion under Fascism, as it remained to be seen if the Vatican would remain autonomous or if, as desired by Fascist ideologue Giovanni Gentile, it would be subordinated to the state.

As the debate regarding the place of Catholicism in Fascist Italy continued, the regime lost no time in appropriating religious themes and icons to better express its ideals to Italians and market them as familiar. This appropriation can be seen in the "cult of the fallen," drawing on the religious notion of the righteous martyr and the transcendence offered to members of the faith (though, again, certainly not unique to Fascism). The appropriation of religious themes persisted throughout the dictatorship and extended beyond the "cult of the fallen." For instance, schoolbooks in Tunisia deified Mussolini through the adaptation of a Catholic prayer in which the "high Duce" was depicted as "our savior," "a valiant soldier" who "came down to Rome," "ascended into the high office," and will preside over "the resurrection of Italy." The prayer further projected Mussolini as an *instrument* of Jesus and the Catholic faith.[65]

Holidays, too, were commandeered to associate Fascist policies with traditional religion. Christmas Eve, for instance, was also named the Fascist Giornata della Madre e del Fanciullo (Day of the Mother and Child), linking the regime's promotion of motherhood with the Christian celebration of Mary and the birth of Jesus.[66] Similarly, Befana, an old woman in Italian folklore who delivers toys to children on the eve of Epiphany (5 January), became Befana Fascista and represented the social programs of the regime.[67] The regime even drew on the popular cult of saints in the construction of the cult of the Duce, particularly that of Saint Francis of Assisi, and Italian saints and

64. Webster, *Cross and the Fasces,* 83, 110; Adamson, "Fascism and Political Religion," 55, 63; and Kertzer, *Pope and Mussolini,* xxi, 27–29.

65. Falasca-Zamponi, *Fascist Spectacle,* 64–65.

66. Ipsen, *Dictating Demography,* 157.

67. Cavazza, *Piccole patrie,* 116–22; and Colin, *I bambini di Mussolini,* 414.

priests were included in the biographies of Italian heroes featured in *Balilla.*[68] The overt associations with religion marked the regime both as traditional and as a rupture with tradition, presenting a break with the secularism of Liberal Italy and a new meaning for conventional religious icons.

Over time, there was a change in tone over how religion was depicted in the pages of *Balilla.* The incorporation of religion initially implied the possibility of coexistence and compatibility between Fascism and Catholicism. After the establishment of the dictatorship in 1925, the appropriation of Catholic language for Fascist purposes became more frequent. One update on the youth groups printed the "Decalogo," or "Ten Commandments," of the Balilla, highlighting one's duty to Italy.[69] Even more telling, when the prohibition of rival youth groups was declared in *Balilla* on 27 January 1927, it was announced that the Catholic Boy Scouts would embroider "O.N.B." on their banners to express their dependence on Balilla groups. The move suggested *subordination,* not coexistence. Far from settled, the stage was set for a tumultuous relationship between state and church in Fascist Italy.

Italian Racial "Superiority" and Imperial Destiny

If Fascism was portrayed as a young movement poised to lead the renewal of Italy, the Italian nation itself was depicted as reaching back to ancient Rome. The connection between Fascism, Italy, and ancient Rome is illustrated in Rubino's tale of Lio. As Lio journeys out into the world, he meets Romulus and Remus, the mythical founders of Rome, who respond to his trumpet's call. The pair come to Lio as children riding upon the she-wolf of Rome and carrying a sign that reads "SPQR" (acronym for the Senate and People of Rome). Immediately recognizing Lio to be a son of Italy, they invite him to drink the milk of the wolf, as they themselves did according to legend. Lio promptly accepts their offer, as shown in figure 1.4. Lio, the embodiment of Fascism and linked to the Italian nation by birth, is thus linked to ancient Rome. As future episodes continually connected Lio and the symbols of the regime to the peninsula's past, *Balilla* established Fascism as an integral and natural component of Italian history while simultaneously projecting its aggressive, imperialistic agenda for the future.

68. Adamson, "Fascism and Political Religion," 69. For biographies of Italian saints and priests in *Balilla,* including Saint Catherine of Siena and Father Giovanni Semeria, see *Il Balilla,* n. 16 (21 April 1927), 3; and *Il Balilla,* n. 10 (10 March 1927), 2.

69. *Il Balilla,* n. 193 (6 January 1927), 6.

SPQR
4 - Il suo latte nutriente
ha un sapore un po' selvaggio,
ma fortifica la mente
e centuplica il coraggio!».

FIGURE 1.4. After being embraced as a son of Italy, Lio is nourished by the she-wolf of Rome as Romulus and Remus look on. "Her nourishing milk has a bit of a wild flavor, but it strengthens the mind and multiplies courage a hundredfold!" *Il Balilla*, n. 195 (20 January 1927), 1.

Mussolini made known his goal of "improving" the Italian race prior to his rise to power. In a speech at the Fascist Congress in Rome in November 1921, he declared, "Fascists must concern themselves with the health of the race by which history is made."[70] To be sure, racial thought was less dominant in the rhetoric of Fascist Italy than in that of Nazi Germany, which, according to some scholars, subordinated all other concerns to that of race.[71] Nonetheless, the language of race was employed by Mussolini and other Fascist leaders from the outset of the Fascist movement, invoking the apparent decline of the white race to strengthen nationalist claims and emphasize the racial link between the individual and the nation.[72]

Mussolini was heavily influenced by the various racial ideas of early twentieth-century Europe. Italian nationalists such as Enrico Corradini conceived of nations as natural communities with continuity over the millennia linked

70. Mussolini, "Il programma fascista," 219.

71. Burleigh, *Racial State*, 23, 305–6.

72. Neocleous, *Fascism*, 31–33; Ipsen, *Dictating Demography*, 67, 70; and McLean, *Mussolini's Children*, 7, 223.

by each generation. However, the Duce was discouraged by the current state of the so-called Italian race. Influenced by the work of Oswald Spengler, Mussolini was concerned that the Italian race was in a phase of decay, having been undermined by Marxism, philosophical materialism, and democracy. Centuries of foreign domination of the peninsula had also stripped the Italian people of their "Roman" virtues: courage, heroism, discipline, and a martial spirit. Despite his pessimism about the Italian people, Futurists such as Filippo Tommaso Marinetti led Mussolini to embrace the ideal of the Italian race as a people imbued with the spirit of conquest. Mussolini sought to utilize the notion of national (and racial) renewal and superiority as a means "to forcibly 'evolve'" Italians into heroic warriors.[73]

The notion of myth enunciated by Georges Sorel was the means through which this transformation would be achieved. According to Sorel, myths "enabled one to transcend a detested present," mobilizing "the masses" and directing them toward action, discipline, and sacrifice.[74] A crucial point here is that myths represent ideals more than truths. A student of Sorel, Mussolini employed historical myths of an idealized past and the myth of Italians' superiority to prepare Italy to "become the dominant nation of the Mediterranean basin and discharge on the African banks the surplus of its population and energies."[75]

The use of historical myths to inspire and condition Italian youth is evident in the pages of *Balilla*. The myth of Italian racial superiority in relation to the people of Africa was common, serving to model the desired mode of interaction, with Italians taking their alleged natural role in leading people from Africa. In "Le trovate di Achille" (Achille's Good Ideas), a boy identified as a Balilla by his uniform interacts with a group of personified African animals, "speaking to them of the practices and customs of the distant civilized countries."[76] That he addresses African *animals* condescendingly conveys a sense that the people of Africa are backward and inferior. The language further marks the African animals as *un*civilized, by emphasizing that "civilized countries" are far away. The animals are depicted as eager to learn from Achille, the giraffe stretching its neck to listen. When a disastrous flood hits, Achille saves the day through his brilliance, and the animals celebrate him. The leading role attributed to Achille (and therefore Italians more broadly) is further normalized for Italian readers by the strip's Catholic themes, with

73. Gillette, *Racial Theories in Fascist Italy*, 37–38.

74. Gillette, *Racial Theories in Fascist Italy*, 38. On the importance of Sorel's notion of myth to Fascist ideology, see Gentile, *Origins of Fascist Ideology*, 3, 356.

75. Mussolini, "Per essere liberi," 106.

76. *Giornale dei Balilla*, n. 15 (27 May 1923).

Achille as a sort of Moses figure, leading the animals and saving them from a flood, who is furthermore associated with Saint Francis by virtue of his ability to talk to animals.

Similar stories serve to continually reinforce this understanding of the relationship between Italian and African people, regularly marking them as *primitivo* (primitive) and as *selvaggi* (savages).[77] No strip better conveys how Fascists envisioned Italians' interactions with the people in Italy's African colonies, though, than that of Attilio Mussino. At the center of Mussino's stories is Pico, a young Italian who travels to Italian Somaliland "to bring civilization to those who do not have it."[78] It is noteworthy that Pico lands specifically in Oltregiuba (presently the state of Jubaland in southern Somalia), a colonial territory ceded from Britain to Italy in 1924 in reward for Italian support during World War I. Pico serves to instruct young readers in Italy's self-proclaimed mission to civilize this recently acquired territory. Interestingly, while "Le trovate di Achille" told the story of a Balilla interacting with African animals and "Un piccolo servo negro" (A Little Black Servant) told of an Englishman instructing an African child, Pico is a young boy who commands the attention of African adults and instructs them in the ways of civilization.

It must be noted that aside from being labeled as Oltregiuba, the setting has no other direct references to Italy's colonies. Rather, the series—much like an earlier strip Mussino had published for *Corriere dei Piccoli* entitled "Bilbolbul"—represents an "imagined geography," where Africa is defined less by empirical fact than by European value judgements and assumptions, marked as distinct from the self-declared civilized countries of Europe.[79] Unsurprisingly, then, the people in the comic bear no resemblance to the Somali people they are said to be, but are drawn in the same racialized style as those in "Bilbolbul," no doubt influenced by European caricatures of African people.

When Pico first lands in this imagined colonial space, he gathers around him "those people still savage," marked as Other by their caricatured features and lack of clothing. He proceeds to tell them of modern forms of transportation in Italy, prompting his audience to create improvised trollies and trains, with giraffes holding up trolley lines upon which people glide in baskets.[80] The following stories are mostly variations of this formula; Pico informs his listeners of some element of European civilization which they then

77. For instance, "Birichino nel paese dei Selvaggi," in *Giornale dei Balilla*, n. 48 (13 January 1924), 12; and "Un piccolo servo negro," in *Giornale dei Balilla*, n. 103 (13 February 1925), 10.

78. *Il Balilla*, n. 11 (17 March 1927), 16.

79. Said, *Orientalism*, 54–55, 59–60, 68–71. On "Bilbolbul," see Sinibaldi, "Between Censorship and Propaganda," 225.

80. *Il Balilla*, n. 11 (17 March 1927), 16.

attempt to imitate, typically with animals. Pico thus is continually framed as well-meaning and altruistically helping people deemed inferior, people who, according to the comic, are eager for his help. The panel provides insight into the virtues and elements of modernity Italians claimed to offer the colonies of Italy, as well as into what the colonized are assumed to lack.

Italian society is positioned as modern and thus superior due to technology such as the radio, as well as flight, represented in this comic in the use of birds for the postal service and transportation. The crude methods through which Italian civilization is adopted prompt the question of whether the colonized in Oltregiuba can embrace modern society, but the stories nevertheless praise the Italian people for bringing these gifts to their newly acquired colony. Despite framing the relationship as "uplifting," little elevation ever occurred in these Italian colonies. Few resources were diverted to the colonies prior to the imperial phase in the mid-1930s, and they were primarily military in nature or for the benefit of Italians. The relationship was marked by exploitation, not development.[81] Nonetheless, Mussino continued to market Italian colonialism as extending the Italian way of life to its colonial territories.

This depiction of African people as Other and "primitive," in need of Italian leadership and only capable of emulating Italian culture, was not new or unique to Fascist Italy. Rather, this was the conventional colonial narrative in European discourse.[82] In this instance, it served to project a claim onto a recently acquired colonial territory while projecting the mission of Italians to civilize the colonies, preparing Italian children for future imperial projects. While there was no way of predicting the war in Ethiopia or the racial laws in the mid-1920s, publications like *Ballila* laid the groundwork that may have made those later developments more acceptable to Italian public opinion.

Normalizing Fascist Violence and Promoting Campaigns

Stories in *Balilla* modeled the behavior Fascists sought to elicit from Italians. The hope, as discussed in the introduction, was to educate children and condition them toward the new norms advocated by Fascism. Yet the pages of *Balilla* also displayed that which the new regime sought to discourage and conveyed the consequences for bad or improper conduct. For instance, a story from April 1924 tells of a group of children attending a puppet show. While most of the children hurry to the performance, Giacomino lags behind.

81. De Grand, "Mussolini's Follies," 132; and Negash, *Italian Colonialism in Eritrea*, 68, 71, 157.

82. Said, *Culture and Imperialism*, xxiii; and Landau, "Amazing Distance," 3.

Annoyed upon arrival that no seats remain, he climbs a tree seeking a better view and, although he means no harm, Giacomino is arrested by a gendarme.[83] While the example of a child arrested for being late is so extreme it seems comedic, it nonetheless conveys the Fascist emphasis on discipline and establishes the use of force to impose the Fascist way of life as normal. The "Marmittone" strip of *Corriere dei Piccoli* discussed earlier does not seem so strikingly anti-Fascist now, with its recurring imprisonment of its protagonist for seemingly minor offenses resulting from incompetence.

Violence was not merely a means to enforce conformity in behavior, but a method to achieve any goal. Fascist campaigns were routinely cast in terms of war or battle, such as the Battle for Grain, during which the Fascist state increased tariffs on imported grain and sought to increase Italian grain production. These national struggles were integrated into Rubino's stories for *Balilla,* representing the Battle for Grain as an actual battle in the comics; when Lio captures a creature named *Ozio* (Idleness) in the grain fields, he and his classmates proceed to beat the creature and declare they will defeat the villain together.[84] The focus on idleness as the villain and the promotion of unity, effort, and violence as the solution echoes Mussolini's call for hard work and obedience from agricultural workers.[85]

Whether to discipline the disobedient or to mobilize Italians to act with the ardor typically reserved for war, violence was glorified in Fascist rhetoric. Drawing on the concept of violence advocated by Georges Sorel, violence was viewed as something that could be *creative*; through the violent destruction of liberalism, democracy, and materialism, Italian society would be reborn. It was not merely a means to an end, but an end in itself, understood as the opposite of the complacent peacefulness of the decadent bourgeoisie.[86] The Great War furthered this notion, glorifying violence and the fallen as martyrs, and proving to many who would later become Fascists that those who fought in the trenches should lead society. The representation of the struggle to increase agricultural yields as an actual battle enabled Mussolini to spotlight heroes, projected the activist nature of the regime, and offered a "rhetorical rehearsal" for the *actual* wars of the future.[87]

---

83. *Giornale dei Balilla,* n. 60 (6 April 1924), 9.

84. *Il Balilla,* n. 33 (18 August 1927), 1.

85. Mussolini, "Ai combattenti della battaglia del grano," 408; and Mussolini, "Ai veliti del grano."

86. Falasca-Zamponi, *Fascist Spectacle,* 29–30; Adamson, *Avant-Garde Florence,* 232, 255, 261; and Gentile, *Sacralization of Politics,* 53–54.

87. Falasca-Zamponi, *Fascist Spectacle,* 148.

"O con noi o contro di noi": Anti-Individualism and Allegiance to the Regime

The Fascist regime demanded complete loyalty as it sought to undertake these endeavors for the nation, which could apparently only fail if they were undermined by those working against it. The mandate for allegiance was encapsulated in the slogan, "O con noi o contro di noi," "Either with us or against us."

In all facets of Fascist society, the emphasis was placed on unity. This emphasis was represented in numerous ways in *Balilla,* such as a strip in which Lio attends school and interacts with his sympathetic but clearly not-yet fascistized teacher, Lieto Core (Light Heart), whom Lio often ends up having to correct. In one 1927 issue, Core begins to lecture the students on the various divisions and regions of Italy in a manner reminiscent of both the geographical features of earlier *Balilla* periodicals and of Edmondo De Amicis's *Cuore* (to which his name is likely a reference). Core's approach to nationalism embodies that of Liberal Italy, according to which all regions of Italy are celebrated as both unique and equally Italian.[88] However, the respect for regional differences prompted in the earlier years of the regime is rejected here, as the teacher is interrupted by a flustered Lio who rushes to the front of the room, stands on a desk and blows his trumpet to announce, "True and good Italians do without divisions because only in UNITY is there true greatness!"[89] His proclamation is met with Fascist salutes from his classmates and a handshake from his teacher. The strip stressed unity while hinting at the concern that teachers brought up in Liberal Italy were not up to the task of educating the new Fascist youth.

Lio's story expresses the Fascist concern for unity and allegiance in other ways as well. Returning to the series on the Battle for Grain, the victory of Lio and his friends against the creatures infesting the grain was not without consequences. The leader of Ozio and these creatures, branded *il Male* (Evil), sends his followers to capture Lio, who is then taken to the "City of Bad Children." The latter is a clear reference to the *Paese dei balocchi* of *Pinocchio* (Land of Toys or Pleasure Island, as it is known in the 1940 Disney adaptation), where poorly behaved children are offered a haven to do as they please,

---

88. In De Amicis's tale of a young boy's school year, Italy's regional differences are presented as something to be praised, such as at a prize-giving ceremony during which boys from all of the regions of Italy are brought on stage to celebrate their differences and their common Italian identity. Similarly, each month includes a story which highlights the virtues of Italians (usually concerning hard work, sacrifice, or patriotism during the war of unification) and focuses on a protagonist from a different area.

89. *Il Balilla,* n. 24 (16 June 1927), 1.

allegedly without consequence. It is assumed that Lio will quickly fall into sin.[90] Lio finds himself in a chaotic society in which people refuse to work, drink their wages, and have succumbed to selfishness and anger. A nearby crowd is enraptured by a speaker preaching words of hate as he holds a puppet labeled *TERRORE ROSSO* (Red Terror) being inflated by a Russian hidden offstage. Lio promptly pops the puppet, for which he is placed in the prison for good children.[91]

Lio escapes from prison after a few daydream-filled stories in which an incarcerated Lio's love of his country is reinvigorated. He rushes to the piazza to speak, but he is met by opposition from a crowd holding signs demanding *diritti* (rights) while he speaks only of *dovere* (duty).[92] Frustrated by the crowd's refusal to listen, Lio calls on the posts of a nearby field which then spring to life and, in brutal Fascist fashion, proceed to beat those in the crowd, and so, "by magic they come to their senses, and everyone listens to Lio." The crowd adopts Lio's ways and now hold signs reading "Long live order" and "Long live duty."[93]

The use of coercion to enforce conformity to Fascist ideals was not viewed as antithetical to liberty, as understood by the Fascist ideologue Giovanni Gentile. According to Gentile, the notion of private interests outside of or in conflict with those of the nation was a liberal fallacy, as there existed a true will common to all members of the community. It is his notion of a universal will that makes it possible to conceive of one man as channeling the will of a nation, as Mussolini, the Duce, claimed to do for Italians. The totalitarian state, then, did not swallow the individual, crushing liberty, but claimed to *enhance* the liberty of the individual by creating the opportunity for the achievement of a people's true will. Since the government knew the true will, the use of coercion to "fix" the will of individuals that did not conform to the national will was deemed justified. Gentile argued that the popular consent necessary for a government to function "may be spontaneous or it may be procured by coercion."[94]

Rubino's tale of Lio in the "City of Bad Children" captures Gentile's philosophy well. A quintessential Fascist tale of struggle, national devotion, and personal sacrifice framed the Battle for Grain primarily as a battle against

90. *Il Balilla,* n. 40 (6 October 1927), 1.

91. *Il Balilla,* n. 41 (13 October 1927), 1; and *Il Balilla,* n. 42 (20 October 1927), 1.

92. *Il Balilla,* n. 51 (15 December 1927), 1.

93. *Il Balilla,* n. 50 (8 December 1927), 1.

94. Gentile, *Genesis and Structure of Society,* 84, 123. Mussolini's support for these ideas can be seen in numerous speeches in which he emphasized that one's duty to the nation came before individual rights. Mussolini, "Siamo tutti servitori della nazione," 147–48; and Mussolini, "Libertà e civilità," 381.

people's unwillingness to work. In the story, however, this idleness was not innate to Italians, but something foreign, instilled by strange creatures who want the grain for themselves. Soviet agents stoke misguided talk of rights. Ultimately, Lio channeled the Fascist glorification of violence and managed to not only force those in the crowd to obey his will but also to "come to their senses." Brutal acts of Fascist repression are therefore normalized and validated for their youthful readers as a means to correct and purify Italians.

Conclusion

Inspired by *Corriere dei Piccoli*'s use of comics during the Great War, the Fascist Party adopted its own form of comics to reach Italian youth almost from the outset of the regime. It is important to note that some of *Balilla*'s earliest comics artists, Rubino and Mussino, came from *Corriere dei Piccoli,* highlighting its influence on *Balilla* and further demonstrating that those creating *Corrierino* shared many values with the new regime. That *Corriere dei Piccoli* was seen as already spreading values aligned with those of the Fascist regime does much to explain why the less radical periodical was allowed to fascistize gradually. Despite the periodical's clear Fascist orientation after 1925, *Corriere della Sera* was not turned into a simple propaganda outlet due to its foreign readership; this same room to maneuver seems to have been extended to its supplemental periodical, *Corriere dei Piccoli.* No criticism of the regime was permitted, as demonstrated by the removal of the Albertini brothers as the directors of *Corriere della Sera.* Yet *Corriere dei Piccoli* was not forced to radically alter its content throughout the 1920s.

Rather than understanding *Corriere dei Piccoli*'s more gradual fascistization as resistance to Fascism, analysis of the content of *Corrierino* highlights the themes in the periodical as embodying the transition from Liberal to Fascist Italy. The periodical expressed many ideas which were not explicitly or innately tied to Fascism, but the traditional, nationalist, and imperialist values depicted in its stories were close enough to support the regime as it was still being established. This is not to say that *Corriere dei Piccoli* was essentially Fascist, but rather that the liberal-conservative nationalist orientation of its director and writers was not innately antithetical to the regime but had numerous points of overlap. This overlap only deepened over the course of the dictatorship, as *Corrierino* adopted more Fascist stories in the 1930s once a new director replaced Spaventa Filippi. When Rubino returned to *Corriere dei Piccoli,* he brought his Balilla, Lio, with him, creating the series "Lio e Dado" to sing the praises of the regime. The series ran between 1933 and 1934 and focused on state campaigns such as those aimed at land reclamation and the elimination of malaria.[95] But the periodical fulfilled a purpose in the regime's cultural project even before this fascistization.

If *Corriere dei Piccoli* smoothed the transition from Liberal to Fascist Italy, linking liberal and conservative nationalists to Fascism, *Balilla* overtly aimed to condition Italian youth. Comics in *Balilla* depicted a stronger emphasis on what were considered core components of the nature of Fascism: solidarity with the regime, duty over rights, and commitment. In the pages of the periodical of the Fascist youth, Fascism's self-conception as a political religion is clear, as is its appropriation of iconography familiar to Italians, particularly that of the Catholic Church. The directors and writers of *Balilla* were thus able to convey Fascism's "with us or against us" mentality, normalize the use of violence, and project ideals of gender and racial norms, all of which attempted to condition Italian youths to the norms of the new regime.

The Fascist state's preoccupation with fascistizing Italian youth to provide a foundation for the future is well established. The attention granted comics and children's periodicals, as well as the messages conveyed within them, demonstrate that comics were recognized as an essential instrument in the struggle to win over and inculcate children with its values.

95. *Corriere dei Piccoli*, n. 28 (9 July 1933), 36.

CHAPTER 2

The Comics Craze of the 1930s

How American Comics Became Anti-Fascist

New illustrated children's periodicals emerged in the 1930s that were visibly different from *Balilla* and *Corriere dei Piccoli.* Predominantly comprised of comics, these weeklies were more akin to American comic books than to Italian periodicals, with their mixture of comics and short stories. The new magazines filled newsstands with American characters such as Flash Gordon and Mickey Mouse (retitled "Topolino," or "little mouse").

Most significantly, these periodicals shed the explicit educational agendas of their predecessors. *Corriere dei Piccoli,* though obviously a commercial endeavor, aimed to reform the working class through spreading middle-class mores.[1] The Fascist youth periodical, *Balilla,* likewise reflected the Fascist obsession with indoctrinating future generations. The weeklies that emerged in the early and mid-1930s, by contrast, were strictly commercial undertakings; as the first issue of *Topolino* boldly stated, "This magazine promises nothing more than to let you spend a few happy moments, to amuse you a little, and has not the slightest idea of being a know-it-all."[2] The abandonment of pedagogical aims represented a shift in how children's periodicals interacted with the rise of youth leisure time. What was once filled with educational though enjoyable stories was now dominated by entertainment. Parents,

1. Carli, "Paola Marzòla Lombroso," 35–38; Fava, "Il progetto culturale," 70–71; and Carabba, *Corrierino, Corrierona,* 17, 18.

2. *Topolino,* n. 1 (31 December 1932), 2, quoted in Meda, *Stelle e strips,* 30–31.

educators, and officials watched with concern as children flocked to the new magazines. A wave of backlash was unleashed alongside this comics craze with which the state would ultimately contend.

By the mid-1930s, some Italian intellectuals were calling for Italianization or even the ban of series from the US. Yet the calls for state intervention did not receive much attention until Italo-American relations deteriorated following the Italian invasion of Ethiopia and the Fascist government's alliance with Germany. A conference on children's literature (discussed in chapter 4) was then held in 1938 to determine the Fascist characteristics of youth literature. The conference coincided with restrictions on comics from the US that were only fully enforced with the entrance of the United States into World War II.

The attacks on comics from the US, rather than simply being indications of Fascism's hostility toward American culture, reflect debates *within* Fascist circles over the question of what a Fascist society should look like. Fascism was an "impossibly heterogenous coalition" of a range of ideological positions that harbored different visions for modern society.[3] Comics from the US introduced Italian youths to an alternative model for society, and some themes were perceived as problematic to many Fascists and non-Fascists alike. Yet other values overlapped with, reinforced, or were nonthreatening to Fascism.[4] American series often featured rather generic storylines that could be framed in Fascist terms, and the adventure stories full of men of action and heroic deeds overlapped with Fascist ideas of the new man and modern society. Analysis of the comics coming from the US identifies some themes which *resonated* with many Fascist officials. Moreover, the periodicals were profitable and were published through the support of the regime. These commonalities, the commercial ties, and the positive relations between the US and Italy initially outweighed the values deemed problematic, which the regime was content to overlook or moderate.

The Fascist state's understanding of and reaction to popular American comics evolved due to the changing priorities of the regime and a developing international situation. It was only as Italo-American relations worsened that the alternative model of modernity offered by the US became increasingly perceived as anti-Fascist, transforming the US from a potential fellow traveler into an adversary. This policy shift demonstrates that these cultural imports were not wholly full of themes counter to the regime. Umberto Eco's argument that American comics spread disillusionment with the regime should thus be approached with caution. So, too, should the framing of the interaction

3. Ben-Ghiat, *Fascist Modernities*, 17.

4. Beynet, "'L'image fasciste de l'Amérique,'" 48, 49; and Bonsaver, *America in Italian Culture*, 208, 222, 223.

between comics from the US and Fascism purely in terms of conflict, as it has been depicted by Fabio Gadducci, Leonardo Gori, and Sergio Lama in their impressive work on American comics in Italy during this era.[5]

The move to suppress American comics in 1938 should therefore not be interpreted as a delayed response or as evidence that the regime had previously neglected these periodicals—a common perspective in Italian studies.[6] Guido Bonsaver has recently adopted this viewpoint as well, arguing, "The huge success of American cartoons between 1932 and 1938 caught the regime sensors with their guard down."[7] The presence in Italy of American cultural products must be positioned within the wider cultural policies of the regime. The state had adopted a policy of relative openness into the early and mid-1930s, with the intention of attracting Italian intellectuals and gaining support abroad. The openness to cultural imports helped meet popular demand for new media, enriched Italian firms handling distribution, and presented a more open image of the regime in contrast to Nazi Germany and the Soviet Union.[8]

This openness did not prevent criticism arising from a variety of Italian intellectual circles, who viewed American society as too materialist and detached from traditions.[9] Anti-Americanism was not shared by all Fascists, however, nor was it unique to Fascist intellectuals. Hostility to Americanism (defined by the *Enciclopedia Italiana* in 1929 as "admiration . . . for American ideas or things . . . in contrast to European cultural traditions") was a sentiment shared by many non-Fascist and even *anti*-Fascist intellectuals.[10] Furthermore, the reaction against American comics extended beyond Italy, suggesting that the issue is broader, related to tensions regarding cultural imports at a time of the reshaping of nationalist identity. The debates within Italy regarding comics paralleled those in other countries, such as France, and

5. Eco, *La misteriosa fiamma*, 147, 234–35; and Gadducci et al., *Eccetto Topolino*.

6. This is most clear in Carabba's study, as he takes 1938 as its starting point. Carabba, *Il fascismo a fumetti*, 7, 41. More recently, Juri Meda and the authors of *Eccetto Topolino* also adopt this perspective. Meda argues that the Fascist regime was concerned with American comics from the start, which makes the 1938 ban appear delayed and yet inevitable. Gadducci et al., by contrast, discuss how American comics were largely left undisturbed until 1938. Meda, *Stelle e strips*, 9; and Gadducci et al., *Eccetto Topolino*, 119, 126.

7. Bonsaver, *America in Italian Culture*, 291.

8. Ben-Ghiat, *Fascist Modernities*, 33–34; Cannistraro, *La fabbrica del consenso*, 7, 69–70; and Stone, *Patron State*, 7.

9. Adamson, "Culture of Italian Fascism," 560–71; Cavallo, *Soffici e Malaparte*, 67–70; Seroni, "Fascismo e riviste letterarie italiane," 548–49; Bossaglia, "Iconography of the Italian Novecento," 52, 54; and Coradeschi, "Novecento Style in Italy," 82.

10. Gentile, "Impending Modernity," 8–9.

echoed assertions of national cinema in opposition to Hollywood in Germany and France during this period.

At the same time, many Fascists—including the Duce himself—had a *positive* image of the US during the early 1930s.[11] The US was seen as dynamic and modern, and Franklin Roosevelt was approvingly perceived as a dictator whose New Deal followed the model of Mussolini's state. The Fascist model attracted the attention and sympathy of many leading American businessmen and powerful brokers of American culture, including key suppliers of comics to Italy, Walt Disney and William Randolph Hearst. Hearst in particular supported Mussolini, even publishing articles by the Duce.[12]

As intellectuals across Europe grappled with the crisis of modernity, some believed European traditions needed protection from the hedonism of the US, while others saw inspiration in the dynamism of American society; this was true within Italy as well.[13] American society and culture became a "mirror" against which European, Italian, and Fascist intellectuals could position themselves, interpreting the version of modernity seen in the US alternatively as a goal, a rival, or a cautionary tale.[14]

This chapter explores the reactions to American comics in the 1930s by focusing on the magazines published by the Nerbini and Mondadori publishing houses, *L'Avventuroso* and *Topolino*, respectively. Both periodicals were immensely popular in Italy and featured major American series, and their owners had deep but complicated relationships with the regime. The first section discusses the launch of these periodicals and details the backlash from critics. The main concern was that American comics created communities of fans centered on entertainment rather than structuring leisure and association around politics, detracting from one's Fascist identity. The second section identifies the themes depicted within American comics that provoked concern from Italian intellectuals—the representations of female sexuality, violence, and the lack of Italian heroes. It also highlights points of commonality. The final section demonstrates the significance of the Italian invasion of Ethiopia in launching the process through which American cultural products became marked as anti-Fascist.

---

11. Bonsaver, *America in Italian Culture*, 209–11, 222; and Gentile, "Impending Modernity," 14, 17.

12. Diggins, *Mussolini and Fascism*, 6, 48, 145–47; and Bonsaver, *America in Italian Culture*, 208, 290.

13. Adamson, "Culture of Italian Fascism," 564; and Gentile, "Impending Modernity," 15.

14. Bonsaver, *America in Italian Culture*, 219, 223.

A New Kind of Periodical: *Jumbo, L'Avventuroso,* and *Topolino*

The new comics magazines that debuted in the 1930s represented a divergence from earlier illustrated periodicals for children, as the emerging comics were primarily profit-seeking enterprises. While the publishers of *Corriere dei Piccoli* or *Balilla* were not unconcerned with profits, they had pedagogical agendas. The original idea for the *Corriere dei Piccoli* came from Paola Lombroso Carrara, daughter of the criminologist and phrenologist Cesare Lombroso, and was primarily inspired by a desire to reform the "crude" lower classes.[15]

Comics in the United States, by contrast, had realized their commercial potential long before the 1930s. Marketing firms seized upon popular characters such as Yellow Kid and Buster Brown to sell products ranging from gum to songbooks. Ultimately, the comic *book* emerged in the late 1920s out of this same entrepreneurial spirit, as comic strips were collected and reprinted on a single page in a tabloid-sized book devoted specifically to the medium.[16]

The success of comics in the United States—and in Britain—must have caught the attention of publishers in Italy, as Italian weeklies with translations of first British and then American comics flooded newsstands. The first such publication was *Jumbo*, launched 17 December 1932. Published by Società Anonima Editrice Vecchi, *Jumbo* was the first magazine to publish true *fumetti,* in the sense that the comics contained speech bubbles—the puffs of smoke, of "fumo," from which the term "fumetto" is derived. The periodical mostly printed British comics, with a small number of Italian originals and comics from the US. Vecchi attempted to assure parents that the stories were educational and moral, but the periodical was marketed primarily to children as "a *giornalino* for you!"[17] Its rapid success (it reached a circulation of 300,000) inspired rivals.[18]

Arguably more significant was *Topolino,* which entered circulation weeks after the launch of *Jumbo* on 31 December 1932. Although comic strips of Mickey Mouse had been published in various American newspapers since 1928 (and in Italian papers since 1930), no journal had yet been based around the character.[19] According to Mario Nerbini, he and his father, Giuseppe,

15. Carabba, *Corrierino, Corrierona,* 18; and Carli, "Paola Marzòla Lombroso," 35–38.

16. Gordon, *Comic Strips and Consumer Culture,* 32, 37, 129–30; and Wright, *Comic Book Nation,* 3.

17. *Jumbo,* n. 1 (17 December 1932), 2; and Gori, "Lucio."

18. Meda, *Stelle e strips,* 28.

19. Grove, *Comics in French,* 127–28. The first Disney magazine published in the US, *Mickey Mouse Magazine,* came in 1935. The French periodical *Le Journal de Mickey* also predated it, first published in October 1934. Mickey's first appearance in Italy, though, was a comic strip printed in *L'Illustrazione del Popolo,* n. 13 (30 March 1930).

were unaware of the strips but were inspired by the success of Disney's short animated films.[20] In any case, Nerbini illustrators Giove Toppi and Antonio Burattini designed strips inspired by Mickey Mouse for the new periodical. Guglielmo Emanuel of King Features Syndicate (KFS) held the rights for the distribution of Mickey Mouse in Italy at the time and immediately contacted the Nerbini firm regarding their failure to obtain the permissions to reproduce the Disney character. *Topolino* became *Il Giornale di Topo Lino,* renamed after the creator Giove Toppi, nicknamed Lino il Topo, and Mickey was modified into a more humanoid mouse.

Fortunately for Nerbini and Italian children, Nerbini and Emanuel quickly reached an agreement, and the original Disney material created by Floyd Gottfredson appeared in *Topolino* beginning on 28 January 1933. That the periodical maintained the speech bubbles from the original American comic strips was significant, as they rendered the accompanying captions redundant. A new graphic language was taking root in Italy, competing with the traditional use of captions still prevalent in *Balilla* and *Corriere dei Piccoli.*[21]

The contract between KFS and Nerbini was significant for another reason: it created a commercial relationship between Mario Nerbini and Emanuel, who proved a tireless advocate of American comics. Following the success of *Topolino,* Emanuel convinced Nerbini to purchase the rights to publish "Tim Tyler's Luck," Italianized as "Cino e Franco," as well as "Flash Gordon" and "Secret Agent X-9." The content of these series was deemed inappropriate for a magazine aimed at young children, though, and so a new adventure-based periodical for older adolescents was created, giving rise to *L'Avventuroso* (*The Adventurous One*). The outcome is not wholly surprising given that the comics were originally aimed at older audiences when published in the United States, and so even this move by Nerbini to target older adolescents did not eliminate all concerns.[22]

With *L'Avventuroso,* Nerbini created the first magazine devoted to adventure comics. Most of these comics were from the US, originally printed in newspapers owned by William Randolph Hearst. The nameplate captured the content of the periodical well through its caricatured depiction of the magazine's villains in the left corner: a Native American, a Chinese man, and an African man. The adoption of American racial categories—easily identifiable to the periodical's adolescent Italian audience—attests to the diffusion of racial tropes through literature and film; it also speaks to the overlap in racial constructions in the US and in Italy. The weekly quickly achieved popularity,

20. Gadducci et al., *Eccetto Topolino,* 93–97; Listri, *Il mondo di Nerbini,* 48; and Meda, *Stelle e strips,* 30.

21. Gadducci et al., *Eccetto Topolino,* 31–34.

22. Bonsaver, *America in Italian Culture,* 287–88.

inspiring numerous competitors, such as Vecchi's *Audace* which printed "Tarzan" and "Brick Bradford."

From Nerbini to Mondadori: The Sale of *Topolino* and the Patronage of the State

Nerbini's dominance of the Italian comics market was short-lived. While *L'Avventuroso* remained the single most popular comic during the Fascist era, reaching at its peak a circulation of 500,000 copies per week, Nerbini did not retain *Topolino* long.[23] For whatever reason, Walt Disney determined that Nerbini was not the right publisher for Disney in Italy, and in 1934 Robert Bennet Martin, director of Disney Enterprises-Italy, contacted Arnoldo Mondadori to discuss Disney books in Italy. A contract was signed on 25 April 1935 concerning illustrated books and the periodical *I Tre Porcellini* (The Three Little Pigs). Mondadori, however, wanted *Topolino*, and Guglielmo Emanuel was soon tapped to mediate the transition of *Topolino* from Nerbini to Mondadori. Mondadori reimbursed Nerbini 300,000 lire for the costs to launch the periodical and an additional 50,000 lire for his stockpile of unpublished Disney material.[24] The relationship between Disney and Mondadori only continued to strengthen, as Walt Disney, his brother Roy, and their wives visited Italy during a European tour in 1935 and spent a day in July at Mondadori's villa on Lake Como.[25]

Nerbini claimed to be untroubled by the sale, which he said allowed him to focus exclusively on the more popular *L'Avventuroso.* Ezio Ferraro has suggested, though, that the sale was more complicated than documents convey, claiming even a payoff to Mussolini. No evidence exists for such a payoff, but, as Leonardo Gori speculates, it is not difficult to imagine that Nerbini turned to his political connections to help him keep his periodical. Mondadori, however, proved to have better-placed friends.[26] Mondadori has largely been acknowledged to be the unofficial publisher of the regime, a position that became ever more entrenched as Mondadori became responsible in 1939

---

23. Becciu, *Il fumetto in Italia,* 85; and Gadducci et al., *Eccetto Topolino,* 91.

24. Contratto tra la Walt Disney Enterprises e la Casa editrice G. Nerbini per la rinuncia da parte di Nerbini dello sfruttamento della figura di "Topolino," Firenze, 25 June 1935. Gadducci et al., *Eccetto Topolino,* 93–94; and Listri, *Il mondo di Nerbini,* 52–53.

25. Bonsaver, *America in Italian Culture,* 290.

26. Gori, "L'editore Mondadori."

for the publication of a number of PNF periodicals, including *Balilla.*[27] Even before then, Mondadori benefitted from numerous contracts to print books of the Fascist *gerarchi.*[28] Already in 1928, the state owed millions of lire to Mondadori for the publications of state documents and school texts, a debt which Mondadori leveraged to have Mussolini personally intervene on his behalf to "encourage" the deferment of debts his firm owed to the Casa di Risparmio di Milano.[29] State support for the Casa Editrice Mondadori was further demonstrated in 1933 by the loan of 4.5 million lire to the firm by the Istituto per la Riconstruzione Industriale, funds which may have enabled the purchase of *Topolino.*[30]

As Mondadori received support from the regime, Nerbini seemed to be losing favor. Despite the compensation offered Nerbini for the loss of *Topolino,* Mario Nerbini was increasingly marginalized from Mussolini, as the Duce repeatedly refused his requests to meet. The rejections predated the sale of *Topolino,* with Mussolini's office ignoring Nerbini as he reached out regarding attacks on *L'Avventuroso* for publishing "adventure stories not adapted for children."[31]

When speculating as to the reasons for Nerbini's apparent fall from grace, one is left to wonder if the root of the issue was Mario Nerbini's association with the earlier, more radical phase of the Fascist movement. Evidence of this appears already in 1927, when the publishing firm, still headed by Mario Nerbini's father, printed anticlerical statements in the periodical *420,* leading to a controversy with members of the clergy. Believing that their Fascist credentials made them unassailable, Giuseppe and Mario were instead rebuked by Private Secretary of the Duce, Alessandro Chiavolini, who told them to

27. Mondadori's biographer, Enrico Decleva, discusses Mondadori's expressions of support for the regime and his connections to it, but speculates that it may have been more to benefit his firm than out of ideological commitments. Decleva, *Arnoldo Mondadori,* 73–75. However, others have stressed the affinity between Mondadori and Fascism. Bonsaver, *Censorship and Literature,* 43; Forgacs and Gundle, *Mass Culture and Italian Society,* 120; and Re, "Women and Censorship," 65.

28. Fabre, *Il censore e l'editore,* 16; and Di Tizio, *D'Annunzio e Mondadori,* 8, 17, 41.

29. Arnoldo Mondadori, Lettera al Prefetto di Bolzano, 26 October 1928, ACS / SPD, CO 1922–43, Serie numerica, B. 1177 / F. 509568-I, Casa Editrice Mondadori, 1, 2; Arnoldo Mondadori, Lettera a Mussolini, 31 October 1928, ACS / SPD, CO 1922–43, Serie numerica, B. 1177 / F. 509568-I, Casa Editrice Mondadori, 3; and Benito Mussolini, Il Capo del Governo a Giuseppe de Capitani, November 1928, ACS / SPD, CO 1922–43, Serie numerica, B. 1177, f. 509568-I.

30. Gadducci et al., *Eccetto Topolino,* 124.

31. *L'Avventuroso,* n. 31 (12 May 1935), 1. "Grande settimanale per tutti." See Meda, *Stelle e strips,* 78.

be "better in tune with the severe discipline of the Party and its intent."[32] At a time when the regime was seeking a concordat with the Vatican, anticlerical publications were problematic. It is likely that Nerbini's association with the radicalism of *squadrismo* proved a liability and that Mussolini's treatment of Mario was emblematic of the regime's shunting of many *squadristi* during the 1920s and early 1930s, when the government adopted a more conservative guise. Mondadori—a Fascist more aligned with traditional forms of nationalism and conservatism—likely appeared more suited to this image.

In any event, Mondadori lost little time in turning *Topolino* into a gem of his publishing house, bringing in Antonio Rubino as the *direttore responsabile.* Slowly, Rubino began to imbue the periodical with a more Italian feel. Even in 1936, once the magazine was firmly under Mondadori's direction, *Topolino* almost exclusively printed American stories, including "Audax," based on the Westerns of Zane Grey, "Tim e Tom" ("Tim Tyler's Luck," creating confusion for readers of Nerbini's "Cino e Franco"), and, of course, "Topolino." Only the final page featured an original Italian story by Guido Moroni-Celsi. The effort to introduce Italian elements was furthered by the efforts of Cesare Zavattini and Federico Pedrocchi, who came on board as the editorial and artistic directors, respectively. Zavattini, who would later make his name as a prominent neorealist screenwriter, and Pedrocchi, the "father of Italian comics," transformed the comics in *Topolino.* In time, Italian serialized novels and comics were added to the periodical, "gli Amici di Topolino" (the Friends of Mickey) fostered correspondence with fans, and the periodical embraced more Italian elements than Nerbini's competing magazines. The persistence of Disney content, though, meant that it remained a hybrid in comparison to more national periodicals such as *Balilla.*

American Comics and the Seeds of a New Type of Consumerism

Many series in *L'Avventuroso* were not warmly received by parents, teachers, or intellectuals, who perceived them as detached from reality and full of dangerous models of female sexuality. Beyond the content, the popularity of comics was particularly distressing to educators, who already lamented the state of education in Italy and feared that this visually dominate media would detract from literacy skills. Writing in 1936, Gherardo Ugolini denounced these comics as lacking any educational or aesthetic value, instead reflecting merely

32. Alessandro Chiavolini, Lettera a Giuseppe Nerbini, 28 December 1927, ACS / SPD, CO 1922–1943, Serie numerica, B. 287, f. 15225-2.5, 2.

"commercially speculative goals."[33] Many obstacles to reading already existed in a country with high rates of illiteracy (about 21 percent in 1931), limited schooling, and the high costs of books, which only decreased in the late 1940s when publishers such as Mondadori began printing mass-produced affordable editions. The lack of affordable books was compounded by the lack of public libraries, with only 13 percent of the 9,148 communes having libraries in 1927.[34]

Low literacy rates did not impede the enjoyment of comics. Gundle and Forgacs note that, based on interviews from the time, "reading" comics and magazines may have often meant "*looking at* these materials, alone or with another person, without being able to understand the written text competently."[35] Comics, as a partially visual media, would have lent themselves to this form of reading and been more accessible to those with limited literacy skills. The relative unavailability of books and the fact that many rural schools ended after third grade—after which students were expected to attend vocational schools but were more likely to start to work—means that comics likely did not detract from literacy skills, as alternatives and reading education were limited.[36] Nonetheless, the popularity of comics and concerns over literacy skills compounded complaints regarding their shedding of an educational orientation.

But this was precisely why Italian youth embraced them. As Giuseppe Trevisani recalls in his account of *L'Avventuroso*'s launch, Italian youth embraced the story because, "All of their journals, all their books, had until that moment been uplifting and instructive. All the content in this rag [*giornalaccio*] finally did not teach anything. . . . It was just fun." Trevisani continues, stating that "Flash Gordon" created a generation gap between the "friends of Gordon" born in 1923 and 1924 (including himself), and those only a few years older.[37] Giorgio Salvucci recalls a similar rallying around *Jumbo*:

> Jum . . . bo, Jum . . . bo, we . . . want . . . Jum . . . bo!!! This cry from a group of boys aged 7 to 10 punctuated the ears of an impatient newsagent back in 1933 (as a protest of the delayed arrival of the weekly issue) along with the attack on the basket of the delivery cyclist—finally arrived—to grab a copy

33. Gherardo Ugolini, "I giornali per ragazzi," in *Scuola italiana moderna* (10 January 1936), 128, quoted in Meda, *Stelle e strips*, 96.

34. Forgacs and Gundle, *Mass Culture and Italian Society*, 36–38; and Talbot, *Censorship in Fascist Italy*, 50.

35. Forgacs and Gundle, *Mass Culture and Italian Society*, 37.

36. McLean, *Mussolini's Children*, 34; and Koon, *Believe, Obey, Fight*, 49.

37. Gori, "Con *L'Avventuroso*."

of the longed-for newspaper, are lived facts establishing the importance of the advent of *Jumbo.*[38]

The generation gap highlighted by Trevisani should not be interpreted at this early stage as a growth of anti-Fascism; disillusionment with the regime did not spread until sometime during World War II, even among those born in 1923 and 1924 who came of age reading "Flash Gordon."[39] Nonetheless, the anecdotes are significant in that they highlight the popularity of these periodicals, which quickly exceeded the circulation of *Balilla* and *Corriere dei Piccoli* despite being similarly priced for only half the number of pages.

Increasingly, the 1930s are recognized as a time during which Italians began to experience mass culture and consumerism. Much of this encounter with mass culture centered on cinema, which accounted for 65 percent of Italian expenditures on entertainment in 1936.[40] Comics contributed to the spread of consumer culture as well. At typically twenty or thirty *centesimi* per copy, illustrated magazines for children were more affordable than tickets at first-run cinemas, which cost about 1.5 lire in 1931.[41] As a result of the relatively affordable price, 1.5 million children's periodicals and comics magazines were sold each week by 1938. Their reach was extended further as the periodicals circulated among friends, allowing those who could not afford them to still read comics. As many as three million read comics each week by 1938 due to this circulation.[42]

Much of this new mass culture came from abroad. Eighty percent of films screened in Italy in the 1920s were imported, most from the US. In 1938, American films represented 63 percent of films screened.[43] The dominance of American culture was in part due to the simple fact that Hollywood and the American comics industry produced material on an unrivaled scale, literally flooding foreign markets as the Motion Picture Producers and Distributors of America actively cultivated the Italian market. Additionally, Hollywood was

38. Gori, "Lucio."

39. Dagnino, *Faith and Fascism,* 189, 198; and Duggan, *Fascist Voices,* xx, 8–9. Ben-Ghiat cautions against reading the generation gap as indicating that the youth was resistant to Fascism. Rather, Ben-Ghiat emphasizes a multitude of "Fascist *modernities.*" Ben-Ghiat, *Fascist Modernities,* 98.

40. Forgacs and Gundle, *Mass Culture and Italian Society,* 5, 28.

41. Forgacs and Gundle, *Mass Culture and Italian Society,* 45. For comparison, the price of a bus ticket averaged 0.5 lire during the 1930s, and the price of a kg of bread averaged 2.06 lire throughout the decade. Scarpellini, *Material Nation,* 110–11.

42. Ferris, "Parents, Children and the Fascist State," 185. Three to four readers have been estimated per copy circulated. Becciu, *Il fumetto in Italia*; and Forgacs and Gundle, *Mass Culture and Italian Society,* 28, 36, 38.

43. Ricci, *Cinema and Fascism,* 61, 68.

considered to have the best techniques, and comics from the US likewise utilized state-of-the-art printing methods. On top of these factors, the US had long been a destination for Italian emigrants, and those who returned or sent word back did much to create an imaginary America as a land of promise in the minds of Italians.[44] American comics benefited from these same trends and reached wide popularity. With these comics and films from the United States came new styles, new notions of acceptable sexual behavior, and words borrowed from foreign cultures. These emerging identities drove wedges between the generations and, potentially, between the youth and the regime.[45]

Just as significant was the democratic ethos of this brand of consumerism. Victoria De Grazia speaks of "consumer democracy" in the US, defined as "a peculiarly American notion of democracy, that which comes from having habits in common," essentially representing a form of voluntary association and identity based on one's entertainment preferences, not politics.[46] It was not necessarily that the stories in the comics themselves supported democratic and egalitarian ideas, but rather that, under the banner of best practices, Mondadori and Nerbini were marketing the periodicals as pure entertainment and making personal tastes the deciding factor in the sale and production of children's periodicals, overriding concerns of civic and moral education, or national interests.

Although this form of consumerism was only developing, tensions between these consumer-based identities and politics emerged. In Italy, political parties often had corresponding leisure organizations, and recreational activities were presumed to match one's political association (a trend that was not unique to the Fascist Party but certainly reached new heights under it). Additionally, the formation of identity and associations centered on consumer goods, periodicals, and comic book heroes contrasted with Catholic notions of solidarity and communities based on traditional ties and obligations.[47] Association around entertainment comics threatened to remove political oversight from leisure. At the conference on children's literature that would occur in 1938, the publisher Enrico Vallecchi lamented that this mode of consumerism encouraged the prioritization of profits over the "spiritual formation of the child."[48]

Indeed, American comics outpaced the Fascist periodical, *Balilla*. The Fascist youth magazine's impressive circulation of 250,000 copies a week is

---

44. Baily, *Immigrants*, 9, 25.

45. Forgacs and Gundle, *Mass Culture and Italian Society*, 2; and Cavazza, *Consumi e politica*, 15.

46. De Grazia, *Irresistible Empire*, 2–3.

47. De Grazia, *Irresistible Empire*, 8, 64.

48. Vallecchi, "Aspetti commerciali del libro da ragazzi," 43–45.

misleading, as the periodical's distribution in schools was unofficially mandated.[49] By contrast, *Jumbo* and *L'Avventuroso* had an average weekly circulation of 300,000.[50] That children tended to prefer *L'Avventuroso, Topolino,* and *Corriere dei Piccoli* over *Balilla* is not surprising; the over-the-top propaganda on Fascist events and campaigns likely appeared tedious to most children.

Nonetheless, the increasing popularity of rivals in comparison to *Balilla* leaves little wonder as to the concern expressed by Fascist officials and intellectuals regarding what the new generation of Italians was reading. Competition drew away from Fascist indoctrination, conflicting with the Fascist ideal of the ethical state. Propagated by Fascist ideologue Giovanni Gentile, the ethical state was to guide the individual to their self-realization and alignment with the national will, as decided by Mussolini, of course.[51] American comics attracting more enthusiastic readers than those sanctioned by the Fascist Party threatened political indoctrination. While the suppression of American comics was far from inevitable, it is also not surprising.

Why, then, did the regime tolerate American films and comics to circulate to such an extent and for so long? The Fascist state's initial cultural policy was one of relative openness, at least when compared to Nazi Germany and the Soviet Union. While opposition was repressed and cultural production was monitored, the regime sought to coopt and attract major institutions and figures. It is significant that the two publishers largely responsible for printing American comics—Nerbini and Mondadori—were longtime supporters of the regime whose ties to Fascism predated Mussolini's appointment as prime minister. Their firms profited from their relationship with the comics industry in the US, not only economically but also in their ability to gradually develop Italian artists within their periodicals as well.

The case of American films in Italy is illustrative here. Mussolini's son, Vittorio, was passionate about cinema and developed ties with Hollywood to learn how to best create a film industry in Italy, Cinecittà, with the ultimate aim to better create Fascist cinema.[52] The toleration of American cultural products in Italy offered opportunities for the enrichment and improvement of Italian industries (though Italian preference for the American products eventually became a problem). Moreover, the regime initially preferred to moderate the content that was considered threatening through methods of dubbing and editing. Theaters also "framed" American movies by playing Fascist newsreels at the start of each screening, in an attempt to imbue the more

49. Carabba, *Il fascismo a fumetti,* 21; and Meda, *Stelle e strips,* 102.

50. Meda, *Stelle e strips,* 28; and Becciu, *Il fumetto in Italia,* 85.

51. Gentile, *Genesis and Structure of Society,* 84, 123.

52. De Grazia, *Irresistible Empire,* 317.

generic Hollywood stories with Fascist values. Like comics, it was only in 1938 that state policies meaningfully curtailed the number of films coming in from America.[53]

Finally, it must be remembered that Italo-American relations were quite positive at the time that comics from the United States appeared in the early 1930s. Many leading American businessmen had a favorable attitude toward Fascist Italy, including American media mogul William Randolph Hearst.[54] Hearst first met Mussolini in 1931 on a trip to Rome and came away with a positive impression. Hearst's politics were complex. Staunchly opposed to monarchies, he nonetheless advocated the need for an executive president to save the US from the Great Depression. He had once supported female suffrage and the eight-hour workday, but he was vehemently opposed to communism's professed egalitarianism and attacks on private property. Fascism, which he considered a reaction to communism, piqued his interests.[55]

Recognizing the attention the Duce captured among the American public, Hearst reached a deal with Mussolini to publish his articles in the Hearst Group papers beginning in 1928.[56] The articles ranged from events in Italy to the dictator's thoughts on the world, though many of them were ghost-written by Margherita Sarfatti, the writer and journalist who was the long-time mistress of Mussolini and influenced his intellectual theories greatly.[57] Despite Hearst's frequent frustration with the often late and esoteric writings he received, Hearst proved willing to accommodate the dictator. In 1928, for instance, he assured Mussolini he would address any concern the regime had regarding the Hearst Group correspondent, Valerio Pignatelli, recalling that "two correspondents of the Hearst newspapers—one in Rome and the other in Paris—were fired because they had shown themselves to be hostile to the politics of Your Excellence," referring to Mussolini.[58] Hearst's support for Mussolini continued until the US entered World War II.

Walt Disney likewise displayed sympathy for the regime and a willingness to work with individuals from Fascist Italy. On the part of Italy, hostility toward American cinema was typically not aimed at Disney, with the exception of *Pinocchio,* condemned as Americanizing an Italian classic.[59] Disney

---

53. Ricci, *Cinema and Fascism,* 5, 7, 63, 68, 71, 142.

54. Diggins, *Mussolini and Fascism,* 145–47.

55. Mugridge, *View from Xanadu,* 30–31, 78; and Procter, *William Randolph Hearst,* 194.

56. Gadducci et al., *Eccetto Topolino,* 120; and Procter, *William Randolph Hearst,* 165.

57. Cannistraro and Sullivan, *Margherita Sarfatti,* 402–5, 407–9.

58. Washington DC Regia Ambasciata d'Italia, Italian Ambassador a Mussolini, 5 November 1928, ACS / MCP, Reports 1926–1944, B. 5, f. 46, William Randolph Hearst.

59. Goggi, "Arnoldo Mondadori," 61–65.

films were credited as works of art in both Italy and Nazi Germany, and Disney was the only Hollywood studio to receive Leni Riefenstahl in 1938. Goebbels even gifted a collection of Disney films to Hitler for Christmas in 1937, which the latter apparently cherished.[60] The anti-Axis propaganda films produced by Disney during World War II did not mean that Disney had always been opposed to the fascist powers.

Early Criticisms of Comics

Many early criticisms lobbed at American comics focused on the fact that they highlighted *American* society rather than Italian. Writing in 1937, Giorgio Vecchietti argued that rather than a ban of American comics, "Gordon must change from American to Italian, from blond to dark, keeping intact his attributes as a bold and proud man." Vecchietti believed Italian authors could draw inspiration from American comics but replace the "cowboys, gangsters, and the Romans of Hollywood" with Italian explorers and soldiers, "the adventures of our colonies and Legionaries in Africa."[61] In the Catholic press, Mario Alfredo Alla similarly decried the lack of Italian heroes. American comics, according to Alla, were "harmful for the education of our Fascist youth" due to "anti-Catholic" and "anti-Roman" themes, which meant they were also "anti-Fascist."[62]

Comics from the United States were a clear target for intellectuals who viewed American culture as crude and destabilizing. This perspective was held most notably by members of the Fascist intellectual movements Strapaese (super-country) and Novecento (twentieth century), as well as by the Catholic Church.[63] While each advocated their own vision for Italian society, these various intellectual positions often rejected the materialism of the US and American notions of egalitarianism. Strapaese and Catholic intellectuals tended to advocate traditional lifestyles over the hypermodernity seen in the US. Novecento intellectuals embraced modernity more, but they too juxtaposed the "high" European culture to the crudeness of American culture.

60. Giesen and Storm, *Animation under the Swastika,* 24; and Ross, *Media,* 315.

61. Giorgio Vecchietti, "*L'Avventuroso,*" in *L'Orto,* n. 4 (April 1937), 3, quoted in Meda, *Stelle e strips,* 50–51.

62. Maria Alfredo Alla, "Religione e morale nei giornali per ragazzi," in *Giovanissima,* n. 9–10 (29 January 1938), 5, quoted in Meda, *Stelle e strips,* 57–58.

63. Adamson, "Culture of Italian Fascism," 560–71; Cavallo, *Soffici e Malaparte,* 67–70; Seroni, "Fascismo e riviste letterarie italiane," 548–49; Bossaglia, "Iconography of the Italian Novecento," 52, 54; and Coradeschi, "Novecento Style in Italy," 82.

The criticism targeting comics from the United States was not limited to Italy. Similar debates occurred in the 1930s in France, Australia, and Canada, with more countries to follow in the decades following World War II. The United States was not immune from such controversy either—albeit without sentiments of anti-Americanism—as educators and religious groups such as the Catholic Church's National Organization for Decent Literature campaigned against harmful material for children (it was not until the 1950s, though, that the debate reached its peak in the US). In each of these countries, educators, politicians, literary critics, and intellectuals expressed concerns that the visual component of comics had a negative impact on literacy, that the crude stories debased culture and kept readers from "real" literature, and that the violence depicted within them desensitized children and fostered antisocial behavior. Outside the United States, intellectuals and artists additionally argued that the popularity of US comics stole jobs from local artists and undermined national culture.

Interestingly, these concerns were voiced by conservatives, ultranationalists, religious organizations, and communists alike. The peculiar alliance formed in anti-comics campaigns—conjoining communists, clergy, and conservatives—highlights that there is something more to this debate than a simple clash between Fascism and American culture, a situation more complex than innately anti-Fascist American comics that would inevitably be censored by the regime. It is worth examining the factors that shaped Italian anti-*americanismo* during the 1930s. France in the 1930s provides a useful comparison.

Discussing the rise of anti-Americanism in France, Joel Vessels argues that such hostilities toward the "invasion" of a foreign culture must be contextualized in the struggles to shape a cohesive French national identity. During the interwar era, French culture was divided between more nationalist, authoritarian trends, on the one hand, and defenders of the Republic, on the other. After World War II, French society struggled to move on from the legacies of Vichy and Nazi occupation as the Fourth Republic gained its footing. Vessels emphasizes that the attacks on American comics in both the 1930s and 1940s should be understood as occurring within a nation attempting to create a sense of a shared national identity.[64]

A brief perusal of the commonalities within the international comics debate shows how concerns regarding comics arose in democracies and dictatorships alike (it is important to note that the French debates on comics predated the Vichy regime). Most concerns were based in a sense of nationalism,

64. Vessels, *Drawing France*, 17.

with the goals of protecting local artists and preventing foreign cultural "contamination." However, in each of these cases, concerns over foreign contamination spiked in particular moments, as countries which once welcomed foreign cultural products suddenly became closed off. Typically, these changes were the product of domestic issues and changes in the international landscape. In the case of Fascist Italy, that change came with the Ethiopian War.

Before that point, though, the state's response to comics was limited because of the varied attitudes among intellectuals associated with the regime toward the US and toward cultural policy. There was a consensus on the need for the regeneration of Italian art and on the idea that such art would have mass appeal among the people and mobilize Italians in some sense for the regime. But how this would be best achieved and what Fascist art might look like was heavily debated.

These disagreements no doubt contributed to the relative openness discussed earlier, both in regard to international culture and to the state's refusal to promote any one art movement in Italy. Instead of choosing one, various aesthetics flourished, so long as they were situated within the parameter of Fascist ideas, a policy Roger Griffin refers to as "totalitarian pluralism."[65] These disagreements compounded as numerous competing cultural institutions existed prior to the establishment of the Ministry of Popular Culture in 1937, including those subjected to the head of government (Mussolini), and those subjected to the prefects. This disunity between various cultural industries and theories contributed to publishers' ability to negotiate with the regime, as whatever cultural polices did exist were fragmented, inconsistent, and often contradictory. What was Fascist or anti-Fascist in the realm of culture in the early and mid-1930s was often unclear.

American Comics and Anti-*Americanismo*

It is within this complicated context that the content of American comics must be assessed. As cultural products of the United States, comics reflected American society. The comic strip emerged from new printing technologies combined with changing lifestyles due to modernization and urbanization. Comics arose "as a humor-based response to the problems of representation faced by a society in transition" and out of a society with a large concentration of immigrants in US cities. Comics in the US began as strips in newspapers to

65. Griffin, "Sacred Synthesis," 6.

stimulate circulation; working-class adults were typically the ideal audience, and it was not assumed that they could read English proficiently.[66]

In Italy, the audience for comics was initially assumed to be children, hence the title of the first popular periodical to print a form of comic strips, *Corriere dei Piccoli,* or Courier of the Children. Italian comics artists and publishers had to reconcile American comics with the transitions taking place in Italian society and to reflect the more overtly moralizing tone adopted by publications such as *Corriere dei Piccoli.*[67]

Perhaps "Topolino" was so well received in Italy because it contained both satirical and moralizing tones. Many episodes of "Topolino" saw the little mouse dealing with harmless shenanigans. But these stories of seemingly pure entertainment were nonetheless often spreading values. In one blatantly moralizing story, Topolino comes across an unattended fruit stand and grabs an apple. His conscience reprimands him and reminds him that stealing is wrong. Topolino shamefully says he was only looking and returns the fruit, for which he is rewarded by the vendor with a free apple.[68]

Not all of American comics had such clear-cut morals, though. Most were fantastical stories, with Westerns, science fiction, colonial adventures, and detective comics gaining particular popularity. Many of the colonial adventures shared much with Fascist racial views, and "Flash Gordon" is perhaps more ambiguous than previously thought. Yet while these stories were not full of egalitarianism and democratic values, the violence and often sexualized women led to concerns in Italy over the depiction of indecency and excess.

Depicting Indecency: Female Emancipation, Sexuality, and "Excessive" Violence

Attitudes toward American women were emblematic of these concerns. Gender norms in the United States and Italy were both undergoing changes, although each retained aspects of so-called traditional roles for women. New Deal policies and rhetoric in the United States, for instance, called upon women to stay at home so men would find jobs during the Great Depression.[69] Yet women also had more opportunities in social, educational, and

66. Gordon, *Comic Strips and Consumer Culture,* 6, 20.

67. Meda, *Stelle e strips,* 19.

68. *Topolino supplemento* (15 March 1934), 1.

69. Melosh, *Engendering Culture,* 1, 81; Allen, *Forgotten Men and Fallen Women,* 22, 98, 99, 101.

economic life in the US, and women's fashion, behavior, and lifestyles were changing. These changes were present in American comics and film.

Despite appearing predominantly in support roles and as love interests for the male protagonists in the comics (thereby upholding gender norms such as deference to men and being presented as more passive), these women were perceived as emancipated and disruptive to social norms by their presence in action comics and their often-sexualized depiction. They were thus labeled in Fascist Italy as the *donna-crisi,* the antithesis of Fascism's depiction of them, which emphasized the virtue of the nationalist and rural woman, who was a mother above all else.[70]

The American comics flooding Italian newsstands were problematic due to their depiction of these quasi-emancipated women. Most problematic was the depiction of seminude women in "Flash Gordon," which graced the cover of *L'Avventuroso* from its launch on 14 October 1934. Gordon, already in the third issue of his interplanetary adventure, encountered such women when he leapt into a balcony to escape from the evil dictator, Ming. To make matters worse, this was no social outcast but the princess, who objected to her father's orders to kill Gordon and helped him to escape, suggesting she was one of those "wicked" emancipated, independent-minded women in addition to being half-dressed.[71]

The regime had already demonstrated its hostility toward the representation of female sexuality in a crackdown of the novel *Sambadù, amore negro* by Mura (pseudonym of Maria Volpi Nannipieri), published in April 1934. The book told of a mixed-race love story, which was not unheard of in Italy but was increasingly labeled problematic by the regime as it prepared for the invasion of Ethiopia and heightened contact between Italians and the people in its colonies. What particularly troubled officials was that the love story was between an African man and an Italian woman, as women in Fascist ideology were to be defenders of Italian racial purity. That the woman *chooses* a relationship with an African man threatened Fascist efforts to control female sexuality because the story portrays a woman with her own sexual desires.[72] The cover displayed these desires by featuring an Italian woman in the arms of Sambadù, earning the illustrator a warning from the police. The scandal ultimately accelerated plans that Mussolini may have already had in mind to centralize cultural production in Italy, no doubt partly inspired by Nazi

70. De Grazia, *How Fascism Ruled Women,* 73; and Willson, *Women in Twentieth-Century Italy,* 61, 70, 85.

71. *L'Avventuroso,* n. 3 (28 October 1934), 1.

72. The Minister of Italian Africa singled out relations between African men and white women in 1940 as "counter to all our moral principles." Ipsen, *Dictating Demography,* 189.

Germany's Reich Ministry of Public Enlightenment and Propaganda. Henceforth, the Ufficio stampa (Press Office) had to approve publications prior to their circulation.[73]

A decree from 3 April 1934 extended these regulations to comics by obliging publishers to send a copy to the Press Office, the Ministry of Interior, and the Prefect's office. The formation of the Sottosegretario per la Stampa e la Propaganda in September 1934 centralized the process under Mussolini's son-in-law Galeazzo Ciano. Its transformation into a full-fledged ministry in June 1935 further strengthened the regime's mechanisms of censorship, as the Ministry assumed the power in October 1935 to sequester any publication.[74]

Mondadori's response in 1936 was to cancel several series from KFS. Nerbini, by contrast, began to modify American stories. Leonardo Gori has shown that in 1935 Nerbini began to have additional clothing drawn on the imported panels deemed indecent.[75] Figure 2.1 shows one of the earliest—and most pronounced—cases of self-censorship through modifying American comics. The additional clothing provided in the Italian version still does not completely cover the women, and the clothing remains skin-tight. The women remained sexualized, sharing more in appearance with Hollywood starlets than with the Fascist ideal of women prepared to bear children. They were the very embodiment of the *donne-crisi* rejected by the regime.[76] Moreover, that the King of the Hawk Men plans to add *another* wife to his harem hardly upholds the traditional notion of marriage (and complicates the idea that these women are emancipated). It is significant, though, that the king is initially a villain, and thus these negative behaviors are associated with Gordon's enemies.

It seems that Nerbini was less concerned that "Flash Gordon" might spread democratic ideas in his challenge to Emperor Ming's rule (discussed more below). Instead, indecency and "emancipated" women warranted the most attention. While the preoccupation with the image of women may perhaps suggest that Nerbini was more within the orbit of traditional Catholic conservatism, much of the censorship during the Fascist period aligned with and was even given religious or moral reasonings, such as the defense of the traditional family.[77] Insofar as women were to participate in Italian civil soci-

73. Cannistraro, *La fabbrica del consenso*, 102–7; and Bonsaver, *Censorship and Literature*, 99.

74. Cannistraro, *La fabbrica del consenso*, 102, 130; and Gadducci et al., *Eccetto Topolino*, 118–19.

75. Gori, "Mandrake il Mago."

76. Talbot, *Censorship in Fascist Italy*, 122; and De Grazia, *How Fascism Ruled Women*, 73.

77. Forgacs and Gundle, *Mass Culture and Italian Society*, 221.

FIGURE 2.1. Nerbini illustrators modified the panel to further clothe the women of King Vultan's harem. The top panel is the original version of "Flash Gordon" published in the US in 1934, while the panel below is that modified for publication in *L'Avventuroso* in 1935. Image comparison from Gori, "Mandrake il Mago."

ety, it was to support the regime and learn its ideology so as to better raise their children to be proper Fascists.[78] They were not meant to be embarking on adventures, even if in secondary roles.

While salacious depictions of women were the primary targets in the moderation of American comics, "excessive violence" was also curbed. This is perhaps best illustrated in an issue of "Mandrake," another popular series in *L'Avventuroso*, originally created by Lee Falk. Often, Mandrake—a magician

78. De Grazia, *How Fascism Ruled Women*, 2, 71, 158, 250; and Willson, *Women in Twentieth-Century Italy*, 70.

who fought criminals by using disappearing tricks, hypnotism, and levitation—is enlisted to investigate mysteries. The series flirted with the horror genre at times, such as in "Mandrake, l'uomo del mistero" (Mandrake, Man of Mystery), in which he finds himself in a dungeon where a lion is chained up and human bones litter the floor. The floor in the original American panels featured mountains of bones, leading to the reduction of the human bones scattered on the floor of the lion's den in the Italian version. The story also includes another "nefarious" modern woman, taking part in dangerous adventures and wearing trousers in place of a skirt or dress. Clearly, America was a corrupting influence on Italian girls.

Images of Africa and Racial Hierarchies

To whatever extent American comics may have disrupted gender norms, they tended to reinforce racial hierarchies. Mandrake, for instance, has a loyal servant who is Black and appears in a cheetah-print sleeveless shirt and wears a fez. Despite his claims that American comics countered Fascist propaganda, Umberto Eco notes that Mandrake's servant, Lotar, appears less like a sidekick or partner and more "as a bodyguard and faithful slave."[79] Many American comics imported into Italy shared similar themes, particularly ones which were centered on adventures in the so-called exotic continent of Africa, whose people were represented as constantly in need of white leadership.

Even the lovable Mickey Mouse embarked on his own African adventures, as in the story "Topolino agente della polizia segreto" (Topolino, Agent of the Secret Police). The comic begins with Topolino selling arms to Yussùf, leader of a tribe in North Africa who plans to use the weapons to become king of the desert by pushing out the foreigners and killing all who oppose him, even his countrymen. Yussùf, who is drawn as human rather than an animal like Topolino and his friends, further illustrates his devious character by betraying Topolino to steal the money with which he purchased the weapons. But this does not bother Topolino, who is a secret agent working for the (French) Foreign Legion, switching into his uniform to set out to stop Yussùf. Lt. Topolino and his men compel Yussùf's forces to surrender, as the weapons Topolino sold turn out to be defective and his forces surround those of Yussùf. True, Topolino has a helpful Indigenous ally in Abid Abu, but he only appears

79. Eco, *La misteriosa fiamma,* 238.

briefly in the series, making the traitorous and cruel Yussùf the main representation of North African people in this comic.[80]

Topolino offers a complex case of American culture in Italy, captured well by this story. Erich Fromm connects Mickey Mouse, a small and relatively powerless creature constantly in danger of being swallowed, to the individual, helpless in the face of the daunting structures of modern life. His continued survival gives readers hope, even if he never escapes the situation entirely. This message can be anti-Fascist, with the individual threatened by overbearing Fascists. And yet, it is not necessarily so, as Mickey Mouse could also represent Italy broadly, a proletariat nation victimized by more powerful countries, a narrative professed by Mussolini himself. Fromm interprets the character neutrally, viewing him as representing modern society and the individual's desire for an "escape from freedom" into either conformity or submission to a dictator, suggesting that many readers of Mickey Mouse may have found some appeal in the notion that Mussolini would relieve them of the burdens of modern life.[81] Furthermore, Mickey Mouse relayed a principle that resonated with Fascist ideals: life is a struggle for survival.

The secret agent story does not exactly fit this mold, as Topolino is an active agent inserting himself into danger. Nonetheless, Topolino, outnumbered by Yussùf's forces, uses his cunning to defeat his foes. On the one hand, it is the tale of a European colonial power winning out over the tribal leader who seeks to drive them out, casting Yussùf as an evil, cruel leader against whom the Europeans are *protecting* the Indigenous people. On the other hand, Topolino is working with the French Foreign Legion, clearly identified by his reference to the "legione straniera" and his French uniform. The story thus clearly promotes imperialism and the supposed benefits of European rule of African people, aligning with the rhetoric regarding Italy's new empire, which had been announced only a few months before the appearance of this story. And yet, the story captured what was perhaps the most significant issue with American comics: the heroes were not Italian but American and, in this case, *French*. The Fascist official and intellectual must have asked, where is the glorification of the Italian forces in East Africa?

Similar colonial tropes appear in Nerbini's *Giornale di Cino e Franco*. "Cino e Franco" originally appeared in Nerbini's *Topolino*, but the duo later received their own periodical. Cino and Franco were two Italianized youths who encountered many adventures in an unspecified region of Africa. The tendency to not specify a location more exact than Africa or at best northern

---

80. "Topolino agente della polizia segreta" runs in *Topolino* from n. 202 (8 November 1936) to n. 206 (6 December 1936).

81. Fromm, *Escape from Freedom*, 131.

or eastern Africa fostered an image of a homogenous continent lacking in distinctions. This unspecified Africa of the comics is othered by the focus on exotic animals and primitive people, sometimes at the same time, as when the duo rode elephants into battle against bandits on ostriches.[82]

The Italian imagining of Africa was shaped partially by Hollywood.[83] It seems comics played a part too, projecting an imaginary Africa ripe for adventure and colonization. Stories of white men protecting African people, animals, and white settlers from those who might wish to do them harm—stories such as "Topolino, Agent of the Secret Police" and the adventures of Cino and Franco—reinforced colonial tropes and the image of Africa as a site of European adventure, exploration, and leadership, while nonetheless failing to emphasize the *Italian* role in this endeavor.

"Flash Gordon": Anti-Fascist Rebel, or Strong Man Defending Western Civilization?

Many scholars have framed American comics imported into Italy as Trojan horses spreading anti-Fascist values, vaccinating Italian youth against the propaganda of the regime. "Flash Gordon" is often pointed to as evidence.[84] Singled out specifically is a series called "Re Gordon contro Ming" (King Gordon against Ming), in which the galactic hero begins in earnest his fight against the tyrannical Emperor Ming of the planet Mongo. In his novel *La misteriosa fiamma della regina Loana,* Umberto Eco ruminates on the Fascist era through a protagonist who suffers from memory loss and uses old newspapers, books, and magazines to piece together his childhood, including his understanding of and relation to the Fascist era. In doing so, Eco stresses the importance of Gordon's struggle against despotism as a counter to stories which promoted unswerving service to the Duce. Eco frames Gordon as distinct from the Fascist heroes who obey Mussolini, arguing that, when reading of his struggle against tyranny, "I could not but recognize in his [Ming's] features those also of the dictator at home."[85]

However, it is important to note that sources supporting this interpretation of "Flash Gordon" were published *after* the fall of the Fascist regime.

---

82. *Topolino,* n. 202 (8 November 1936), 8.

83. Ben-Ghiat, *Italian Fascism's Empire Cinema,* xiii.

84. Giulio C. Cuccolini, "L'americanismo de L'Avventuroso & co," in *Dick Fulmine: L'avventura e le avventure di un eroe italiano,* ed. Gianni Bono and Leonardo Gori (Motta: Milano, 1997), 28, quoted in Meda, *Stelle e strips,* 94.

85. Eco, *La misteriosa fiamma,* 235.

Natasha Chang is correct in their analysis of *La misteriosa fiamma* when arguing that Eco's interpretation is heavily shaped by his contemporary era, situating it within the narrative that Italy was a nation of anti-Fascists somehow immune to the charms of Fascism. As Chang explains, Eco's view is perhaps more about *forgetting* the Fascist era than uncovering and analyzing it.[86] Fascist indoctrination and education greatly diminished the critical thinking skills of the generation that grew up reading this series, and this generation lacked political alternatives to the regime, making the formation of these connections less likely.[87] Eco himself acknowledges—in the sentence following the one quoted above—that this interpretation of Gordon as anti-Fascist was formed in hindsight, stating, "I certainly could say [that Gordon fought Fascism] now, rereading, not then."[88] It is probable that many making these arguments are adding new meaning to the stories of their youth, as new experiences offered new lenses of interpretation. The image in Italy of Gordon as an anti-Fascist was likely formed during and after World War II, no doubt shaped by the ban on American comics and the increasing difficulty of dismissing the brutality of the Fascist regime.

But Fascist Italy was likely not the inspiration for the author, Alex Raymond, as he created Ming. The tyrannical emperor seems better situated within the hostility toward Asian countries associated with the so-called Yellow Peril hysteria of the first half of the twentieth century, hostilities often expressed by Raymond's employer, Hearst.[89] Ming—named likely in reference to the Ming Dynasty of China—was depicted with yellow skin and sported the "Fu Manchu" mustache, as in the panel in figure 2.2. This mustache came to symbolize wickedness in Western culture through the character Dr. Fu Manchu in the 1930 film, *Mask of Fu Manchu,* based on the works of Sax Rohmer. Rohmer's work both captured and helped spread anti-Chinese sentiments through references to the "unemotional cruelty of the Chinese," who apparently are unphased by assassinations or even infanticide, attesting to the threat embodied by Dr. Fu Manchu, who seeks the destruction of Western civilization.[90] It is likely that the cruelty exhibited by Emperor Ming draws on Rohmer's work and expresses a fear of Asian expansionism more than anti-Fascism.

86. Chang, "Forgetting Fascism," 108, 110, 112.

87. Koon, *Believe, Obey, Fight,* 232, 234.

88. Eco, *La misteriosa fiamma,* 235.

89. Hearst, "Democratic Party," 461; Hearst, "Exclusion of Asiatics." For comparison, see Mugridge, *View from Xanadu,* 139; and Procter, *William Randolph Hearst,* 211.

90. Rhomber, *Insidious Dr. Fu Manchu,* 140; Mayer, *Serial Fu Manchu,* 37, 44, 52, 60; and Chang, "Forgetting Fascism," 118.

FIGURE 2.2. Ming has captured Flash Gordon's love interest, Dale Arden, and plans to make her his wife. Note that Ming and his subordinate are depicted as yellow with slanted eyes and that Ming has a Fu Manchu mustache. "La distruzione del mondo!!," *L'Avventuroso,* n. 5 (11 November 1934), 1.

The Asian nature of Ming's empire would have been recognizable to Italians, as indicated by Eco's comment that Ming is marked as "diabolically Asiatic" by his name and features.[91] Rohmer's books were translated into Italian beginning in 1931, and European works had long depicted the Chinese as uniquely cruel.[92] Yellow Peril in Europe was rooted in centuries-old fears of a Mongolian invasion and was further ignited by the 1901 European colonial concessions in China following the Boxer Rebellion. Many Italian journalists and politicians racialized the Chinese people and represented them as backward and cruel.[93] Anti-Asian sentiments again grew in the mid-1930s as Japanese public opinion initially condemned the Italian invasion of Ethiopia. Mussolini promoted the image that Asians represented an existential threat to Europeans against which Italy must act.[94] Emilio Bodrero, a member of the Chamber of Deputies, advocated Western cooperation against the rising threat in Asia.[95]

---

91. Eco, *La misteriosa fiamma,* 234.

92. Mayer, *Serial Fu Manchu,* 21. On the European representation of the supposed cruelty of people from China, see Iannuzzi, "Cruel Imagination," 199–204.

93. Liu, "Italian Literary and Cinematic Representations," 223–24, 226.

94. Clarke, *Alliance of the Colored Peoples,* 110, 114, 120; and Hofmann, *Fascist Effect,* 91–94.

95. Gentile, "Impending Modernity," 18.

"Flash Gordon" and the nefarious Ming must be placed within this American and European anti-Asian hysteria. Although Gordon struggled against authoritarianism, Ming's name, caricatured skin color, and Fu Manchu mustache all marked him as Asian. The authoritarian empire, then, is not that of the Fascist regime, but draws on Western orientalism to create a stereotyped form of barbaric "Asiatic despotism," against which the white "strong man" Gordon battles.

Indeed, Gordon, Mandrake, and even "Topolino" were all men of action akin to those advocated by the regime. Mandrake (a scrawny magician) and a little mouse may seem odd embodiments of strong men, but they, like Gordon, prove capable, crafty protagonists who never retreat from a challenge, act fast, and resolve all situations to their advantage. The strong man basis of the (super)hero comic does not automatically make them Fascist. The political messages within these comics are defined by the systems which they defend.[96] However, unlike the superhero comics of the late 1930s and early 1940s, in which Wonder Woman, Captain America, and the like defend American democracy, The Phantom and Mandrake defend individuals, uphold private property, and solve murders—nothing Fascist but nothing *adverse* to Fascist values either. In discussing Mandrake and "Secret Agent X-9," Eco acknowledges this by stating that they "do not seem particularly revolutionary."[97] As for Gordon, although he is embroiled in a war against tyranny, the sort of society he is fighting *for* is unspecified. He is not a warrior for American democracy. He is, arguably, a white savior, who arrives on a technologically more advanced planet and nonetheless leads the challenge to the rule of the yellow-skinned Ming.

Subversive, anti-Fascist readings of "Flash Gordon" are one possible interpretation. The fantastical ultramodern cities of the future in "Flash Gordon" ran counter to the Strapaese movement's notion of *italianità* based in traditions. The rampant technology and the emancipated, sexualized women also chaffed with the morals of the Catholic Church and seemed to confirm its image of the US as a Sodom of vice. However, many of these negative values were associated with Ming's empire, against which Gordon fought. The predominant theme remained heroic masculinity fighting against autocratic and Asian rule, drawing on racial ideas of the people of Asia. It seems unlikely that Italian readers would interpret "Flash Gordon" as anti-Fascist unless they were already encountering anti-Fascist sentiments.

96. Arnaudo, *Myth of the Superhero*, 71, 73.

97. Eco, *La misteriosa fiamma*, 238.

The Ethiopian War as a Turning Point

While some of the content detailed above clashed with Fascist sentiments, much did not or was at least ambiguous. The change in Italian cultural policies which resulted in restrictions targeting American comics in the late 1930s are best explained when situated within the shifting international context due to the Ethiopian War. Many educators had lamented the lack of educational content in comics or denounced them as crude literature, but American comics and culture broadly were only branded as anti-Fascist following the deterioration of Italo-American relations following the Italian invasion of Ethiopia. There were exceptions, such as members of the Strapaese movement who rejected *any* artifacts of the American way of life, but these intellectual circles had little hold on the regime in the early and mid-1930s. Mussolini remained open to the US, and the policies of state cultural institutes reflected this openness, whatever individuals may have felt about American comics.

Mussolini's attitude changed by 1937.[98] In response to the Italian invasion of Ethiopia in 1935, President Roosevelt invoked the 1935 Neutrality Act to deny the sale of US arms to Italy. His administration did not implement a formal embargo but declared that the US government would not protect American trade with Italy and called for a moral embargo by American companies to not send war-related materials.[99] Roosevelt feared Italy's actions in Ethiopia threatened world peace, a concern exacerbated by Italy's subsequent involvement in the Spanish Civil War. From that point on, Roosevelt became critical of the Fascist totalitarianism and made it clear in his 1936 State of the Union address that he favored the democratic powers of Europe and the containment of fascism in Germany and Italy.[100] Roosevelt's criticism of Fascist Italy soured the Duce's opinion of the man he once considered a like-minded dictator.

Mussolini nonetheless remained open to limited cultural exchanges with the US, even approving a venture by his son, Vittorio, to coordinate a joint project with a Hollywood studio in 1937. However, it was not just Roosevelt's opinion of Mussolini that changed, but much of US public opinion, and Vittorio found Hollywood to no longer be inviting. Many studios closed their doors to him as his erstwhile collaborators bowed to mounting pressure to break ties with representatives of Fascist Italy. Perhaps this personal humiliation was the final straw for Mussolini, or perhaps the incident merely drove home to the Duce that public opinion in the US had turned against his

98. Gentile, "Impending Modernity," 17.
99. Schmitz, *The Sailor*, 54.
100. McCulloch, "FDR as Founding Father," 225–26.

regime.[101] In either case, Mussolini adopted in 1937 the anti-American viewpoint of many Italian intellectuals, denouncing the United States as "a country of N*****s and Jews."[102]

The Ethiopian War stimulated changes within the regime and Fascist ideology as well. The 1938 *leggi razziali,* for instance, radicalized Fascist racial theories, codifying anti-Semitism and racial hierarchies and resulting in the expulsion of Jewish Italians from the PNF and the military. The law prevented "Arian Italians" from marrying Jewish or African people. The reasons for these changes are debated and varied, but the influx of white settlers into Italian East Africa certainly prompted a sense that relations between Italians and Indigenous people living in the colonies must be policed.[103]

In part, the radicalization of Fascist ideology and policy was driven by the increasing entanglement between Nazi Germany and Fascist Italy, as Mussolini moved further away from the democratic powers that he believed had hypocritically rebuked Italy's invasion of Ethiopia. The deepening of ties with Nazi Germany further deteriorated those with the United States, prompting the Italian ambassador to the US to note in February 1937 that in the event of a conflict between the democratic and fascist powers, the US would undoubtedly side with the democratic ones, even if that included the Soviet Union.[104] As Italy was losing support abroad, the regime shifted toward autarchy, and the image of Italy as a nation gloriously standing alone began to appear in the pages of *Il Balilla.*

The transformation in 1937 of the regime's cultural institution into the Ministero per la Cultura Popolare (Ministry of Popular Culture, MCP) resulted from this radicalization of Fascist policy. The new minister, Dino Alfieri, began to pressure publishers to develop more Italian stories in their periodicals as Mussolini embraced the anti-*americanismo* of intellectuals affiliated with Strapaese, Novecento, and the Vatican. In August, Giovanni Calò, the director of the Centro didattico nazionale di Firenze, called explicitly for state intervention.[105] The stage was set for the 1938 suppression of American

101. Bonsaver, *America in Italian Culture,* 365, 368, 371, 376.

102. Gentile, "Impending Modernity," 23.

103. Ben-Ghiat, *Italian Fascism's Empire Cinema,* 170; and Livingston, *Fascists and the Jews,* 13.

104. Correspondente dell'Ambasiata d'Italia, "Contegno dell'opinione pubblica americana," 4 December 1936, B. 7, F. 78, Reports USA, ACS / MCP, Gabinetto, Reports 1926–1944; Fulvio Suvich, "Stati Uniti—Politica italiana," 4 February 1937, B. 7, F. 78, Reports USA, ACS / MCP, Gabinetto, Reports 1926–1944; Fulvio Suvich, "Atteggiamento dell'opinione pubblica americana nei riguardi dell'Italia," 14 May 1937, B. 7, F. 78, Reports USA, ACS / MCP, Gabinetto, Reports 1926–1944.

105. "Meridiano di Roma" in August 1937, quoted in Meda, *Stelle e strips,* 98.

comics, which briefly resulted in their almost-complete disappearance from Italian comics magazines. But it was only then, after the establishment of official restrictions by the MCP, that American comics truly became anti-Fascist.

Conclusion

Attitudes regarding American society and culture among intellectuals connected to the Fascist regime evolved during the 1930s. Most Fascist intellectuals were likely united in criticizing the perceived emancipation and hypersexualization of women in American comics. The technology and the futuristic settings of many stories also conveyed an image of unchecked modernity that was bound to be rejected in whole by ultratraditionalists, particularly the Strapaese movement. But, as stated in the introduction, Fascism was not a monolithic or static ideology. Rather, it is perhaps more accurate to speak of various Fascisms during the 1930s, which only began to coalesce with the radicalization of the regime after the Ethiopian War, when the parameters of Fascist ideology narrowed.

Before the break in Italo-American relations, it was not clear whether the American model of modernity, itself undergoing changes in the 1930s, would be antithetical to that advocated by the regime. While intellectuals associated with Strapaese and the Vatican rejected the society depicted in American comics, others seemed intrigued, ready to take in part of the American model while modifying or rejecting the rest. Censorship and modifications, then, were preferred as means to moderate American comics. Even so, they lacked Italian heroes and Italian settings.

Above all, it was the new mode of consumerism associated with American comics that troubled the regime, displacing politically and educationally oriented magazines with entertainment comics. But this was not enough to pin American comics as anti-Fascist, yet. The reception and treatment of American comics evolved over time, and the deterioration of Italo-American relations with the Italian invasion of Ethiopia and Italy's alliance with Nazi Germany were the turning points in the process by which American comics gained their anti-Fascist status.

CHAPTER 3

Il Vittorioso

The Church Responds

Before the Fascist state reacted to American comics with its string of decrees and regulations, the Catholic Church responded by launching a comics periodical to compete with those from the US. *Il Vittorioso* (The Victorious), as the magazine was called, is a remarkable chapter in the history of Italian comic books. It is notable for many reasons, not least of all because it brought joy to millions of readers over decades of publication. More than that, it played a significant role in shaping a particularly Italian style of comics, as one of the earliest publications to print only original stories and characters created by Italian artists. Many of these illustrators and writers became major names, such as Benito Jacovitti, who for many became synonymous with *Vitt,* as fans affectionally called it. Gianluigi Bonelli also worked on *Vitt* in the late 1930s before establishing his own publishing house after World War II that would print classics such as *TEX.*[1]

The popularity and influence enjoyed by the periodical from its origin in 1937 until the publication of its last issue in 1966 has led many to discuss its significance beyond the comic book industry. *Vitt* has been praised as "a popular culture enterprise" which helped build a common national language and culture."[2] Others go further: "For thirty years, the pages of the periodical

1. Meda, *Stelle e strips,* 51; Preziosi, *Il Vittorioso,* 115–16; and Vecchio, *L'Italia del Vittorioso,* 11.

2. Marco Tarquinio, forward to *L'Italia del Vittorioso,* 3, 4.

contributed to nourish the widespread culture of our country, giving form and principals to the way in which many young readers see the world and operate in it."[3]

Its founders in Gioventù Italiana di Azione Cattolica (the Italian Youth of Catholic Action, GIAC) had hoped *Il Vittorioso* would become such a periodical, as they intended from the beginning that it would be a vehicle to provide wholesome entertainment that also spread Catholic values. The GIAC leadership rejected what they considered the immorality of popular children's periodicals, particularly those printing comics from the US. The periodical was to be an *all-Italian* rival to American comics. At the same time, *Il Vittorioso* was born out of the conflict between Catholic and Fascist youth organizations. Ironically, despite its rivalry with *Il Balilla, Il Vittorioso* depicted an image of compatibility between Fascism and Catholicism.

The significance of *Il Vittorioso* to its readers and to Italian culture has led to a debate regarding its representation of and relationship to Fascism. Scholars such as Giorgio Rumi and Ernesto Preziosi have downplayed the significance of any themes which overlapped with Fascism, arguing they were concessions made in order to avoid censorship and sequestration.[4] Sabrina Fava similarly asserts the *subversive* nature of the magazine, as producers of *Vitt* incorporated keywords of Fascist rhetoric but shaped them to relay alternative and even oppositional values.[5] *Vitt* thus becomes, as Giorgio Vecchio has called it, a "latent seat of conflict with Fascism."[6]

Not all scholars who have commented on *Il Vittorioso* accept this view. Writing in 1971, Leonardo Becciu emphasized the Fascist undertones present in the periodical, arguing that *Vitt* could not help but be sympathetic to Fascism due to the Catholic Church's official position of collaboration with the regime.[7] Juri Meda has made similar points: cognizant that anti-Fascist Catholics were involved in its printing and thus never reducing it to mere Fascist propaganda, Meda nonetheless concludes the periodical "cannot be in any case considered an expression of Catholic youth anti-Fascism, because—as

3. Editor, "Ai Lettori," Vecchio, *L'Italia del Vittorioso*, 5.

4. Rumi, "Un'occasione di riconoscimento"; Preziosi, *Il Vittorioso*, 79, 156; and Preziosi, "Luigi Gedda e la stampa," 258–64.

5. Fava, "'Il *Vittorioso*,'" 652.

6. Vecchio, *L'Italia del Vittorioso*, 13.

7. Becciu, *Il fumetto in Italia*, 203–5. Around the same time, Carabba described *Vitt* as formed "with high and noble pedagogical pretenses, but grave and clear compromises with the Fascist regime," and presented the *giornalino* as "aligned with the commands of the MCP." Carabba, *Il fascismo a fumetti*, 278.

Becciu argued—in it, 'the fermentations of opposition never appear, even though they were spreading among Catholics.'"[8]

The debate over the nature of *Vitt* under Fascism mirrors the broader debate of the relationship of the Vatican to the Fascist regime. Traditionally, there have been two opposed positions. The first maintains the "irreducible incompatibility" of the two; the second speaks of the relationship in terms of "collusion" and positions the Vatican as the "center of coordination and guidance of the most reactionary forces."[9] More recent studies have emphasized the complexity of the relationship, acknowledging that conservative Catholic circles found much in Fascism that aligned with the objectives of the Church but also highlighting sources of conflict between the two.[10] This fraught relationship was embodied in the Lateran Pacts of 1929.

Adopting this nuanced perspective, I demonstrate that the periodical was entangled with the Fascist project and conveyed close links between Fascism and Catholicism, but that *Vitt* was simultaneously an attempt to compete with the Fascist indoctrination of Italian youth. The focus of the periodical was clearly educational and religious, and it numbered among the Vatican's experiments with mass culture to grow its Christian base. The periodical consequently helped create a foundation for the Church's influence in Italian society after the fall of Fascism.

However, this should not be interpreted as a sign that GIAC was planning for a time after Fascism, or that it was hostile to the regime either openly or in subtly subversive tones. At the same time that GIAC sought to present the Church as an alternative point of reference for Italians, many of the ideas and themes depicted in *Il Vittorioso* were held in common with Fascism. Even when such themes were the result of Fascist enforcement, the authors and editors interpreted Fascist agendas through a Catholic lens. More importantly, whatever hesitancy, debate, and tensions existed behind closed doors, Fascist values incorporated into *Il Vittorioso* presented an image of compatibility and thus offered legitimacy to the regime.

This chapter is primarily interested in *how* GIAC engaged with the rhetoric and realities of Fascism, as the stories presented an image of Italy that

---

8. Meda, *Stelle e strips*, 62.

9. Dalla Torre, "Azione Cattolica e fascismo," 297; and Rossi, *Il manganello e l'aspersorio*, 17–21.

10. Ceci, *Vatican and Mussolini's Italy*, 129, 301; and Kertzer, *Pope and Mussolini*, xxx, 27, 50, 163, 388–89, 405. The nature of this relationship is contested. Ceci and Kertzer speak of an alliance while others, such as Robert A. Ventresca, argue the term "alliance" is inaccurate as it implies "doctrinal-ideological complementarity that did not exist to the extent (or of a kind) that Ceci, Kertzer and others maintain." Ventresca prefers *modus vivendi* to stress accommodation and common interests. Ventresca, "Vatican and Mussolini's Italy," 148, 151.

aligned with the Fascist nationalist and imperialist project. Whether coerced or not, the presence of Fascist themes normalized the regime, fostered a notion of a Catholic "wholesome" Fascism, and linked the mission of Fascism with the Italian nation. So, while the periodical itself represented a source of conflict and competition with the regime, any conflicting views within *Il Vittorioso* represented a site of *contestation* rather than a subversion or a source of opposition; the debate was not framed between two opposing forces, but as a dispute *within* the accepted parameters of the worldview held by Fascists and the authoritarian faction of the Catholic Church. This dispute largely hinged on the meaning and role of Catholicism in Italian society and its empire, but also had implications for the desired attributes of the "new man."

The first section discusses the relationship between the Vatican and the regime, highlighting both their commonalities and the tensions between them. The next section explores the objectives behind the formation of *Il Vittorioso.* The final section analyzes the themes present within issues from the first year of the weekly. It should be noted that this chapter focuses on the adventure stories in *Il Vittorioso,* even though the periodical had a mixture of comics and stories more geared toward children and religious education. However, it is these adventure stories that best demonstrate the sources of entanglement with Fascism, as well as its limitations.

The Tenuous Alliance between the Vatican and the Fascist Regime

The allure of Fascism for the conservative wing of the Vatican centered on the similarity of their structures and priorities. Mussolini ceased anticlerical pronouncements as Fascism transitioned into a formal party and promised to address the concerns long held by the Catholic Church, and the authoritarianism of Fascism aligned with the Vatican's own hierarchical vision for society. The Vatican under Pius X (pope 1903–14) and Pius XI (pope 1922–39) adopted an authoritarian and centralized route toward modernization, despite Pius XI following his predecessor Benedict XV (pope 1914–22) in embracing a degree of mass politics.[11] Shaped by "an ideological and totalizing Catholicism" exacerbated by the Great War, a particularly "militant and intransigent" faction arose within the Vatican and its lay social organizations which extolled the values of heroism, discipline, action, obedience, and leadership.[12] This faction

11. Webster, *Cross and the Fasces,* 78–79.

12. Dagnino, *Faith and Fascism,* 1, 2; and De Giorgi, "La Chiesa totalitaria," 44.

was additionally concerned with internal enemies, which predominantly targeted socialists in the twentieth century and, later, the looming specter of *americanismo.*[13]

Fascists shared these characteristics and concerns, and there were many points of intersection between the authoritarian faction in the Vatican and the Fascist regime: anti-communism, opposition to liberal parliamentarism, a defense of traditional values, and a common vision of a hierarchically structured society. This hierarchical society rejected class struggle, aiming to unify all members of society. While Fascism aimed to achieve this harmony through nationalism and the Vatican through religion, the myth of Italy as a *Catholic nation* bridged their approaches by emphasizing the Catholic foundation of the Italian nation, shaping its traditions, values, and history. Tension remained between Fascism's extreme nationalism—which placed Italy above other nations—and the Church's universalism, as did the state's attempts to *nationalize* Catholicism. This tension was greatly reduced at key moments of Catholic support for the regime, such as with the expansion of the Italian Empire through the invasion of Ethiopia, and what the Vatican viewed as the defense of Catholic Europe in the Spanish Civil War.[14] But, even before these moments, Mussolini successfully cultivated an image of the regime as an ally of the Church against those who threatened its vision for society.[15]

Not all Catholics supported collaboration with the regime. The Church's principles of love, forgiveness, and charity hardly aligned with Fascism. Alongside the authoritarian tendency within the Catholic hierarchy existed a more progressive one open to social and economic reform. Pope Leo XIII (1878–1903) laid out the devotion of the Church to social well-being and development in encyclicals such as his 1901 *Graves de communi re* (while remaining opposed to both liberal democracy and socialism).[16] It was this tradition and Benedict XV's relative openness to mass politics that validated claims by moderate Catholic intellectuals that Fascism and Catholicism were incompatible philosophically.[17]

Claims of the incompatibility of Fascism and Catholicism abounded on both sides. Mussolini himself had originally pronounced anticlerical ideas. Most notable among Catholic critics of the Fascists was perhaps Luigi Sturzo, a leading figure in the Catholic Partito Popolare Italiano (PPI), who rejected

13. De Giorgi, "La Chiesa totalitaria," 43, 46–47.

14. Moro, *Il mito dell'Italia cattolica,* 268, 298.

15. Ceci, *Vatican and Mussolini's Italy,* 65; De Cesaris, "Catholic Church and Italian Fascism," 154–55; and Kertzer, *Pope and Mussolini,* 27.

16. Corrin, *Catholic Intellectuals,* 59.

17. Ceci, *Vatican and Mussolini's Italy,* 67; and Corrin, *Catholic Intellectuals,* 7.

Fascism and was exiled as a result. Sturzo denounced members of the PPI who abandoned the party and joined or indirectly supported the Partito Nazionale Fascista (PNF). But factions in both the Fascist Party and the Catholic Church saw enough commonality that collaboration was possible and enabled the pursual of their own agendas.[18]

The appeal of Fascism to the clergy was in part driven by a shared sense of moral decay and a desire to regenerate Italian society.[19] Their projects for the renewal of society provided an avenue for collaboration, but was just as much a cause of tension: Catholics, for instance, envisioned religion and the Vatican as taking the lead in this national rejuvenation and considered Fascism's totalitarian claims and sacralization of politics as a threat to Catholicism.[20] Even where overlap existed, as in the promotion of large families, the underlying motivations differed.[21]

Despite reservations, Fascism's anti-socialism and hierarchical structure convinced Pius XI and many ecclesiastical hierarchs that a relationship with the regime would further Vatican interests. Mussolini took advantage of the rift between Liberal Italy and the Vatican caused by the process of unification, which stripped the papacy of the Papal States and ended its privileged status in education and civil life. Convinced that the Fascist state could enlist the Church as a pillar of the state, Mussolini promised to restore the authority of the Vatican. To such incentives was also added the violence of the blackshirt squads against Catholic organizations, prompting legitimate fears that opposition would further imperil the authority of the Church. Pius XI withdrew support from the PPI and extended it instead to the PNF, continuing to defend the regime even during the infamous Matteotti crisis.[22]

The ability of the regime and the Vatican to collaborate was enshrined in the Lateran Pact in 1929. The Church finally recognized the unified state of Italy and the loss of the Papal States in return for the acknowledgement of Vatican City as an independent enclave in Rome, an indemnity for its lost territories, and Catholicism named as the religion of Italy. The significance of the Pact varied between Fascists, who thought it would fascistize Catholicism and subordinate the Church to political objectives, and members of the Church

18. Ceci, *Vatican and Mussolini's Italy*, 79–80; Griffin, "'Holy Storm,'" 217, 220; Kertzer, *Pope and Mussolini*, 29; and Pollard, "'Clerical Fascism,'" 433.

19. Dagnino, "Catholic Modernities in Fascist Italy," 330–31; Griffin, "'Holy Storm,'" 222; and Pollard, "'Clerical Fascism,'" 435.

20. Gentile, "New Idols," 162; and De Cesaris, "Catholic Church and Italian Fascism," 159.

21. The Catholic Church viewed the need for a greater number of births in moral terms rather than as a means to increase national strength. Ipsen, *Dictating Demography*, 75–77.

22. Kertzer, *Pope and Mussolini*, 27, 50–51, 74–77; and Webster, *Cross and the Fasces*, 83, 110.

who believed Fascism was undergoing a Catholicization.[23] To the Vatican, the Lateran Pacts turned Italy into a confessional state and safeguarded the Church's independent sphere in Italian society. But, for the regime, the Catholic Church had been successfully enlisted in its mission for society.

As discussed in chapter 1, the regime regularly appropriated religious themes and liturgy to bolster its own authority and prestige. However, despite tensions, there were many who identified as Catholic *and* Fascist, including Mussolini's brother, Arnaldo. Luigi Federzoni, president of the senate and member of the Fascist Grand Council, spoke of Catholicism as *the* basis of Italian nationalism.[24] Whether genuine or manipulative, these acts of appropriation and sites of overlap fostered support for Fascism and amounted to a legitimation of the Fascist state for millions of Italian Catholics.

Behind this public display of collaboration, the different understandings in the nature of the relationship between these institutions laid the foundation for tensions that would remain throughout the dictatorship. An essential site of conflict was the status of Catholic youth groups and the education of young Italians.

Catholic Youth Groups

The organization that would ultimately publish *Il Vittorioso* had its roots in an association founded in 1868 by Count Mario Fani and Count Giovanni Acquaderni. Committed to the defense "of Catholic dogma and morality, of the religious liberty of the Vicar of Christ," La Società della Gioventù Cattolica Italiana (the Society of Catholic Italian Youth, or SGCI) aimed to maintain and expand the authority of the Catholic Church in Italy despite its diminished political power following the unification of Italy.[25] After unification, the Church's influence became *parziale,* shared with that of the state.[26] SGCI aimed to pursue the political and social agenda of the Vatican at a time when the Church abstained from direct participation in Italian political life.

Numerous similar Catholic organizations emerged during the nineteenth century. As a part of his broader moves to unify Catholic organizations, Pius X centralized their administration under Vatican control and aggregated the

23. Gentile, "New Idols," 148, 162; and Moro, *Il mito dell'Italia cattolica,* 140.

24. Moro, *Il mito dell'Italia cattolica,* 30, 103.

25. GIAC, La Società della GCI, 1925, ISACEM / Fondo GIAC / Serie 5, B. 780, Appunti-Articoli sulla storia della SGCI, dal 1925–28, 1.

26. De Giorgi, "La Chiesa totalitaria," 41.

organizations in 1904 as Azione Cattolica.[27] Catholic Action (AC) was tasked with organizing Catholic lay activities aimed at spreading the Church's social mission and remained firmly under the supervision of the Church hierarchy. The SGCI was integrated into this new structure and granted authority over youth organizations. SGCI was reorganized in 1931 as the Gioventù Italiana di Azione Cattolica, with a separate section for boys between ages ten and fifteen called the Aspiranti (the Aspiring).[28] AC was most active under Pius XI, who gained the title of "Il Papa dell'Azione Cattolica."[29]

One of Pius XI's priorities in pursuing the Lateran Pacts was the protection of Catholic youth groups. When the Fascist state disbanded all competing youth groups in 1926 to push Italian youths toward its own organization, the Opera nazionale Balilla (ONB), Catholic youth organizations alone were spared. Ongoing negotiations leading to the Lateran Pacts enabled this exception, but Pius XI was unable to protect all Catholic organizations; the Catholic Boy Scouts engaged in activities claimed by the ONB and was thus dissolved in 1929.[30] Sports events and physical activities were to be exclusive to the ONB. The AC focused its youth initiatives on founding private schools, organizing events and lectures, and growing the Catholic press, including magazines and books.

The Lateran Treaty and the acceptance of Catholic youth groups did not, however, end conflicts between church and state. Article 43 of the Concordat confined such organizations to the "spread and fulfillment of Catholic principles," meaning activities of explicit spiritual and religious nature. Tensions persisted as the overlap of religious and educational activities with political issues led to allegations in the Fascist press that GIAC was intervening in activities reserved for the ONB. Hostilities between Fascist and Catholic student associations escalated to the level of street violence in 1931.[31] Pius XI criticized the violence and the intervention of the Fascist state in Catholic education in his encyclical *Non abbiamo bisogno*, going so far as to denounce statolatry. Mussolini did not wish the conflict to escalate further, and the pope was similarly inclined to reach a compromise and protect the Vatican's recent gains.[32]

---

27. Weber, *Cross and the Fasces*, 13.

28. GIAC, Statuto-Regolamento della Gioventù di Azione Cattolica, 4 November 1932, ISACEM / Fondo GIAC / Serie 5, B. 780, Statuto-regolamento della Gioventù cattolica approvato il 4 novembre 1932, 3–4, 8.

29. Malgeri, "La riforma di Pio X," 23–26; and Moro, "Pio XI," 39, 44.

30. Ponzio, *Shaping the New Man*, 39, 45.

31. Malgeri, *Stato e Chiesa in Italia*, 151, 153; O'Brien, "Italian Youth in Conflict," 630; and Kertzer, *Pope and Mussolini*, 159.

32. Corrin, *Catholic Intellectuals*, 233; and Adamson, "Fascism and Political Religion," 56.

Although a truce was reached, the PNF increasingly stacked the deck in favor of its own youth groups and agendas. Religion was frequently neglected in Balilla groups and only genuinely included about once a year despite the official policy that religious education was to be incorporated. Religious education was likewise deprioritized in schools, often absent entirely, leading to complaints from the clergy. In 1938, many priests lamented that the ONB inhibited not only their participation in the activities of the Balilla, but also the participation of boys in religious services by holding demonstrations on Sundays.[33] GIAC considered other means of reaching Italian youth.

The Formation of *Il Vitt*

The relationship between the Vatican and the Fascist state was characterized by cooperation and conflict. The two shared much in their visions for Italian society and aligned regarding those they deemed enemies. But they were bound to clash over claims to leadership in Italy. As Fascism called for a radically new society and form of politics, the primary goal of the Catholic Church remained "the reconquest of de-Christianized Catholic countries."[34] Luigi Gedda, president of GIAC from 1934 to 1946 and key in founding *Vitt*, was emblematic of this mission, and *Il Vittorioso* was born in the context of the Church as both the ally and the rival of the regime. The periodical was therefore never a straightforward piece of Fascist propaganda.[35]

When adopting the format of a *comics* periodical, GIAC took inspiration from an unlikely source: American comics. Many Catholic intellectuals had numbered themselves among those who condemned comics imported from the US as vehicles for the spread of American values, namely, the valorization of a modernity defined as "a savage capitalism" that privileged individual enrichment over traditional morality.[36] In addition to the dubious messages present in comics, Catholic intellectuals were skeptical of the pedagogical value of an image-dominant medium. As one author lamented (ironically in an ad announcing the illustrated periodical *Il Vittorioso*), the centrality of "illustrated cartoons with few words" was viewed as a "march backward, from words to the *pupazzo* [dummy], from sustained narrative to stuttering;

---

33. Griffin, "'Holy Storm,'" 163–64.

34. De Giorgi, "La Chiesa totalitaria," 45.

35. Fava's understanding of *Il Vittorioso* as something "beyond Italian Fascist propaganda" is accurate in this sense, and her findings that *Vitt* instilled Fascist values with alternative Catholic meanings must be taken seriously. Fava, "'Il *Vittorioso*,'" 653, 662.

36. Meda, *Stelle e strips*, 81.

or should we say from civilization to barbarity?" As the piece continued, however, it became clear that the author was most disturbed that the stories told of "heroes with foreign names."[37] GIAC had decided to make use of this medium that threatened to take Italians "from civilization to barbarity" for wholesome stories centered on Italian characters. Interestingly, GIAC's plan mirrored the suggestions of journalist and Fascist intellectual Giorgio Vecchietti, who advocated Italianizing comics rather than banning them outright.[38]

The Vatican and its lay auxiliary organization had already made use of youth periodicals prior to the advent of comics in Italy. The Aspiranti, for instance, had their own periodical (*L'Aspirante*) starting in 1928, and Pius XI supported "publications that can contribute to the better formation of youth."[39] However, *L'Aspirante* was aimed at existing members of GIAC and concerned the operations of the association, while the organization's other periodical, *Il Giornalino,* targeted children, not older adolescents. The leaders of GIAC—Luigi Gedda in particular—believed the association needed a new periodical to compete with rivals.[40]

The first announcement regarding the launch of *Il Vittorioso* came during a meeting of the Consiglio Superiore della GIAC on 28 June 1936. The periodical was presented as having the potential to "replace the numerous examples of comics, almost all copied from abroad and somewhat questionable from the educational point of view."[41] A newsletter two weeks later promoted *Il Vittorioso* to the Presidents of the Diocese as an illustrated periodical "for all boys" and as a "necessary supplement of the organizational weekly *L'Aspirante* and a powerful weapon of conquest."[42] The magazine was not reserved for members of GIAC, then, but was intended to appeal to *all* Italian youths. Although GIAC took advantage of the Church's networks to distribute *Vitt,* it was also sold at newsstands, and GIAC developed strategies to extend its reach beyond existing Aspiranti.

Framing *Vitt* as a "weapon of conquest" alluded to the ongoing cultural struggle between the Church and the regime to be the dominant educative force for the next generation of Italians. Yet the anxieties held by leaders of

37. "Un quotidiano di Roma si domanda: Che cosa diamo da leggere ai nostri ragazzi? Noi rispondiamo: 'Il *Vittorioso*,'" *Gioventù Nova* XIII, n. 46 (8 December 1936): 41.

38. Meda, *Stelle e strips,* 97.

39. Presidenza Centrale della GIAC, Circolare ai Presidenti Diocesani di 4 luglio 1932, ISACEM / Fondo della GIAC / Serie 3, B. 522 / Circolari 1930–37, GIAC, 1, 4.

40. Vecchio, *L'Italia del Vittorioso,* 11.

41. Consiglio superiore della GIAC, Riassunto del Consiglio Superiore, 28 giugno 1936, ISACEM / Fondo della GIAC / Serie 3, B. 522, Circolari, 1935–36, 1.

42. Presidenza Centrale della GIAC, Circolare della GIAC, 10 luglio 1936, ISACEM / Fondo della GIAC / Serie 3, B. 522 / Circolari, 1935–36, 2.

GIAC concerning the sway of American comics on Italian youth was shared by the Fascist regime. In this way, *Vitt* aligned with the agenda of the Fascists to promote and defend *national* culture. *Il Vittorioso* was presented as "completely ours, which is to say *Italian*." A full year before the decrees from the Ministry of Popular Culture that sought to eliminate American influences, Gedda declared "we have no need to resort to foreign designs and inspirations—in contrast to the spirit of Italian traditions—to find material and wholesome adventures that exalt the heroism of the pioneers of the faith and the Patria."[43] GIAC did not adopt this policy to support the regime, but the move highlights how GIAC and the Fascist state understood culture and comics as a means to establish a dominant cultural influence that shaped and oriented Italian social life. Both perceived American comics as a threat and advocated an "Italian approach" to comics rooted in Italian stories and Italian heroes, and inspired by Italian visual and literary traditions, including the use of captions rather than speech bubbles.

The periodical's mission of conquest, Gedda's confidence the periodical would succeed, and the apparent sanctity of their work all contributed to the selection of the title, *Il Vittorioso*, "The Victorious." The name had religious connotations, with ads connecting the periodical to "la Regina delle Vittorie" (the Virgin Mary), who was to protect the endeavor and ensure its success. Other ads emphasized "that the Victorious is He, Christ the Lord" and that it was a "victory of the spirit."[44] The religious connotation of the name is evident and clearly evokes the mission behind the venture: to attract children to GIAC and spread religious virtues. Even the nationalist tones of the periodical were wrapped in Christianity, stating in a bulletin to GIAC leaders that *Vitt* would illuminate children so that "they grow pure, strong, and generous in ever greater love for God and for country."[45]

However, the title had multiple layers. Advertisements for *Il Vittorioso* in 1936 issues of *L'Aspirante* emphasized the periodical's evangelizing goal, but they also connected the periodical to Africa Orientale Italiana (Italian East Africa, AOI). A photograph of a missionary surrounded by children from Africa under the Italian tricolor, for instance, had a caption stressing his

43. The emphasis is from the original. Presidenza Centrale della GIAC, Circolare della GIAC, 10 luglio 1936, 2. The first memos from the Ministero della Cultura Popolare addressing the need to nationalize heroes and focus on Italian subjects came in May 1937. Gadducci et al., *Eccetto Topolino*, 154.

44. "Ora viene il bello," *L'Aspirante* (Roma), n. 45, 22 novembre 1936, 1; "Pubblicità per 'Il Vittorioso,'" *L'Aspirante* (Roma), n. 47, 6 dicembre 1936, 1. The December issue of the Bollettino Dirigenti stressed the centrality of the "spirito": "È lo spirito che doma e piega la materia, è lo spirito che crea la santità e l'eroismo." Bollettino Dirigenti, 1 dic. 1936, 280.

45. *Bollettino Dirigenti*, 1 dicembre 1936, 277.

commitment to spreading the "love of the great Italian Patria" "even down here in Africa."[46] More pointedly, another declared the periodical was "entitled with a marvelous, splendid name, worthy of the young men of Fascist and Imperial Italy: 'Il Vittorioso'!"[47]

The connection between Italy's recently declared empire and *Il Vitt*'s title has been downplayed in the past as a concession to Fascist cultural policies.[48] Writing in 1946, Gedda states that the selection was a "wink at the triumphalist climate that stirred the country" following the declaration of the empire and, moreover, was a means to "deflect the attention of the censors."[49] Certainly, the influence of the regime's mechanisms of censorship should not be downplayed. The Vatican, fearful Catholic Action would again be targeted by the regime, informed clergy and lay organizations in 1931 to conduct themselves accordingly so as to "not provoke any possible reaction on the part of the Fascists."[50] Yet an overemphasis on censorship neglects the genuine overlaps between the regime and the Vatican. Moreover, it is important to note that Gedda's memoir was only published *after* the fall of Fascism and that the declaration of the empire in East Africa was well received by Catholics in Italy, many of whom viewed it as an avenue through which to bring Christianity, equality, and justice to the people of Africa.[51]

Regardless of the reasons, the empire was present in the title and would routinely serve as the backdrop of stories published in *Il Vittorioso*, entangling the periodical in the regime's project of empire building. Gedda fully understood the need to make *Vitt* appealing to Italian children—*all* Italian children, even those who were not a part of GIAC or particularly religious. He believed this could be achieved by printing *Italian* stories with *Italian* heroes. These stories would draw inspiration from the Italian past, but they would also "adhere to the reality of boys today," which in part meant Africa Orientale Italiana.[52] It was even reflected in the periodical's nameplate, which featured

46. "All'ombre del tricolore," *L'Aspirante* (Roma), n. 46, 29 novembre 1936, 1.

47. "Eh, eh, . . . ma non la sai la novità?!," *L'Aspirante* (Roma), n. 47, 6 dicembre 1936, 2.

48. Ernesto Preziosi, for one, asserts that the name was not inspired by Fascist nationalism and imperialism, but religious devotion. Preziosi, "Gedda e la stampa," 258.

49. Luigi Gedda, 18 April 1948, *Memorie inedite dell'artefice della sconfitta del Fronte popolare* (Milano: Mondadori, 1998), quoted in Preziosi, "Gedda e la stampa," 259–60.

50. Quoted in Malgeri, *Stato e Chiesa in Italia,* 155.

51. Dagnino, "Catholic Modernities in Fascist Italy," 322; and Kertzer, *Pope and Mussolini,* 229.

52. Presidenza Centrale della GIAC, Circolare della GIAC, 10 July 1936, ISACEM / Fondo della GIAC / Serie 3, B. 522 / Circolari, 1935–36, 2.

a bust decorated with a crown of laurels, used during the Roman Empire to adorn the emperor, indicate an imperial official, or honor a soldier or hero.[53]

While *Il Vittorioso* was a multifaceted periodical, it was framed in part around Italian imperialism and nationalism, as is illustrated by the 1936 *Bollettino Dirigenti* incorporation of the notion of *italianità*, speaking of "a purifying wave of Italianness" that would "exalt God and country with a spirit, personage, adventure, and illustrations 100 percent Italian."[54] Although centering this notion of *italianità* on Italy as "the cradle of Christianity" offered an alternative to Fascism's emphasis on the Rome of the Caesars, it was not necessarily antagonistic and nonetheless incorporated the rhetoric of Fascism.

Defining the Traits of *Il Vittorioso*

The periodical produced by GIAC was a combination of serialized novellas and comics, as well as features that included games, ads, and information on Church activities and Catholics around the world. Many of the comics were printed in full color, while black and white images accompanied the serialized novels and features. From the beginning, *Il Vittorioso* developed its own style of comics, relying more on captions but incorporating speech bubbles in select stories. This balance gradually shifted in favor of captions, well before any mandates from state cultural institutes. Likewise, the illustrators demonstrated a knack for experimenting with the arrangement of images, often breaking out of the simple arrangement of panels to create a creative flow with numbered captions to identify the sequence. Its composition was carefully curated to target children ages ten to fifteen (the age group of the Aspiranti), though GIAC truly desired for it to appeal to *all* Italian youth.

From the first issue, the editors sought to define the victorious in the broadest of terms: "We, Italians, are victorious!" Moreover, "Our victory is grand and will be ever grander."[55] The response conveys that this *Vittoria* is to be understood in more than religious terms, expressing a great sense of nationalism, with Mussolini's proclamation of the empire in May 1936 at the center.[56] The connection is further illustrated by an editorial in the first issue

53. *Il Vittorioso*, n. 1 (9 January 1937), 1.

54. *Bollettino Dirigenti*, 1 dic. 1936, 280.

55. "Radio Vitt," *Il Vittorioso*, n. 1 (9 January 1937), 2.

56. Leonardo Becciu asserts that *Vitt*'s stories "reached tones of intense nationalism," particularly those regarding AOI. Becciu, *Il fumetto in Italia*, 200. This contrasts starkly with Preziosi, who distinguishes the patriotic tendencies of *Vitt* from the nationalism in Fascist periodicals. Preziosi, *Il Vittorioso*, 112–13, 143.

discussing the Balilla Lorenzo Fusco who, at thirteen, enlisted in the Italian army and participated in the October 1935 invasion of Ethiopia, receiving a medal and a photograph with Mussolini. Demonstrating the layers of the title, Fusco is praised for both his bravery and his love for his mother. GIAC incorporated Catholic values to contest and broaden what it meant to be "victorious" and a good Italian by emphasizing love and respect for one's family and parents. Nonetheless, the reader is left with the impression that it is Fusco's service to the empire that provokes the author to write that, upon seeing Fusco, "I said to myself: 'Here is a *Vittorioso*!'"[57]

Il Vittorioso was forced to operate within the evolving parameters shaping cultural production discussed in chapter 2. Policy changes in 1934 required publications—including children's periodicals—be submitted to the Ufficio stampa, the Ministry of Interior, and the Prefect's office prior to their distribution to ensure their alignment with the directives of the regime. Cultural institutions did not yet officially require the printing of Fascist propaganda, but editors and authors adopted practices of self-censorship to limit their periodicals' risk of suspension. Furthermore, GIAC editors were certainly aware of the criticism of comics for not depicting Italian stories, particularly as Catholic intellectuals participated in these debates.

The issues of *Vitt* published under Fascism were undeniably shaped by ministerial restrictions and guidelines. It was unthinkable that *Vitt* could print stories that were *anti*-Fascist. However, that is not to say that GIAC was compelled to print stories that mirrored Fascist propaganda. In other words, although writers could not oppose Fascism in their stories, they did have agency in the stories they decided to tell and the themes they emphasized. While *Vitt* regularly emphasized religious themes and the Catholic foundation of many of the regime's achievements and campaigns, it nonetheless promoted state campaigns to readers and thus offered validation for the Fascist state.

Praise for the Empire

References to the empire were prevalent in the periodical's first issue and did not differ starkly from those of the regime (or from traditional colonial tropes, for that matter). The serial "Sangue Africano" (African Blood) told of an Italian secret agent in present-day Libya prior to the Italian invasion in 1911. The agent intended "to expose the plan of Arab resistance," framed not as an honorable defense of one's country but as led by "fanatical Muslims." Hinting at

57. "Un Pensiero," *Il Vittorioso*, n. 1 (9 January 1937), 3.

the regime's rhetoric that Fascism would be the defender of Islam, an Arabic captain who refuses to participate in the resistance says to his compatriots, "The Italians don't fight against Islam, they fight the Turkish government!"[58]

Such stories in *Il Vittorioso* drew on Mussolini's self-proclaimed status as "the sword of Islam." Following the brutal suppression of resistance to Italian colonial rule in Libya, Fascist policy adopted a tactic of reconciliation, supporting the building of mosques and the teaching of Islamic education. The state invested in local newspapers and radio broadcasts to project an image of Italy as the friend of Muslims. It was, in essence, an attempt to distract from the Fascist atrocities in colonizing the region, attract support, and develop a tool for challenging British and French rule in North Africa.[59]

Respect for Islam seems counter to the Vatican's objective of spreading Catholicism, understood by Catholic missionaries as *the* core of European empires' supposed civilizing mission in Africa, inseparable from bringing justice and peace.[60] However, religious deference may have also aligned with Vatican authorities' favored strategy of gradual conversion of Muslims; in Somalia, for instance, missionary activities aimed to convert Muslims by displaying the generosity of missionaries and the opportunities afforded by the Catholic faith.[61]

The complexities in the rhetoric on Islam coming from the regime and from the Vatican highlight the potential tensions between the Vatican and the colonial project. On the one hand, in August 1935, a few months before the Italian invasion of Ethiopia, Pius XI is said to have declared that the proposed invasion would be an "unjust war." However, his circle of advisors, including Eugenio Pacelli (the future Pius XII), watered down his remarks into vague commentary which the regime later manipulated into words of support. Many in the Church hierarchy—indeed, many Catholic Italians—supported the invasion as an opportunity to spread Catholicism. Pius XI's disapproval before the war changed into silence once the war began. In contrast, Catholic clergy around the world lent support for the expansion of the Italian Empire, including in the US, where Italian diplomats and Catholic priests endeavored to counter American disapproval of the war.[62]

---

58. "Sangue Africano," *Il Vittorioso*, n. 1 (9 January 1937), 2.

59. Fiore, *Anglo-Italian Relations*, 37; Labanca, "Italian Colonial Internment," 27; and Wright, "Mussolini, Libya," 124–25.

60. Foster, *Faith in Empire*, 142–44.

61. Scalvedi, "*Cruce et Aratro*," 149.

62. Kertzer, *Pope and Mussolini*, 214–16, 221, 223; and Coppa, *Politics and the Papacy*, 103.

FIGURE 3.1. The final panel of the comic "L'informatore fantasma." *Il Vittorioso*, n. 40 (9 October 1937), 3.

Entanglements with the regime and the prospect of spreading Catholicism led the Vatican to overlook Fascist abuses and war crimes.[63] The pope's hesitancy at the start of the invasion turned to criticism of the hypocritical Western empires, and the Giornata della Fede (Day of the Faith) on 18 December 1935, just weeks after the invasion was launched, was accompanied by a speech in which the bishop of Aqui declared the war a triumph "at the side of the cross of Christ to bring religion and civilization to barbarian peoples."[64] The *Vittoria* brought glory to Italy and God alike, minimizing the distinction between Italy as a Catholic nation and Catholic nationalism.[65] The identification of the victories of the Italian nation with Fascism was depicted in *Vitt* in the ending of the comic "L'informatore fantasma" (The Phantom Informant) which tells the tale of a victory in Ethiopia and ends with a panel centered on the *fascio* (see figure 3.1), marking it as a *Fascist* victory, rather than a Catholic or even an Italian one, conflating these and emphasizing the role of Fascism and the Duce.[66]

As the goal of spreading Italy's empire became entangled with increasing the reach of the Church, *Il Vittorioso* called on *all* Italians to participate in the empire-building project. In the first issue of "Fior di Loto" (Lotus Flower), a young orphan boy named Italo living in Shanghai is emboldened by a radio

63. Larebo, "Empire Building and Its Limitations," 84. Some Catholic Italians remained staunch in their denunciation of the invasion of Ethiopia, among them Luigi Sturzo. Chamedes, *Twentieth-Century Crusade*, 198.

64. Moro, *Il mito dell'Italia cattolica*, 277.

65. Moro, *Il mito dell'Italia cattolica*, 268. On the overlap between the Catholic Mission and colonial educational policies under Fascist Italy, see Negash, "Ideology of Colonialism," 112–13.

66. *Il Vittorioso*, n. 40 (9 October 1937), 3.

broadcast "which proclaimed to the world the decisive will of Italy" and spoke of the "young infantrymen who prepare to fight in Abyssinia." He hastily boards a ship to AOI to join the colonial project, only to be swept up in his own *avventure cinesi* when his trip is interrupted and he meets up with Paolo, an Italian explorer.[67] Similarly, Ugo Sandri is an Italian living in America who leaves his family in the comic "Il fedele Dubat" (The Loyal Dubat) to further the mission of empire.[68] These stories conveyed that *all* Italians numbered among the "victorious" by nature, regardless of their geographic location.

Again, there is alignment with the regime. By 1928, an estimated nine million Italians lived abroad, prompting the regime to initiate programs to "maintain a national spirit among Italian expatriates." Calls for repatriation increased following the Ethiopian War.[69] The comics in *Il Vittorioso* reflected Mussolini's claim on Italians throughout the world and the notion that all Italians, even those abroad, owed their loyalty to the regime. Italo and Ugo modeled this sense of belonging and commitment to the nation by responding to the call and rushing off to join the soldiers in Ethiopia. Regardless of where one lived, they remained Italian.

As more and more Italians were expected to head to the Italian colonies, readers needed to be familiarized with the racial hierarchy intended to shape interactions in the empire. In addition to being brave, strong, and dutiful, Italian protagonists in *Vitt* were depicted as natural-born leaders, particularly in relation to Indigenous people. Indigenous people, whether of Asian or African ethnicity (or, in one case, Native American), are often present in supporting roles, serving as guides or baggage carriers, as in "Il cuore della foresta" (The Heart of the Forest) and "Fior di Loto." Italian protagonists in both stories tower over their Indigenous companions, visually conveying the dominance of the Italian people.[70] Yet even the young protagonists who lack a physically commanding stature are granted such authority; when young Paolo is captured in "Fior di Loto," his Native guide, Feng, still defers to Italo as the "piccolo padrone" (little master).[71] Again, there is similarity to the model of interaction between Italians and colonized peoples depicted in *Balilla*, as discussed in chapter 1, which projected the innate leadership of all Italians, including in reference to Italian children over adult African men.

67. *Il Vittorioso*, n. 1 (9 January 1937), 8.

68. *Il Vittorioso*, n. 16 (24 April 1937), 3.

69. Ipsen, *Dictating Demography*, 62, 91–92.

70. There are many examples of this visual trope. For one, see *Il Vittorioso*, n. 4 (30 January 1937), 1.

71. *Il Vittorioso*, n. 6 (13 February 1937), 1.

These comics legitimate the supposed preeminence of Italians through their technological superiority. Italian mastery of technology is most evident in "Il cuore della foresta," in which an Italian scientist has been kept against his will by an African tribe in a white tower where he has a great wealth of technology at his control that only he understands how to use.[72] In more realistic stories, Italian technological superiority is exemplified through advanced military aircraft that are essential to the Italian victory in many comics, as with the planes pictured in the final panel of "L'informatore fantasma." The technology of Indigenous enemies, on the contrary, is depicted as "primitive," with those attacking routinely termed the *selvaggi,* or "savages."[73]

And yet, with this advanced technology, the Italian heroes are not there for their own gain, but to help the Indigenous people. Paolo, for instance, uses Italian weaponry to defend a local village. Fabio, the protagonist of "I predoni del Kansas" (The Raiders of Kansas) is similarly trying to protect the Native Americans terrorized by American bandits. Enraged by the killing of a young Native American, Fabio declares, "The area needs to be purged of those wastes of society who dishonor whites and render life impossible in these regions."[74] The story places American imperialism in stark contrast to the apparently benevolent colonialism undertaken by Italians in Africa, as if to ask, by what right do other Western states criticize Italy's invasion of Ethiopia?[75]

Il Vittorioso was therefore not immune to the common perception in Italy that Italians were *brava gente* (good people) and uniquely gentle colonizers. The alleged benevolence of Italy's imperial project is further depicted in *Vitt* through the trope of the *ascaro fedele.* The supposed loyalty of *ascari* (colonial soldiers) was used to assert the claim that the colonized *wanted* to be a part of the Italian imperial program.[76] The myth is most explicitly incorporated into the comic "Il fedele Dubat," in which a former *Dubat*—referring to the white turbans worn by colonial troops from Italian Somaliland—rescues a downed Italian pilot. The colonized, then, can also be victorious, so long as they accept the professed benevolence of Italian colonialism and serve loyally. Those who resist are cast as insidious rebels to be eliminated, allegedly for the benefit of the colonized. Representing the relationship between the colonized and the colonizer in this manner reassures readers of its beneficial nature

---

72. *Il Vittorioso,* n. 46 (20 November 1937), 1.

73. *Il Vittorioso,* n. 18 (8 May 1937), 1. African warriors, for instance, are depicted shirtless and with large shields and spears, and as attacking in a disorderly fashion. *Il Vittorioso,* n. 14 (10 April 1937), 1.

74. *Il Vittorioso,* n. 34 (28 August 1937), 1.

75. Meda, *Stelle e strips,* 55.

76. Von Henneberg, "Monuments, Public Space," 64.

while nonetheless affirming the alternatives for those colonized: "Serve or be destroyed."[77]

The depiction of Italian colonialism in *Il Vittorioso* thus largely adhered to its depiction in Fascist sources. Italian protagonists are routinely commanding *ascari*, protecting villages, engaging in development projects, and resisting slavery and oppression. Colonized peoples are depicted as benefitting greatly from Italian rule, and Italians who further the imperial project are ennobled.

Even those Italians who perished in the effort are projected as victorious, treated as righteous martyrs. The act of martyrdom becomes blurred with the Fascist cult of the fallen in the pages of *Il Vittorioso*, such as when one of the protagonists of "L'informatore fantasma" dies with the final words, "I . . . am done for . . . but . . . I am content . . . to have done . . . my duty. . . . Addio . . . long live . . . Italy."[78] This overlap between the Catholic and the Fascist idealizations of sacrifice indicates not only commonality but also the way in which each position drew on the rhetoric and belief of the other, attempting to prioritize their own values. While in many ways the Fascist idea represented an appropriation of a Catholic idealization of sacrifice, *Vitt* incorporated Fascism's cult of the fallen in depicting those who fell in defense of the nation as defenders of Christ.[79]

The entanglement here highlights how the stories and themes within the periodical could at times contest Fascist values and definitions. Among *Vitt*'s feature "Precursori dell'Impero" (Precursors of the Empire) was Guglielmo Massaia, a missionary spreading Catholicism to Ethiopians prior to Italian occupation of the country. He is eventually exiled by the emperor, who believes Massaia intends to enslave Ethiopians. Massaia responds:

> I bring the true truth of Christ and the great civilization of Rome: you have nothing to lose, indeed everything to gain from the work of evangelization that I and my companions carry out among your people. Your kingdom will be great and powerful if civilization illuminates it with its light and religion warms it with the flame of love. If you refuse civilization, you will lose everything.[80]

The Church's evangelizing mission and its role in the colonies is thus emphasized, as it is above when our heroes in "Fior di Loto" were saved by Italian

77. This choice at the core of the victim's experience of colonialism is emphasized by Edward Said. Said, *Culture and Imperialism*, 168.

78. "L'informatore fantasma," *Il Vittorioso*, n. 40 (9 October 1937), 3.

79. Gentile, *Sacralization of Politics*, 17, 18.

80. *Il Vittorioso*, n. 28 (17 July 1937), 7.

missionaries.[81] The stress on the role of Catholics in building Italy's empire, as well as on the importance of spreading Catholicism in the colonies, represents a significant if subtle departure from Fascist ambitions in Africa.[82] Nonetheless, this distinction still amounted to support for the Fascist project. As stated in the introduction, this distinction cannot be considered a subversion of Fascist values, but a contestation of the meaning of the empire that occurred *within* the accepted parameters of the Fascist worldview.

The Defense of Catholic Europe

The theme of sacrifice, discussed above in relation to the empire, is most prevalent in stories of the ongoing Spanish Civil War. Viewed by Fascists and Catholics alike as a struggle against communism, the Spanish Civil War was among the deepest points of convergence between Fascists and Catholics.[83] The simplifying of the Republican forces into *i rossi* (the reds), or else *i comunisti* or even at times *i russi* (casting Republicans as agents of Russia) mirrored the position of some in the Vatican leadership that the Popular Front in Spain amounted to no less than a communist attempt at world revolution.[84] Brief informational sections such as "Cosa fanno i ragazzi nel mondo?" (What are the children of the world doing?) kept attention on the conflict by relaying that, in the provinces still under the control of the *rossi*, "all the churches have been destroyed and the religious have been killed, [but] many continue to secretly practice Christianity."[85] The war was quickly termed a war of religion.[86]

The Spanish Civil War unleashed atrocities that validated the concerns of Pius XI. Republican forces killed hundreds of priests, monks, and nuns and desecrated Catholic sites. The Vatican, though, had opposed the Republican forces even before these horrendous acts, and used such outrages to justify acts of brutality and carnage carried out by Franco's forces, seen as the defenders of Christ.[87] The perception and reality of a Church under attack

81. *Il Vittorioso*, n. 8 (27 February 1937), 1.

82. Dagnino, "Catholic Modernities in Fascist Italy," 332.

83. Pollard argues that "the Spanish Civil War was undoubtedly *the* major moment of encounter between Christians and fascists." Pollard, "'Clerical Fascism,'" 441.

84. Chamedes, *Twentieth-Century Crusade*, 173.

85. "Cosa fanno i ragazzi nel mondo?" *Il Vittorioso*, n. 1 (9 January 1937), 3; and "Armata del cielo," *Il Vittorioso*, n. 52 (31 December 1937), 7.

86. Moro, *Il mito dell'Italia cattolica*, 298; and Casanova, *Spanish Civil War*, 51.

87. Kertzer, *Pope and Mussolini*, 243. On the religious tensions in the Spanish Civil War and the atrocities committed on both sides, see Casanova, *Spanish Civil War*, ch. 2.

that required defending *by any means necessary* created a foundation for the Catholic Church's uneasy alliance with Fascism; although the two conflicted in numerous ways, *Il Vittorioso*'s reporting of the Spanish Civil War shows that its primary nemeses were socialists, perceived as an existential threat to religion.

Readers of *Vitt* could rest assured, though: the *nazionali* forces of Franco were fighting back, albeit at great personal sacrifice. In "Arriba España!," the Reds capture the colonel's son and attempt to ransom him in return for the surrender of the entrenched *falangisti* (the Spanish fascist group). The colonel, distraught, "fixating on the crucifix attached to the wall, responds: 'My son, I order you to die . . . Be worthy of your father! Long live Spain!" Lined up to be executed, the son cries out, "Arriba España! Viva Cristo Rey!"[88] *Vitt* used these stories to connect religion and the nation, projecting an image of Catholic Spain similar to the Catholic nation of Italy, with the Francoist forces defending their faith. The connection between Catholicism, the Spanish nation, and fascism was emphasized by the regular references to the Spanish forces as *falangisti.*

Readers did not get a depiction of the Spanish Civil War in the comics of *Il Vittorioso* until the following year, when Kurt Caesar launched "Il Legionario." The series focused on the exploits of Italian fighter pilot Romano, who volunteered to defend Francoist forces. No discussion is had as to *why* Romano is there, as *Il Vittorioso*'s coverage of events in Spain makes an explanation unnecessary. The only statement is in the summary of the series, which states that Romano and the Italian volunteers fight "for the triumph of civilization and of religion."[89]

The final panel of the series (see figure 3.2) embodies Romano's fight to defend Catholicism, as well as the entanglement between religion and national identity. As Romano returns to Italy, he flies over the symbols of the faith and the Patria: St. Peter's Square is pictured on the right, while the partition on the left displays the Monumento Vittorio Emanuele. The monument honors Victor Emmanuel II, the first king of unified Italy, and its inclusion does reflect the ties between the Church and the Italian Patria. Interestingly, though, it is the *king,* not Mussolini, who is highlighted as the symbol of Italy. The Palazzo Venezia, which housed Mussolini's office, is barely pictured in the bottom left across from the monument. Such panels underscore the complicated relationship between the Church and state, highlighting tensions as to sources of authority and identity.

---

88. "Arriba España!," *Il Vittorioso,* n. 14 (10 April 1937), 7.
89. *Il Vittorioso,* n. 17 (30 April 1938), 1.

IN UN MATTINO DI SOLE GIUNGE ALLA CITTA' ETERNA E SORVOLA I SIMBOLI DELLA FEDE E DELLA PATRIA.
FINE DELL'EPISODIO

FIGURE 3.2. "Romano reached the Eternal City on a sunny morning and flew over the symbols of the faith and of the Patria." *Il Vittorioso*, n. 45 (12 November 1938), 1.

GIAC's focus on the monarchy rather than Mussolini in figure 3.2 may have been an attempt to remind readers that the Church and the monarchs of Europe had long defended Catholicism, and that Fascism was an ally in this effort but was not acting alone. *Il Vittorioso* often presented the historical role of the Vatican in defending and unifying Europe. In the story "Ottobre 1571: Lepanto," Pius V amasses an armada by rallying the various European kingdoms to protect Europe from the Ottoman Turks, emphasizing the Catholic foundations of European unity and security. The Italian states took a leading role in this story (particularly the House of Savoy—the dynasty that would preside over the unification and remained the kings of Italy until 1946). The story thereby stressed the peninsula's historical role in controlling the Mediterranean Sea to protect European liberty.[90]

These stories demonstrate the entanglement of Catholic and Fascist goals, as seen with *Vitt*'s depiction of the empire. The story promotes Fascism's imperial ambitions of dominating the Mediterranean as *mare nostrum* (our sea) and claiming for Italy a leading role in Europe. Yet the emphasis is on the *Catholic* states of Europe, with which many in the Church hoped Fascist Italy would forge an alliance.[91] According to the tale of Lepanto and the editors' reporting on the Spanish Civil War, GIAC understood Catholicism as the very

90. "Ottobre 1571: Lepanto," *Il Vittorioso*, n. 44 (6 November 1937), 7.

91. Webster, *Cross and the Fasces*, 113.

basis of European civilization, the core which at once legitimized Italy's leading role but which also required renewal and to be spread throughout Europe once again. Moreover, while Italy may have a favored role, Catholicism was understood as *universal,* not nationalist (though, again, the distinction was often lost due to Italy's "position at the centre of Catholicism").[92]

Once more, *Il Vittorioso* offers a key distinction in the understanding of Italian (and European) society and of the foundation of Europe. But this contestation regarding the place and meaning of the Catholic Church in Italy and Europe did not prevent collaboration in advocating for the defense of European civilization, the pursual of *mare nostrum,* or the staking out of Italy's leading role in Europe.

Protecting Traditional Gender Roles

In defining the victorious, the producers of *Il Vittorioso* projected exemplary models of masculinity and femininity. The Italian (Catholic) man was devoted to God and the Patria, which were in many ways considered inseparable. When this Patria and its religious traditions needed defending, Italian men were to drop everything to answer the call, as the young orphan boy Italo did in "Fior di Loto," and Romano did as a volunteer fighting to defend Catholic Spain in "Il Legionario." More than defending these values, the Catholic man was to *spread* them.

The idealized man in *Vitt* was strong, capable, and a man of God. He had to place family, nation, and religion above himself, as well as be prepared to join the honored list of martyrs through sacrifice. While he had to be ready to fight, he was not to be cruel. Whenever possible, Italians in the pages of *Vitt* showed mercy to their enemies, such as in "Fior di Loto" when Feng asks for forgiveness after attacking Paolo and Italo. Spared by Paolo, Feng becomes a loyal guide who ultimately dies to save his Italian companions.[93] Moreover, their mission in these lands was not selfish gain or mere thrill seeking; instead, it was to uplift the people by spreading justice and, above all, Catholicism.

The emphasis placed on devotion to God and the virtue of mercy represented a marked difference from the violent and aggressive Fascist man. The stories in *Il Vittorioso* did not often give way to the demonization of the enemy as Fascist propaganda did, instead tending to represent enemies as misguided. The Catholic new man was instead to be pure in both his heart

92. Dagnino, "Catholic Students at War," 291.

93. *Il Vittorioso,* n. 20 (22 May 1937), 1.

and his intentions.[94] The Vatican, GIAC, and *Il Vittorioso* wanted a Catholic, wholesome Fascism. However, while this distinction between the *uomo nuovo* of Fascism and that of the Church was significant, it did not prevent the Catholic soldier from fighting in the Spanish Civil War, the campaigns in Africa, or later in World War II.[95]

The stories of *Vitt* discussed above predominantly focused on men and imagined Italian boys as the ideal audience, like most illustrated periodicals at the time. Female characters were relegated to supporting roles, such as Lidia in "I predoni del Kansas," whose primary role as the damsel in distress who sets the protagonist, Fabio, on his journey to save her and the Native Americans from insidious American bandits. Liliana has a similar role in "Il cuore della foresta." Even so, the two characters attest to the changing gender roles for women, as they are participants in these stories and taking on adventures typically reserved for men.[96] Lidia, after being saved by Fabio, aids in defeating the bandits, albeit primarily through the gender-approved role as a nurse.[97] Liliana challenges traditional gender roles simply by joining her brother, Marco, on an expedition to the Congo to find their father.

However, the two characters ultimately uphold gender norms more than they challenge them. Both are clearly granted support roles and are positioned often as the object which needs rescuing. Moreover, both Lidia and Liliana function as the foil for the male heroes; it is primarily through their expressions of fear that readers understand the stakes of the situation and thus the bravery of the men.

The presence of women in these stories is also framed as out of the ordinary. Liliana is only in Africa because a sign has been found of her father, who has been missing for years. She is, furthermore, under the protection of her brother. Likewise, Lidia's first appearance in "I predoni del Kansas" is because she was kidnapped by the bandits who killed her father. At the end of the story, Lidia settles down with her new spouse, Fabio.[98] Liliana, too, marries her guide and frequent savior, Alfredo. While *Il Vittorioso* did incorporate women into its stories, it was in secondary roles and under the assumption that the ultimate victory for Italian women was marriage and the start of a family.

94. Dagnino, "Catholic Students at War," 297.

95. For more on the "Catholic soldier," see chapter 5 and also Dagnino, *Faith and Fascism*, 195–98.

96. Lombardi-Diop, "Pioneering Female Modernity," 152.

97. *Il Vittorioso*, n. 29 (24 July 1937), 1.

98. *Il Vittorioso*, n. 37 (18 September 1937), 1.

Reception

The promotions throughout 1936 and the reliance on preexisting associations within AC to distribute the periodical resulted in a successful start for *Il Vittorioso*, which reached a circulation of 97,000 in February 1937.[99] Circulation fluctuated greatly over the next months, dipping to 85,000 in September before climbing again throughout the fall.[100] *Vitt* was presented as a great success in GIAC's periodicals, as conveyed by the comments from retailers expressing the need for more copies to sell because children found it "beautiful, charming, and exciting!" Parents, too, declared it "just the paper we wanted!"[101] *Vitt* received praise from Catholic intellectuals as well, apparently no longer concerned that the media of comics was highly visual. The Catholic journalist Natal Mario Lugaro, for instance, commended the periodical for its ability to be educational while rivaling other magazines in the sense of aesthetics and quality.[102]

Most importantly, *Il Vittorioso* was gaining readers throughout the peninsula. Each week, editors responded to a handful of readers who wrote in. Letters hailed from Italy's various regions, including the recently annexed territories of the Istrian peninsula. Editors' responses to readers provide a glimpse into the range of readers. While many who wrote were the young males GIAC envisioned as its ideal audience in the meetings of 1936, letters also came from girls like Giuseppina Maritati from Apulia. *Il Vittorioso*'s audience was not limited to youth either. Replying to Pio Cavalleri of Verona, the editors write, "You read *Vitt* even at the age of 80? Still another *evviva*!"[103]

Despite the relatively strong launch, *Vitt* trailed rival illustrated periodicals. The periodical of the ONB, *Il Balilla,* averaged a weekly circulation of about 250,000 copies (aided by its quasi-obligatory distribution in schools), and *L'Avventuroso* distribution typically reached around 300,000.[104] Enthusiasm for *Vitt* continued to grow throughout the year, reaching a weekly circulation of 102,000 by the end of the year, but this number fell short of the

---

99. Consiglio superiore della GIAC, Processi verbali dell'assemblea, febbraio 1937, ISACEM / Fondo della GIAC / Serie 3, B. 495, Processi verbali dell'assemblea 2,1935–11,1943, 36.

100. Presidenza Centrale della GIAC, Il Vittorioso, 1938, ISACEM / Fondo della GIAC / Serie 3, B. 523 / Circolari, 1937–38, 3.

101. Il Campanaro, "I trionfi del 'Vittorioso,'" L'Aspirante XIV, n. 3, 24 gennaio 1937, 2.

102. "Ciò che dice un quotidiano del Vittorioso," Gioventù Nova XV, n. 1, 8 gennaio 1938, 4, quoted in Preziosi, *Il Vittorioso,* 135.

103. "Radio Vitt," *Il Vittorioso,* n. 31 (7 August 1937), 2. Cavalleri is not alone, either, as Mario D'Aquino of Chieti reveals that his grandmother "avidly reads the 'sempre + bello' at over ninety years of age!" "Radio Vitt," *Il Vittorioso,* n. 48 (4 December 1937), 2.

104. Becciu, *Il fumetto in Italia,* 85; and Carabba, *Il fascismo a fumetti,* 21.

ambitions of the leaders of GIAC. Continued efforts to promote the periodical—including GIAC hosting a "*Vitt* Week" to celebrate the magazine the week before Christmas—ultimately proved fruitful, as by mid-June of 1938, *Vitt* had 12,019 subscribers and a weekly circulation of 121,500, at which level the periodical remained fairly steadily into World War II.[105] Despite this impressive achievement that demonstrated the success of the periodical's first year, a report by the Presidenza Centrale della GIAC on *Vitt*'s circulation lamented the fact that the weekly reached only 5.48 percent of the total amount of Italian adolescents (which it recorded as 2,215,177).[106] It seemed there was still a long way to go to reach GIAC's goal of a periodical for all Italian youth.

Conclusion

As *Il Vittorioso* found its footing in its first years of publication, it became clear that the victorious were, broadly speaking, *all* Italians. These victorious Italians were to be selfless, devoted to Catholicism but also to the Italian Patria. They were to honor Italy by serving in the defense of Europe and in the spread of the Italian Empire, and, through doing so, defend and spread the faith. The two were intertwined. The story of "il balilla Fusco" discussed above demonstrates how *Vitt* portrayed this entanglement by showing that those affiliated with the Balilla and Fascism more broadly were capable of living a victorious life.

Vitt was not, however, simply a source of Fascist propaganda. Stories in the periodical emphasized the virtues of friendship, family, and religion. While this study focused on adventure comics, many other comics depicted cooperation, brotherhood, and morality.[107] GIAC also placed its own spin on stories and endeavored to distinguish *Vitt* from its competitors and to represent a uniquely *Catholic* vision for society. The editors and writers of GIAC thus offered a vision of Fascist Italy which contested that envisioned by many Fascist officials by placing the Vatican at the forefront and advocating a tamed, *Catholicized* Fascism that was more universal and in service of the Church.

105. Presidenza Centrale della GIAC, Il Vittorioso, 3; Presidenza Centrale della GIAC, Dati statistici, maggio 1940, ISACEM / Fondo della GIAC / Serie 3, B. 523 / Circolari, 1939–40, 2. One report of the Consiglieri Centrali della GIAC in February–March of 1942 records the circulation to have reached as high as 150,000 copies, but no other documents have recorded it as this high. Consiglieri Centrali della GIAC, Traccia da seguire in occasione della Giornata Regionale da parte dei Consiglieri Centrali (febbraio–marzo 1942), 1942, ISACEM / Fondo della GIAC / Serie 3, B. 524, Circolari, 1941–42, 1.

106. Presidenza Centrale della GIAC, Il Vittorioso, 2.

107. Fava, "'Il *Vittorioso*,'" 662.

GIAC launched *Vitt* to project this vision for society, to compete with the Fascist and American illustrated periodicals, and to continue its mission of the *conquista* of the Italian youth. Its nature as an educational endeavor positioned it within the cultural struggle taking place between the regime and the Vatican, which was after all often centered on competing youth organizations and the education of Italy's children.

While the periodical was meant to spread Catholic teachings despite restrictions from the Fascist state, it must be remembered that *Il Vittorioso* also grew out of several concerns which the Catholic Church held in common with Fascist intellectuals. Foremost among these were anxieties over the American way of life as depicted in popular comics from the US. Gedda and the writers of *Vitt* sought to provide an alternative model of modernity for their readers. This model emphasized the Catholic roots of Italian identity, the need to spread and defend the Catholic faith, and the defense of traditional gender roles. These goals led to support for the regime's efforts to contain socialism, to defend Catholic Europe, to expand Italian colonialism, and to return the Italian (Catholic) nation to a leading role in Europe.

In depicting Italians and Italian society in this manner, *Il Vittorioso* engaged in Fascist rhetoric, attempting to define key ideas according to the principles of the Church. Yet the contestation over the meaning of the empire, of sacrifice for the nation, and the foundations of the nation took place within the parameters of the Fascist worldview rather than in opposition to it. The result was the depiction of a traditional and wholesome vision of Italy centered on Catholicism that nonetheless suggested to readers a sense of compatibility with the nationalist and imperialist endeavors undertaken by the Fascist state.

CHAPTER 4

Produced by Italians, for Italians

Autarky and Popular Culture

The popularity of American comics and the emergence of *Il Vittorioso* amplified the attention paid to comics by Italian intellectuals and Fascist officials. Debates about comics reached a new intensity around 1938 as the shifting policies of the regime prioritized *bonifica culturale,* or the reclamation of Italian culture. Numerous trends motivated this new course in cultural policies, including the souring of international opinion of Italy following the Ethiopian War, the rapprochement with Nazi Germany, and the sense that Italy's relative openness in cultural policies was not sufficiently fascistizing Italians.[1]

The restrictions imposed on comics by the Ministero della Cultura Popolare (MCP) in 1938 mandated Italian settings, Italian characters, and a focus on the nation's past and present. American icons like Flash Gordon disappeared, and comics became overtly propagandistic. Italian comics were to follow and embody Fascist principles, such as those enshrined in the 1938 Racial Laws. The MCP regulations did much to Italianize comics and insert more explicitly propagandistic themes into these stories. However, comics from the US persisted, as publishers such as Mondadori and Nerbini negotiated for greater tolerance or sought ways to *subvert* the policies, meaning that the objective remained unrealized. Nonetheless, cultural officials seemed willing

1. Bonsaver, *Censorship and Literature,* 102–8.

to accept this ideological impurity so long as the Italianization of names and settings allowed the MCP to *claim* the achievement of its campaign.

Intervention began in 1938 as the MCP targeted foreign translations. Dino Alfieri, who had taken over as Minister of Popular Culture the previous year, spoke of "the need to develop Italian stories" to replace those of foreign origin.[2] The continued publication of American comics led Alfieri to issue a circular on 19 July:

> Since it is my intention to proceed with the utmost determination in confronting publications for children not inspired by the educational principles of Fascism and considering that this problem assumes no less political importance than other publishing sectors, I *formally invite you* to remove *within three months* all stories or comic strips imported from America or imitating American comics, as well as any of anti-educational theme.

To ensure that publishers understood that this was an order and not a request—despite the language of invitation—Alfieri clarified at the end of the memo that any publications which failed to accommodate this "repeatedly expressed will of the Ministry" would be suppressed.[3] Because the MCP had the authority to sequester publications, such memos from the MCP regulating comics amounted to the expansion of censorship. Nerbini suspended "Flash Gordon" soon after Alfieri's July memo.

Three months later, educators, authors, and editors met in Bologna for the National Convention for Children's and Youth Literature to discuss the *bonifica* of Italian literature for children. The conference was hailed as a hallmark of the corporatist system in that it gathered (state-approved) representatives from all professions concerned with the "substantial and urgent problems of children's and youth literature."[4] The selected nature of the guests suggests they largely shared the objectives of the MCP, but it should be noted that the publicity afforded the convention required attendees to display loyalty to Fascism and its cultural mission.[5]

The conference speakers reviewed the state of children's literature, discussing what it was and, more importantly, what it *should* be. Many speakers followed Enrico Vallecchi's assertion that the printing of comics based purely on

2. Alfieri spoke on 21 May 1937 of "il dovere di svolgere soggetti italiani." Gadducci et al., *Eccetto Topolino*, 154.

3. Alfieri to Nerbini (19 July 1938 MCP), in Gadducci et al., *Eccetto Topolino*, 167. The first emphasis is mine; the second appears in the original as underlined text.

4. *Convegno Nazionale per la letteratura infantile e giovanile*, 5.

5. Sinibaldi, "Between Censorship and Propaganda," 51.

metrics of popularity and profitability ran counter to the Fascist objective of "educating" Italian youth. Such an approach to publishing, moreover, clashed with traditional Italian children's literature, which had always been situated in the goal to "make Italians."[6] American stories, with their foreign heroes, "corrupting" values, and portrayal of Italian Americans as gangsters detracted from these goals. Pedagogue and writer Nazareno Padellaro expressed these sentiments best: "Better it be mediocre books by mediocre authors who are Italian, than famous books by famous, but foreign, authors."[7]

Presenters at the conference argued that children's literature needed to be *functional,* educating children toward a Fascist philosophy of life.[8] Five common themes emerged as speakers defined the values desired in Fascist literature: deference to the patriarchal family and authoritarian state; racial superiority; the glorification of Italy's past; heroism; and dedication to duty, be it military or one's work.[9] Religious faith could perhaps be added to these themes, the importance of which was emphasized by nearly all attendees and was often listed *first.*[10]

These talking points—reducing foreign influence and defining Fascist culture—aligned with and legitimized the regime's preoccupation with *bonifica culturale.* The newfound fervor around cultural reclamation in part arose from a hegemony crisis of the regime, which prompted concerns among officials regarding the limited penetration of a Fascist way of life into Italian society.[11] While the regime's earlier policies might have been successful in attracting intellectuals to the regime, they were less successful in generating a distinctive popular culture. The Fascist regime thus lacked a uniquely "Fascist" culture to shape Italians and foster consent, as the culture present in Italian society was a mixture of Catholic, conservative, American, and Fascist values and themes. The bloc these various cultural influences created through their overlapping points provided only a fragile and unstable foundation for the regime.

The changing context and evolving priorities of the state furthermore necessitated a shift in policies. As the regime's imperial expansion and racial legislation soured international relations, foreign culture became a larger issue. Foreign translations of all kinds were suppressed, and publishers such

---

6. Sinibaldi notes that children's literature in Italy largely arose with the emergence of the unified Italian state and that it became embroiled with the desire to "make Italians" and shape a national identity and character. Sinibaldi, "Dangerous Children," 54.

7. Padellaro, "Traduzioni e riduzioni di libri," 42.

8. Sinibaldi, "Between Censorship and Propaganda," 52–55.

9. Sinibaldi, "Between Censorship and Propaganda," 50, 57.

10. See, in particular, Marinetti, "Accademico d'Italia"; Giovanazzi, "Gusti letterari dei ragazzi"; and Fanciulli, "Il giornalismo per i ragazzi."

11. Scotto di Luzio, *L'appropriazione imperfetta,* 268.

as Mondadori increasingly had to defend the continued publication of foreign books, let alone comics.[12] Imports of American films and comics were limited due to deteriorating relations between Italy and the US.[13] The state became unwilling to tolerate rivals such as "Flash Gordon," with which its own comics periodical had proved unable to compete. The suppression of American comics remained the only solution.

After the convention, the MCP announced the "complete abolition of all material of foreign importation, making exception for the creations of Walt Disney, which are separate from the rest for their artistic value and substantial morality." All stories *inspired* by foreign culture were also banned, and children's periodicals were to decrease the number of pages devoted to comics. Going forward, stories for children (comics or otherwise) were to have "an educative function, exalting Italian heroism, especially of the military, the Italian race, and the past and present of Italy."[14]

Authors and publishers explored ways to adhere to these new directives while maximizing profits, hoping to appeal to children while meeting the standards established by adults.[15] While many Italian publishing houses had already been developing stories that drew on Italian history and cultural traditions, each was forced to invest more in creating an "Italian style" of comics that focused on glorifying the Italian past and present.[16] Colonial stories, already popular, became more frequent features in these magazines, now centered on the Italian Empire in East Africa, and were more explicit in their Fascist themes. The first section examines the colonial adventure comics that predated the 1938 decree and demonstrates the resulting change in tone. The second section focuses on stories which praised Italy through its past, with series on the Risorgimento and Italian unification, which had appeared in comics prior to this point but with little frequency.

The final section examines the persistence of American comics. Even in its most centralized form under the MCP, the cultural system constructed

---

12. Arnoldo Mondadori a Gherardo Casini (16 December 1938), FAAM / AME, Fasc. Ministero della cultura popolare, 1, Sf.2, dal. 5.5.1938 al 31.12.1939; and Arnoldo Mondadori al Duce (14 maggio 1940), ACS / SPD, CO 1922–43, Serie numerica, B. 509568/I–II Milano. Casa Editrice Mondadori, 509568/II Varia.

13. Ricci, *Cinema and Fascism,* 68.

14. "Il Convegno per la letteratura infantile e giovanile (Bologna, 9–10 novembre)," in *Giornale della libreria,* n. 47 (19 November 1938), 327, quoted in Meda, *Stelle e strips,* 126–27; and in Gadducci et al., *Eccetto Topolino,* 187.

15. Zohar Shavit notes that this balance is a common struggle in children's literature, not unique to literature under Fascist Italy. Shavit, *Poetics of Children's Literature,* 36–37, 93.

16. Sinibaldi, "Between Censorship and Propaganda, 47; and Forgacs, *Italian Culture,* 79–80.

by the Fascist state remained dependent on personal relations and prone to uneven enforcement. Therefore, while Italianization *would* occur, the ability for publishers to negotiate with state officials endured. Many American comics returned after brief suspensions in the years following the passage of the restrictions in 1938, restyled with Italian names and more Italian features. State officials nonetheless appeared satisfied, boldly declaring cultural *bonifica* had been carried out. Yet the persistence of American series in any form, whatever the claims of the state, represented the *subversion* of state policies and a challenge to the state's declared cultural autarky. It was during this period that comics imported from the US adopted a truly anti-Fascist nature due to their official status of being banned.

Colonial Adventures and the Ethiopian War

The decrees of 1938 represented a new phase in the Italian comics industry. But publishers were not entirely unprepared to develop Italian original comics. Even the comics magazines responsible for printing American comics—Nerbini's *L'Avventuroso* and Mondadori's *Topolino*—had been experimenting with comics created by in-house authors for years. Colonial stories had been popular throughout the 1930s, so it is not surprising that many of these Italian comics embraced the genre, especially following the Italian invasion of Ethiopia and the increased attention granted to the empire. Although both *L'Avventuroso* and *Topolino* included comics by Italian authors and artists, two concerns remained to which the MCP and the presenters at the convention felt compelled to respond in 1938: many of these comics were not set in Italian colonies, and the popularity of American comics overshadowed those that did. Examining these earlier Italian comics deepens our understanding of the 1938 intervention.

The first colonial stories printed in the periodicals of Nerbini and Mondadori were primarily set in *British* colonies rather than in Italian ones. The first issue of *L'Avventuroso,* for instance, contained "Dal deserto alla jungla" (notice the quasi-Anglicization of the spelling of the Italian "giungla"). Set in 1865 Egypt, the comic focused on the British defense of work on the Suez Canal. These stories drew inspiration from English and American adventure comics, but also Italy's own rich tradition of adventure stories.

The most important and successful author in the Italian tradition of adventure stories was Emilio Salgari, whose voluminous body of work remained avidly read in the Fascist period. Salgari's stories always centered on the "exotic" and "mystical" components of foreign lands and colonial adventures, which rendered Italy's own colonial possessions inadequate sites because claims of uplift and actual interaction with the lands and people demystified these locations.[17] His most successful stories were set in British India and centered on local *resistance* to British imperial rule, advocating the righteous revolt against oppression.[18]

In 1936, Salgari's stories were adapted to the medium of comics in *Topolino* as a part of Antonio Rubino's desire to expand the Italian originals printed in *Topolino.* Rubino had been hired in 1935 to serve as *direttore responsabile,* a position he held until 1940. Cesare Zavattini (the future neorealist screenwriter who was hired in 1936 as the editorial director of *Topolino*) and Federico Pedrocchi, the periodical's artistic director, were essential to Rubino's vision.

Adaptations of Salgari's works appeared in *Topolino* in June 1936, illustrated by Guido Moroni-Celsi. The adaptations launched with "I misteri della jungla nera," part of Salgari's Indo-Malaysia series, often referred to as the Sandokan series.[19] The series focuses on Tremal-Naik the hunter and his endeavors to rescue a British woman held captive by a cult. Although this story pits the protagonist against Indigenous villains, Tremal-Naik ultimately teams up with Sandokan the pirate, who has sworn revenge against the British for killing his parents and seizing his family's kingdom. Tremal-Naik's imprisonment by British governor James Brooke positions the British as the overarching antagonists of the series.

Despite this resistance to European colonialism, the adaptations of Salgari's work were safe bets because they appealed to young Italians and remained likely to obtain the approval of Italian intellectuals. In Giuseppe Fanciulli's critique of adventure comics at the conference in Bologna, he was careful to stress that he neither wished to condemn the adventure genre itself nor the great works of the *maestro* Emilio Salgari.[20] However, Salgari was not without his critics. Fascists officials struggled to reconcile the tensions inherent in drawing on Italy's literary past while emphasizing a *new* Fascist culture. In the case of colonial literature, Fascist officials desired the depiction of the new "reality" of Italian colonialism, with particular attention to the alleged development of African territories through the construction of infrastructure,

17. Palumbo, "Orphans for the Empire," 226.

18. Scotto di Luzio, *L'appropriazione imperfetta,* 209.

19. Laura, "*Topolino*: Indici generali." Salgari's *I misteri della jungla nera* was originally serialized in 1887 under the title "Gli strangolatori del Gange" in the periodical *Il Telefono di Livorno.* Leonardo Becciu suggests that Salgari's work was ideal for adaptation into Italian comics during this time, due to its rich dialogue and "exotic" characters and locations. Becciu, *Il fumetto in Italia,* 111.

20. Fanciulli, "Il giornalismo per i ragazzi," 165–66.

schools, and farms. Salgari's novels represented imperialism as a space of adventure and excitement, not a site of civilizing work.[21]

Surprisingly, no problem was made of the fact that the hero, Sandokan, was not European and that he struggled *against* a European power. Salgari's work had been revived and claimed by Fascist intellectuals, with his novels touted as foreshadowing Italian imperialism and embodying the hostility leveled at the British Empire following the invasion of Ethiopia. Unlike the self-professed image of Italian colonialism, Fascists cast the British Empire as the embodiment of oppression.[22] Moreover, even without Italian heroes, Salgari regularly offered legitimation for white colonial rule in his works.[23] The comics adaptation thus survived and continued to be published in *Topolino* until the periodical was suspended in 1943. Increasingly, though, both Mondadori and Nerbini incorporated more explicitly Italian stories into their periodicals.

Pedrocchi's "Saturno contro la Terra"

The two main publishers of American comics initially took widely different approaches to Italian stories. Where Nerbini placed stories in the Italian Empire directly, Mondadori's creative team of Federico Pedrocchi and Zavattini developed fantastical adventures centered on Italian heroes, such as the science-fiction comic "Saturno contro la Terra" (Saturn against the Earth). Published in 1936, the innovative sci-fi comic enhanced Pedrocchi's already significant contributions to the Italian comic industry, which are so momentous that he is often remembered as the "father of Italian comics."[24] The series is at times credited as the first originally Italian sci-fi comic, but that honor belongs to the series "S.K.1" by Guido Moroni-Celsi. "Saturno" does hold the distinction of being the first Italian comic to be sold in English in the US market, though.[25]

Zavattini and Pedrocchi's creation is heavily shaped by the context in which it was produced. The influence of American comics such as "Flash Gordon" is evident, and yet the series reflected the rising tensions between

21. Palumbo, "Orphans for the Empire," 227, 47; and Scotto di Luzio, *L'appropriazione imperfetta*, 202–3.

22. Palumbo, "Orphans for the Empire," 226; and Becciu, *Il fumetto in Italia*, 111. In 1928 the Minister of Public Instruction emphasized Salgari's contribution to the heroic education of Italy's younger generations, a view advocated again in 1937 by Silvio Zavatti. See Scotto di Luzio, *L'appropriazione imperfetta*, 220.

23. Palumbo, "Orphans for the Empire," 226.

24. Carpi, *Cesare Zavattini direttore editoriale*, 29–30; and Becciu, *Il fumetto in Italia*, 104.

25. Dini, "Saturno contro la Terra."

Italy and the international community which resulted from the invasion of Ethiopia. The outrage sparked in the US and the broader international community resulted in an unofficial embargo of war materials sent to Italy from the US and sanctions from the League of Nations.[26] The condemnation of the invasion of Ethiopia by countries with their own vast empires (namely France and Britain) was viewed as hypocritical in Italy and fueled calls for economic and cultural autarchy, accelerating the development of *Italian* comics.[27] The centrality of Italian characters, who act virtually alone in defense of the earth from the ambitions of the dictator of Saturn, Rebo, reflects the real-world isolation of Italy.

As with other comics, "Saturno" is ambiguous, as the denouncement of dictatorship on the planet Saturn could be an indictment of Mussolini's dictatorial rule in Italy. Yet the series is undeniably marked by Fascist rhetoric. For instance, "Saturno" begins with the protagonists, Marcus and Ciro, discovering the approach of a projectile launched from Saturn. Marcus, an accomplished scientist dressed in a robe reminiscent of ancient Rome, and Ciro, a muscled and dark-haired man sporting a black shirt, represent the blending of Italy's mythic past and the Fascist new man in accordance with Fascist propaganda.[28] The parallels to Fascist Italy continue as Marcus announces this discovery to an eager audience from a balcony, a frequent occurrence from the Duce.

As the story continues, the two figures demonstrate Italy's leading role in the world as they form a plan to save the earth. Interestingly, only the French scientist, Leducq, challenges Marcus's plan, but his rejection is clearly prompted by a jealous wish to lead the world's forces. Leducq is proved wrong, as his plan ultimately fails. Ciro, on the other hand, is aided by his German friend, Bastian. However, if this is to be taken as a nod to the increasing reproachment between Fascist Italy and Nazi Germany, it is limited by the fact that Berlin is included in the devastation of all major cities. Figure 4.1 depicts the destruction that is unleashed when Emperor Rebo of Saturn sends giant animals and catastrophes to demolish London, Berlin, Paris, New York, and Moscow.

Only the cities of Italy are saved by the well-equipped and courageous Italian military. In time, Marcus and Ciro manage both to cripple Rebo's base on Saturn and to stop the animals from raging across the world. The two are paraded through the streets as saviors of the world, in a fashion familiar to anyone acquainted with images of Mussolini touring Italy and its colonies. The

26. Schmitz, *The Sailor,* 54.

27. Becciu, *Il fumetto in Italia,* 98.

28. Zavattini, Pedrocchi, and Scolari, *Saturno contro la terra,* 3.

FIGURE 4.1. Berlin, Paris, and New York are destroyed in Rebo's attack on Earth in an issue published 17 June 1937. Zavattini, Pedrocchi, and Scolari, *Saturno contro la Terra*, 22.

FIGURE 4.2. Marcus is paraded through the streets in an issue published 15 July 1937. The caption reads, "Long live Marcus! Long live the saviors of the world!" Zavattini, Pedrocchi, and Scolari, *Saturno contro la Terra*, 25.

car, seen in figure 4.2, is even drawn to look like the Alfa Romeo convertible in which Mussolini often rode.

The first volume ends with Marcus giving a speech from a balcony worthy of the Duce himself, declaring, "And now our watchword must be: reconstruction! . . . Italy, cradle of world civilization, has won and will set the examples, as always, of what miracles order and discipline are capable of!!"[29]

While the story was neither set in the Italian Empire nor dealt explicitly with Fascism, Pedrocchi and Zavattini integrated themes of Italian nationalism and Fascism into the comic. Indeed, "Saturno contro la Terra" is ultimately a story of the regeneration of the world led by Fascist Italy.[30] The series was popular and ran for many years, but the fantastical setting, the clear influence of American comics such as "Flash Gordon," and the ambiguous messages of the comic meant that the series was likely not what attendees at the convention in Bologna envisioned in their desire for "real" Italian stories lacking foreign influences.

Celebrating the Italian Empire

Other comics did explicitly focus on the Italian Empire. The appearance of comics set in Italy's colonies accelerated surrounding the regime's imperial turn. Focusing on the empire followed guidelines from the Fascist cultural institutions to focus on the "war and on the fighting and heroic spirit of the Italian people."[31] Nerbini's *L'Avventuroso* was first in this regard, capturing Fascist imperial ambitions in Ethiopia in "La prigioniera del Ras" (The Prisoner of the *Ras*) by Guido Moroni-Celsi.[32]

Launched on 15 September right before the Italian invasion of Ethiopia in October 1935, the story begins with two Italian boys, Gianni and Luciano, hunting in an Ethiopian forest. They follow an Abyssinian who promises to guide them to better game but are captured by a tribe of raiders led by Ras Bula instead.[33] Over the following issues, the boys discover that a tribe from modern-day Kenya called the Samburù have taken an Italian girl by the name of Rossana. The Samburù are slavers and are revealed to be the true enemy of the series, as they pose problems for the Italians and Abyssinians alike. Ras Bula forms an unlikely alliance with the Italian forces to save Rossana before

29. Zavattini, Pedrocchi, and Scolari, *Saturno contro la Terra,* 25.
30. Pasquero, "Federico Pedrocchi," 79.
31. Forno, *La stampa del Ventennio,* 67.
32. Gori, "La nascita."
33. *L'Avventuroso,* n. 49 (15 September 1935), 1.

she is sacrificed.[34] During the rescue mission, Ras Bula is killed as he throws himself in front of the young Italian girl to shield her from a bullet. The final words of the Ras are praise for Italy, leaving the Italian protagonists to declare him a hero.

Believing that Italian leadership ennobled Bula, one of the boys states, "These men would become heroes if under Italian rule!" prompting a Fascist colonial official to reply, "Let us vow that Italy, in her interests and those of humanity, will know how to destroy the barbarism of these lands."[35] If American comics played an integral role in the construction of an Italian imaginary Africa, Italian adventure comics gave more explicit shape to that imagery by foregrounding *Italian* characters and colonial territories, all the while engraining the notion that Italian rule was benevolent.

The Ethiopian invasion featured prominently in *Balilla* as well, which was purely propagandistic and thus established the expectations for children's periodicals. Throughout the mid-1930s, *Balilla* increasingly turned to issues of foreign policy, and Italy's supposed imperial destiny became a regular fixture of the youth periodical. Ethiopia was depicted as a barbaric land, with seminude hunters with crude weapons tracking exotic animals, and a place in which slavery was ever-present.[36] Images and drawings depicted the bravery of Italian soldiers and the *ascari* (colonial troops) who fought alongside them. Colonial troops, particularly from Eritrea, figured heavily in reports on the Ethiopian war, and the myth of the *ascaro fedele* (loyal *ascaro*) symbolized the supposed benevolence of Italian colonialism: Italians were apparently "elevating" Eritreans by teaching them how to use modern technology and improving their lands, inspiring those colonized by Italy to loyally fight for the Italian flag. In the same way, the myth highlighted the promise of what would ultimately become of the people of Ethiopia.[37]

Topolino only began to incorporate such overtly imperialistic comics in 1937. By this point, the fulfillment of the Fascist imperial expansion in Ethiopia had garnered great popular support.[38] "Il bandito dell'Amba Uork" was set in Africa Orientale Italiana (Italian East Africa, or AOI) and centered on

34. *L'Avventuroso*, n. 57 (10 November 1935), 1.

35. *L'Avventuroso*, n. 58 (17 November 1935), 1.

36. "Ethiopia barbara," *Il Balilla*, n. 1 (2 January 1936), 3.

37. Ben-Ghiat, *Italian Fascism's Empire Cinema*, 128; and Moyd, *Violent Intermediaries*, 20.

38. Forlenza and Thomassen, *Italian Modernities*, 74; and Duggan, *Fascist Voices*, 260, 264, 274–76. It is important to note that the enthusiasm and consent around achievements of the regime were always structured by repression and that, additionally, Renzo De Felice, who argues that the mid-1930s were a peak of consensus around the regime, acknowledges the tenuous and short-lived nature of this spike in enthusiasm around the occupation of Ethiopia. De Felice, *Gli anni del consenso*, 597, 616.

FIGURE 4.3. Bandits flee to the mountains as one yells, "Let's flee! The Italians are following us!" In the next panel, Captain Folgore is a looming presence exuding strength, determined to quell the bandits. "Il bandito dell'Amba Uork," *Topolino*, n. 215 (4 February 1937), 11.

the Italian, strong, Fascist officer Folgore, who sets out to establish order by defeating bandits hiding in the mountains.[39] His towering presence is conveyed in figure 4.3. Folgore is accompanied in his task by loyal *ascari* and emphasizes the Italian army's ability to bring order to the newly conquered area, supposedly for the benefit of the local people.

Comics set in the Italian colonies—such as *L'Avventuroso*'s "La prigioniera del Ras" and *Topolino*'s "Il bandito dell'Amba Uork"—embodied the realism desired by the MCP and the speakers at the 1938 convention in Bologna. However, these comics were not representative of the majority of comics, nor were they the most popular. In a study of the reception and popularity of children's magazines of the 1930s, Kate Ferris evaluated essays written in 1935 by Venetian school children, in which they discuss their favorite comics. What she found was that while about fifteen of the forty-five children did write on comics of war and empire, two-thirds of the children made no mention of Fascism, and most expressed a preference for fairy tales, fantasies, "Topolino," and the games printed in children's magazines.[40] In *La misteriosa fiamma della regina Loana,* Eco poignantly raises the question, "Who lived in my dreams?," the heroes of Fascist stories, or those from American comics?[41] Fantasy and science-fiction comics from the United States—while not innately adverse to

39. The series, written by Luigi Motta, was illustrated first by Edgardo dell'Acqua and then by the Italo-German artist Kurt Caesar. Edgardo dell'Acqua would illustrate many of the original comics that later appeared in *Topolino,* and Caesar illustrated the most explicit "war comics" for *Topolino* during World War II, as well as Romano, the legionnaire adventure and war hero for *Il Vittorioso.*

40. Ferris, "Parents, Children and the Fascist State," 194.

41. Eco, *La misteriosa fiamma,* 147.

the regime—were crowding out and overshadowing the overtly Fascist comics. As tensions with the United States escalated in the second half of the 1930s, this situation become untenable.

The Impact of the 1938 Decrees on Italian Stories

Following the 1938 decrees from the MCP, Galeazzo Ciano (now Minister of Foreign Affairs but formerly Minister of Press and Propaganda) initially assured representatives of King Features Syndicate (KFS) that the new dictates only targeted crime stories, and that comics such as the colonial adventure "Tim Tyler's Luck" would be unaffected.[42] Ciano proved incorrect, and publishers had to find replacements for their American comics. Publishers therefore had to accelerate and expand efforts to develop Italian stories, and, in a break with the Italian originals that predated these decrees, the stories had to be more overtly integrated within Italian settings and aligned with Fascist rhetoric.

Many of these Italian originals nonetheless continued to visibly draw on American counterparts. Indicative here is *Topolino*'s "Gino e Gianni." The series centers on two youthful male protagonists, Gino and Gianni, who bravely embark on adventure in the African continent not unlike "Tim Tyler's Luck." The series by Rino Albertarelli proved an adequate replacement and ran for 177 issues.[43]

The publication of more colonial stories aligned well with the desires of Alfieri, the MCP, and the attendees of the convention in Bologna, who wanted more Italian stories and "real" narratives. It should be noted, though, that the realism advocated by Fascist intellectuals remained an *imagined* or *mythic* reality, more aligned with propaganda. The noble heroism of Captain Folgore and the myth of the *ascaro fedele* were pleasant stand-ins for a brutal imperialist war that deployed chemical weapons.[44] Reality in these comics meant

42. Gherardo Casini to Mario Nerbini, 15 September 1938, quoted in Gadducci et al., *Eccetto Topolino*, 170.

43. "Gino e Gianni" was not Albertarelli's only success, either. He also illustrated several series written by Pedrocchi, and Albertarelli himself had previously created and designed "Kit Carson, cavaliere del West," which established many of the tropes and visual styles of Italian westerns, influencing those which followed, such as *TEX*.

44. The use of chemical weapons in the invasion of Ethiopia was not acknowledged by the Italian government until 1996. Chemical weapons were also deployed in the Fascist "pacification" of Libya, as were concentration camps. Del Boca, "Myths, Suppressions, Denials, and Defaults," 20, 25. On the use of chemical gas and other atrocities committed by the Italian army in Ethiopia, see Sbacchi, "Poison Gas and Atrocities," 47–53.

real *geographical* settings and Italian endeavors: an Africa with real rivers, foliage, and animals, but a stereotyped people that reflected the objectives of the regime. Unconquered Africa thus appeared barbaric and savage, while Italian colonial spaces had to be projected as spaces of security wherein "the Italian colonizer knew they did not have to be afraid."[45] This depiction of African colonial territories glossed over the realities of brutal acts of repression in the name of "pacification," and the lack of genuine prospects for the education and betterment of the colonized peoples.[46]

Setting comics in the colonies further embodied the regime's new efforts to regiment the interactions between Italians and African peoples in the colonies. The Council of Ministers published the Racial Manifesto in July 1938, followed in October by the enactment of the Racial Laws. These laws distinguished Jewish and African people from Italians, placed limits on the civil, political, and professional lives of people of Jewish and African heritage, and forbade marriage between these demographic groups. Memos from the MCP in August 1938 instructed journals to "continuously carry out racial propaganda."[47] Publishers increasingly printed comics depicting the supposed inferiority of African people alongside the professed benefits of Italian rule.

Writers for *L'Avventuroso,* for instance, replaced stories of imperial Britain or France with those in Italian East Africa. "L'eroe di Gimma" praised the victory of Italy's heroic soldiers in Ethiopia, who were cast in the role of liberators while the Abyssinian defenders, by contrast, were *predoni,* or "raiders." The massacre of Abyssinian soldiers at the hands of Italians with modern weaponry—depicted in panels within these stories—was framed as the defense and extension of civilization.[48]

The story which replaced "Flash Gordon" on the cover of *L'Avventuroso* exemplified this trend. Adapted from Edilio Napoli's novel *I tre di Macallé,* the series of the same name began with the 1896 siege of Macallé, a humiliating loss in Italian colonial history. The Abyssinians are shown as cruel in their victory, but three Italians escape with the help of a faithful *ascaro.* The three Italians continue to "uplift" Abyssinians over the following decades. Ultimately, they gain enough support and decide to march on the capital, only to find the Italian army is already attacking. The "liberators" take the capital, marking the start of the empire. With shouts of "Viva l'Italia!," the three protagonists

45. Scotto di Luzio, *L'appropriazione imperfetta,* 206. Patrizia Palumbo makes a similar point. Palumbo, "Orphans for the Empire," 226.

46. Duggan, *Fascist Voices,* 283–84; and Negash, "Ideology of Colonialism," 110–11, 115.

47. Forno, *La stampa del Ventennio,* 150.

48. *L'Avventuroso* (January 1937).

cheer the retreat of the Abyssinian army as an Italian officer and *ascari* raise the Italian tricolor.[49]

The depiction of Italians as brave and benevolent liberators intent on spreading civilization to colonial territories was not new to Italian children's periodicals. The long-established popularity of adventure novels set in colonies made colonial adventures an obvious setting for comics, even before the MCP's dictates of 1938. However, these stories became more frequent and more explicit in their messages. As the state intervened in the comics industry, the Italian Empire became a safe setting for new stories. The emphasis on the empire in Fascist propaganda and the passage of the Racial Laws signaled that imperial comics which depicted Fascist victories and Italian leadership over African peoples would be well received by cultural officials. Moreover, publishers benefitted from the historic popularity of the genre and the public support given the imperial project.

Italy's Glorious Past

Another setting Italian writers turned to in their need to find new Italian settings is the peninsula's past glories. Unlike colonial comics, these stories had been uncommon in most Italian illustrated periodicals, with the exception of *Balilla* and, to a lesser degree, *Il Vittorioso*. A series published in the first year of *Vitt*, for instance, depicts the First War of Unification of 1848.[50] The efforts of the House of Savoy to liberate Italian territories from the Austrians and unite them is praised, which is interesting since the Vatican had been cautious of Italian unification and of a war that pitted Catholic Kingdom of Sardinia against Catholic Austria.[51] Despite the ultimate failure of the campaign, the sacrifice of Italian soldiers is praised, as is the young prince Vittorio Emanuele, who becomes the first king of the Kingdom of Italy.

After the 1938 decrees, though, stories like this became regular features. One of the more frequent historical settings adopted by both *Topolino* and *L'Avventuroso* was the Italian Risorgimento, a movement throughout the nineteenth century in which there was a "resurgence" of Italian national consciousness as it was actively promoted in literature, theater, and intellectual work. The movement culminated in the unification of Italy.

49. *L'Avventuroso*, n. 235 (9 April 1939).

50. "Agli ordini del Re" (At the Orders of the King) was published in *Il Vittorioso* from 1 August to 8 October 1937, spanning issues 31 to 40.

51. Sperber, *European Revolutions*, 135. The House of Savoy was the ruling dynasty of the Kingdom of Sardinia.

Most notable among these stories was "La primula rossa del Risorgimento," created by Zavattini, Pedrocchi, and Pier Lorenzo De Vita, and published in *Paperino* ("Donald Duck," another of Mondadori's periodicals) in 1938 and 1939. Set in Milan in January 1848, the story tells of the Cigar Revolt, when Milanese patriots resisted Austrian rule by boycotting new taxes on tobacco, as well as the resulting anti-Austrian uprisings. The stage is set as "the patriotic Milanese await the moment to rise up against the Austrians who oppress them with a cruel and intransigent government."[52] The introduction casually connects the north and south of the peninsula by stating that the uprisings in the south and in Sicily have emboldened patriots in the north. The renouncement of foreign rule of the peninsula and the implications that there is *one* Italy align the story with the Fascist narrative of the Risorgimento.

The comic, like so many, is open to many interpretations. According to one reading, the story is *anti*-Fascist in nature, because the Austrian oppression is identifiable with that of the Fascist regime. The tactic of Marshal Radetzky and his men to turn patriots into informers who infiltrate the patriotic societies is akin to the network of informers developed by the Fascist police, the OVRA.[53] In this reading, resistance to oppressive rule is the most prominent theme.

However, it is significant that the resistance is to *foreign* rule, and the story embraces the sort of nationalism emblematic of Fascism. Proud Milanese patriots stand strong against the Austrians' proposals to betray their compatriots stating, "Better to die than serve you corrupt masters!" When the revolt has temporarily driven the Austrians from the city, the only Italian traitor, Predi, lies in bed lamenting his betrayal of his fellow countrymen and announces, "I will die of shame" before promptly doing so in the next panel.[54]

The story focused on the spread of the Risorgimento and Italian nationalism, which drive Italians to action. The protagonist, Stefano, goes to great lengths to free imprisoned patriots and, in doing so, diffuse these ideas and connect compatriots. His actions and sacrifices continually inspire others to join the cause of "Giovine Italia" (Young Italy), with the wagon driver swearing his desire to break ties with the *croati,* as a good Milanese himself.[55] The Milanese patriots ultimately arm themselves, and the fighting spills out into the streets, with the formation of barricades characteristic of the age of revolution. Milan is freed from Austrian subjugation after five days of fighting, and

52. Zavattini, Pedrocchi, and de Vita, *La primula rossa del Risorgimento*, 1.
53. Gadducci et al., *Eccetto Topolino*, 264.
54. Zavattini, Pedrocchi, and de Vita, *La primula rossa del Risorgimento*, 1, 39.
55. Zavattini, Pedrocchi, and de Vita, *La primula rossa del Risorgimento*, 7.

Stefano is honored as a hero. The rebirth of the (temporarily) liberated Milan embraces the Fascist ideal of Italian palingenesis.[56]

"La primula rossa del Risorgimento" is additionally careful to uphold traditional gender roles, even as it praises women who participate in defending the nation. Gloria—Stefano's fiancée—displays her bravery by not telling Radetzky's men everything when they question her about Stefano, but she is also the one who ultimately needs rescuing after she is arrested by the police. Stefano risks much in attacking the policemen to save her.[57] The final panel is of their marriage, an ending common to adventure stories in *Topolino*, *L'Avventuroso*, and *Il Vittorioso* alike. This formula upholds gender roles in that the male and female leads end up together, validating the characteristics of the protagonist as desirable to women. But it also seems to offer a distinction between the adventures of a girlhood or a women's young adult years, during which she can participate in the national life to some extent, and womanhood, defined by family life. Marriage at the end of adventure series symbolized this transition.

The message of "La primula rossa del Risorgimento" is ambiguous and contested. Seemingly aligned with the MCP's objectives of more Italian stories that advocated Fascist values, there is nonetheless a critique of oppression which might indict Fascism and Austrian rule alike. The presence of the Mazzinian slogan of Young Italy, "Dio e Patria" (God and Country), throughout the story enhances the ambiguity. Though a committed nationalist, Giuseppe Mazzini was a quintessential liberal democrat whose views were not easily appropriated by Fascists. Additionally, the slogan's placement of God *before* country was a consistent point of contention between the Catholic Church and the Fascist regime, who argued between "Fede e Patria" and "Patria e Fede."[58] The issue even arose at the Bologna Conference, during which many Fascist intellectuals defined Fascist literature as orienting itself toward God and the Patria. Yet the historical importance of the slogan in mobilizing Italians for the unification of Italy renders it difficult to interpret as anti-Fascist, and it further aligned with the regime's efforts to appropriate the Catholic Church and claim it as a source of legitimation.

Less ambiguous in its meaning was "I ragazzi di Portoria" (The Boys of the Portoria) in the Nerbini periodical *Giungla!* The story focused on a precursor to the resurgence of Italian nationalism: the anti-Austrian revolt in Genoa on 5 December 1746 sparked by eleven-year-old Giovanni Battisa Perasso, better known as "Balilla." Balilla and his friend regularly display the courage,

56. Gadducci et al., *Eccetto Topolino*, 264.

57. Zavattini, Pedrocchi, and de Vita, *La primula rossa del Risorgimento*, 11, 16–18.

58. Moro, *Il mito dell'Italia cattolica*, 98.

righteousness, and generosity of Genovesi, and lead the way in resisting foreign rule.[59]

The authors took steps to make the connection between their story and Fascist rule more explicit. At the end of "I ragazzi di Portoria," the vision of an old Italian woman predicts the terrors of the French Revolution, which will be ended by the arrival of *un italiano,* Napoleon, who would briefly bring order to Europe. She spoke of *la giovine italia* and of Giuseppe Garibaldi and the *re galantuomo* (Gentleman King, a reference to Victor Emmanuel II) who would unify Italy.

That she spoke of these two by name and not Mazzini is telling. Garibaldi, though an advocate of democracy, was a "man of action" and martial hero who installed himself as dictator in Sicily before the unification of the Kingdom of the Two Sicilies with the Kingdom of Sardinia to create the Kingdom of Italy. Victor Emmanuel was the king under whom Italy was first unified and whose family remained Italy's ruling dynasty. These figures more easily integrated into the Fascist narrative of the Risorgimento than did Mazzini. In any event, these figures were framed as mere precursors to Mussolini, a great man who the woman foretold would rise to quell the chaos sowed by the "wicked seed" spread in Italy after the Great War. The old woman's predictions were accompanied by panels displaying crowds cheering the Duce and lines of Balilla parading as they sang the Fascist anthem, "Giovinezza."[60]

The main difference in the stories after the 1938 MCP dictates was the explicitness of their Fascist orientations. While periodicals such as *L'Avventuroso* and *Topolino* had begun printing more Italian stories years earlier, many of which aligned with Fascist values, the 1938 decrees left publishers no choice but to develop more Italian stories which more overtly aligned with Fascist values. These new stories left little unsaid, highlighting their *italianità* and emphasizing their alignment with Fascist principles for the young readers and the censors alike.

American Comics Persist

Publishers of comics demonstrated resourcefulness as they substituted American comics with ones more clearly aligned with the regime. The process was complicated, though, partially because the extent and timeline of the suppression was initially unclear. Despite initial impressions that the ban would be

59. "I ragazzi di Portoria," *Giungla!,* reprinted in Carabba, *Il fascismo a fumetti,* 209.
60. "I ragazzi di Portoria," *Giungla!,* reprinted in Carabba, *Il fascismo a fumetti,* 220.

more narrow and gradual, Nerbini received a letter from Gherardo Casini of the MCP on 15 September 1938 accusing his firm of continuing American stories under Italian names, "anti-educational [stories] without any reference to the Fascist way of life."[61] Nerbini was forced to halt his American series and inform Guglielmo Emanuel that he had been instructed "to renounce all American features still running in my newspapers, without any exclusion even for the most inoffensive ones." When John Brogan of KFS contacted Emanuel for clarification, he received a response from Casini that the MCP intended the complete removal of American comics. However, Casini claimed this was not forced upon publishers by the state: "The principal publishers (Nerbini of Florence and Vecchi and Mondadori of Milan) willingly adhered to the transformation of their periodicals in a more educational and Italian way." Stating that publishers were allowed to finish certain ongoing stories of foreign origin, Casini insisted, "The Ministry had not used coercive methods but obtained the convinced adherence of publishers."[62]

Some editors likely did welcome the decrees, including those of *Corriere dei Piccoli* and *Il Vittorioso.* Editors of *Il Vittorioso* championed the move toward cultural autarchy, praising their periodical as a pioneer: "The motto of the campaign of autarky is 'Let's do it ourselves!' *Il Vittorioso*—above all in its intentions—is at the head of its field, with its stories, drawings, etc., all Italian."[63] Alfieri's calls for state intervention were enthusiastically embraced by Catholic intellectuals, who lambasted American comics as "absolutely contrary to the spirit with which the regime intends to educate Italian youth" and even called for the boycotting of American comics and films.[64] The decrees of the MCP could only aid *Il Vittorioso* insofar as they harmed its main competitors.

One firm which did not survive the changes was Vecchi, publisher of one of the earliest comics magazines in Italy that helped launch the comics craze, *Jumbo.* Overshadowed by competitors and now further hobbled by MCP

61. Gherardo Casini to Mario Nerbini, 15 September 1938, quoted in Gadducci et al., *Eccetto Topolino,* 170.

62. Mario Nerbini to Guglielmo Emanuel, 17 September 1938; John A. Brogan to Guglielmo Emanuel, 21 September 1938; Gherardo Casini to John Brogan, 20 ottobre 1938. Gadducci et al., *Eccetto Topolino,* 170, 171, 174.

63. "Autarchia!" *Il Vittorioso,* n. 47 (26 November 1938), 7.

64. "Verso la vera autarchia! Con una magnifica circolare il Ministro Alfieri vieta le indecenze di tanti giornali illustrate," in *La vita cattolica,* n. 2, 6 January 1938, quoted in Meda, *Stelle e strips,* 98; and "I nostri ragazzi leggono . . . ," in *La madre cattolica,* fasc. V (May 1938), 179, quoted in Meda, *Stelle e strips,* 99–100.

restrictions on foreign comics, Vecchi pivoted to other European markets and sold his adventure periodical, *Audace,* to Mondadori.[65]

Nerbini found himself in a strained position as well. Above all, Nerbini was preoccupied with how to reduce reliance on American stories without alienating a readership that had developed precisely because of those stories. When *L'Avventuroso* came under criticism in 1935 for its reliance on American comics, Nerbini had argued that the firm made much of its profit from these stories and "would not survive" without them.[66] The situation had changed little by 1938, and Nerbini was loath to abandon their most popular—and profitable—series. Accommodating such concerns, Alfieri assured publishers in November 1938 that the Italianization of children's periodicals would be conducted "with necessary gradualness" to lessen the financial blow.[67] However, Italianization *would* occur.

The editors of *L'Avventuroso* resigned themselves to this fate and attempted to explain the coming changes to their audience in mid-November:

> Our periodical has gradually eliminated almost all of the American illustrations from its pages: only two of the twelve pages are currently occupied by works by non-Italian artists, *but even these will disappear at the end of their episodes in progress.* We are sure that our Italian readers appreciate this innovation of ours in favor of the battle for autarky[. . . .] And we hope—no, we are sure—that other publishers of magazines will follow the same line without exception.[68]

The statement was at once self-praising and defensive. Editors framed the change as Nerbini's own initiative in support of the battle for cultural autarky, and the statement boasted the progress *L'Avventuroso* had already made toward this goal. At the same time, by pointing to the state's campaign, the editors implied that, as good Fascists, readers could not be upset with the change, which clearly aligned with the regime. Finally, Nerbini called on other publishers to do the same, informing readers that the magazine's rivals should also be dropping their American stories. This final line seems like a jab at Mondadori, whose "Topolino" was exempt from the MCP directives, and perhaps reflected resentment at the uneven enforcement of the policies.

---

65. Gadducci et al., *Eccetto Topolino,* 67, 230; and Pasquero, "Federico Pedrocchi," 78.

66. Segretaria Particolare del Duce, Rapporto sul Editore Mario Nerbini di Firenze, magg. 1935, ACS / SPD, CO 1922–1943, Serie numerica, B. 287, F. 15225-1.5 Varia 1926–1937.

67. Gadducci et al., *Eccetto Topolino,* 160.

68. Editore, "Ai lettori," *L'Avventuroso,* n. 215 (20 November 1938), 3.

Exemptions for Mickey Mouse

Nerbini's resentment was justified, as the Mondadori Publishing Firm did not find itself in the same dire straits as its competitors. True, it had eliminated "Audax" and several other popular American comics in 1938. In September, the "Tim e Tom" series rebranded as "I piccoli coloniali" concluded, effectively eliminating all American imports except for "Topolino" and "Paperino" (Donald Duck). But the Disney material remained safe.

The reasons for *Topolino*'s relatively secure position seem multiple. Regarding the Disney material itself, it has been said that Mickey Mouse was exempt because he was beloved by Mussolini's children, Romano and Anna Maria. While Romano has confirmed in interviews that he did not understand the suppression of American comics, that he and his sister loved Mickey Mouse, and that he said as much to Fernando Mezzasoma (then Director General of Italian Press), Romano dismisses claims that he and his sister were the reason for this exemption.[69] It is possible, though, that their affinity for Disney endeared Mussolini to the characters or provided him with a familiarity to mark the content as harmless to or even supportive of Fascist values, as "Topolino" stories consistently upheld traditional values and notions of racial hierarchy. But this view that Disney stories were wholesome, traditional, and of artistic value was shared in many European circles, Fascist and non-Fascist alike.

Similarly, Disney stories embodied many themes that were common to Fascist series, including racial tropes. The series "Topolino e Robinson Crusoe" is exemplary of this overlap. In the series, Topolino is granted a role in a Robinson Crusoe movie. The movie becomes more than an act when Crusoe and Topolino's boat is separated from the film crew during a storm and the two are truly stranded on an island. As in the original story, the two encounter a Black boy living alone on the island, conveniently already of the name "Venerdì" (Friday). Crusoe refers to him as a *selvaggio* (savage) and a *furfante* (scoundrel) and fears that there might be others nearby. Venerdì's appearance is highly caricatured—even by the standards of the highly caricatured world that is Disney cartoons—and he is further othered by the bizarre way in which he completes the tasks Topolino assigns him.

Topolino is continually perplexed to discover that Venerdì's "helpers" are, in fact, animals. Initially, Topolino believes Venerdì is lying when he says these animals can help. But the mouse soon finds out that Venerdì is completing

---

69. Intervista a Romano Mussolini, edited by Francesco De Giacomo (1995) in Gadducci et al., *Eccetto Topolino*, 406–7.

his tasks well. Here, the story both upholds racist hierarchies and stereotypes (Venerdì can command animals) and subverts them in the sense that Topolino is forced to acknowledge that Venerdì's ways work, a fact he is more than happy to convey to the still-skeptic Crusoe.

Whatever limited subversion there may be in the form of Venerdì's competence, though, is undermined by his exotic nature and is completely undone when Topolino and Crusoe later encounter other Indigenous people of the island. The Indigenous tribe is depicted with heavily caricatured features, and, keeping in line with colonial tropes of the era, they turn out to be cannibals who wish to eat the two.[70] The two ultimately escape and are relieved when Venerdì points to a ship off the coast of the island. They construct a signal fire to ensure their rescue.

Later in 1940, Topolino attempts to "civilize" Giovedì ("Thursday," who is either a new character or underwent a name change) in the series "Topolino e il selvaggio Giovedì" (literally "Topolino and the Savage Thursday," though the original US title was "Education for Thursday"). Exploits entail Topolino preventing Giovedì's attempts to eat Pluto. Disney stories presented an exotic Africa that integrated well into a periodical full of stories of Italian colonialism and claims of uplift.

Alignment with Fascist values in "Topolino" was not sufficient to convince all Fascist intellectuals to support the exemption for Mickey Mouse. During the comics debate in the late 1930s, Fascist journalist and politician Ezio Maria Gray frequently wrote to Mondadori questioning the reliance on comics. Gray could not understand why Mondadori published comics over the publication of children's books by his wife, Corinna Teresa Ubertis, the accomplished poet and novelist who wrote numerous children's books under the pseudonym Térésah. Gray pushed Mondadori "to consider that not all children are already idiotic; there are, fortunately, oases of poetry and good taste among them and therefore there can and must still exist a good children's book alongside the 'comics system.'"[71] Gray's resentment became more palpable the following year as Alfieri's intentions to enforce restrictions on American comics deepened, and Gray again reached out to Mondadori asking, "Why not take up the work of what is the best writer for children that you have had: Térésah?"[72]

But "Topolino" weathered Gray's protests. Mondadori had entangled his firm with the Fascist cultural project and fostered connections with officials. Rubino, Zavattini, and Pedrocchi had also sufficiently aligned the periodical

70. *Topolino*, n. 350 (7 September 1939).

71. Ezio M. Gray a Arnoldo Mondadori, Undated 1938, FAAM / AME, Fasc. Gray, Ezio M.

72. Ezio M. Gray a Arnoldo Mondadori, 19 November 1939, FAAM / AME, Fasc. Gray, Ezio M.

with the objectives of the MCP, successfully marketing the periodical as Italian and increasing its series by Italian artists since 1937. Most importantly, the regime had long demonstrated a preference for the Milanese publisher. Mondadori greatly benefited from loans and state intervention on its behalf. Additionally, the publishing firm had developed deep ties with individual Fascist leaders through the Italian culture of *raccomandazione*, a system of clientage networks based on the exchange of favors and a sense of mutual obligation to aid one another.[73] These favors took multiple forms, such as requests from Gherardo Casini and Dino Alfieri that Mondadori publish the books of specific authors or that Mondadori hire the son of Casini's friend.[74] Although Mondadori occasionally refused such requests, he benefited greatly from consenting. *Raccomandazione* represented a relationship that grew stronger with each exchange, meaning that the more Mondadori obliged these requests for favors, the more likely Casini, Alfieri, and others with similar such requests would continue to send his firm potential publications or grant Mondadori further leeway in, for instance, *Topolino.*

The regime's preference for Mondadori was cemented in June 1939 when the Fascist Party began the process through which the Mondadori Publishing House would be entrusted with the publication of three Party periodicals, *Il Balilla, Donna fascista,* and *Passo romano.*[75] Despite official circulation numbers of 250,000 copies per week, *Il Balilla* was struggling. It did not rank high in the essays of Venetian students writing about their favorite comics and stories, and it was not self-sustaining but instead cost the Party money. The move was accompanied by the formation of a new periodicals entity run by Mondadori, the Anonima Periodici Italiani (API), a significant step toward Mondadori's long-held goal of dominating the Italian publishing industry and the Fascist policy favoring cartelization.[76]

---

73. Evangelista, "Particular Kindness of Friends," 415.

74. Gherardo Casini a Arnoldo Mondadori, 12 ottobre 1937, FAAM / AME, Fasc. Fasc. Ministero della cultura popolare, 1, Sf.1, dal. 3.8.1933 al 25.4.1938; Dino Alfieri a Arnoldo Mondadori, 22 ottobre 1937, FAAM / AME, Fasc. Fasc. Ministero della cultura popolare, 1, Sf.1, dal. 3.8.1933 al 25.4.1938; Gherardo Casini a Arnoldo Mondadori, 17 febbraio 1938, FAAM / AME, Fasc. Ministero della cultura popolare, 1, Sf.1, dal. 3.8.1933 al 25.4.1938. These requests for the publication of other people's works were likely a part of this larger network of *raccomandazione,* representing favors Casini and Alfieri were rendering to others.

75. Al Sig. Consigliere Delegato Milano della Casa Editrice A. Mondadori Sede di Roma, 16 Giugno 1939, FAAM / AME, Fasc. Partito Nazionale Fascista.

76. As early as 1928, Mondadori wrote to Mussolini that "the creation of a strong editorial group, in addition to representing an economic force operating in the country, would, as Your Excellency can see, be of enormous importance for the development and direction of culture in Italy." Arnoldo Mondadori a Benito Mussolini, ACS / SPD, CO 1922–43, seria numerica, B. 509568/ F. 1—1923–1937. On the state's preference toward cartelization, see De Grand, *Italian Fascism,* 84, 162; and Pinto, *Nature of Fascism Revisited,* 93.

With a combined circulation of fourteen million copies annually, the decision to entrust the Party's periodicals seemed a stroke of luck for the Milanese publisher. However, the real reason for the transition was that the periodicals were, in fact, *failing*, particularly *Il Balilla*. With the assumption of the printing of *Il Balilla*, the API also assumed the losses of 200,000 lire accumulated by the Party's youth periodical. The Party, meanwhile, stood to earn 70 percent of subsequent profits for the periodical should the API rescue the sinking ship.[77] It is likely that Mondadori did not believe taking on *Il Balilla* was a good financial move in and of itself, but that this was instead an exchange which would further the development of his periodical empire and provide additional leeway with his flagship children's magazine, *Topolino*.

The exemption granted to Disney material was monumental for Mondadori's periodicals. But it should be remembered that Zavattini and Pedrocchi did much to develop the Italian stories in *Topolino* and its fellow periodicals well before the MCP decreed the suppression of American stories.[78] These efforts paid off as the periodical continued to thrive despite the disappearance of all American series not based on Disney material.

The Return of American Comics in *L'Avventuroso*

Nerbini, by contrast, struggled, as his periodicals were afforded no exemption. Moreover, although Nerbini had begun developing Italian originals earlier than Mondadori, the Italian originals in *L'Avventuroso* were often imitations of American comics that served as fillers. This was problematic because Nerbini therefore lacked established Italian series to fall back on when the MCP rejection of Italian series too clearly inspired by American comics resulted in a severe purge of the magazine. The stories that replaced these series which had formerly driven the periodical's popularity simply did not hold up. The sale of *L'Avventuroso* plummeted from its average weekly circulation of 300,000 copies down to 100,000 by 1940.[79] Nerbini thus scrambled to stay afloat while Mondadori continued to sell relatively unimpeded.

In 1939, Nerbini reached out to Emanuel about the possibility of modifying the American stories from KFS to make them more Italian. The owner of

77. Arnoldo Mondadori, Pro-memoria per il duce, 13 maggio 1940, ACS / SPD, CO 1922–43, Serie numerica, B. 509568 / F. II Varia.

78. As noted above, this cultural project was already underway in 1935 under the direction of Antonio Rubino. It accelerated in 1936 with the efforts of Zavattini and Pedrocchi. Laura, "Topolino: Indici."

79. Gadducci et al., *Eccetto Topolino*, 222, 232.

KFS, Hearst, proved unwilling to allow such modifications of KFS copyrighted material. Relaying this news to Nerbini on 14 July 1939, Emanuel sympathized with the Florentine publisher's situation and said that, as a representative of KFS, he "could not authorize the execution of the project" to bring back American stories in altered forms.[80] Nerbini proceeded with his plans regardless.

The popular American series "L'Uomo Mascherato" ("The Phantom") had been among those to cease publication around the same time "Flash Gordon" disappeared. In July 1939, three days after receiving the letter from Emanuel, the masked hero was the first series to return. Redesigned by Nerbini illustrator Roberto Lemmi, "Il Giustiziere Mascherato" appeared in issue 249 of *L'Avventuroso.* Figure 4.4 compares the modified hero to the original Phantom. The story is credited to the writer Emilio Fancelli, but it is clearly a modified "Phantom" story.[81] The characters remained largely the same, including the protagonist's love interest, Diana. But our hero has changed costumes, shedding his usual red in favor of a green hood and a larger red eye mask. Could Nerbini have imagined this change would prevent the censors from recognizing this modified American hero?

In truth, it seems highly unlikely that the censors did not recognize the series for what it was. In February of 1939, the MCP had dictated that all publishers send eight copies of publications to the offices of their regional prefects for preventative censorship. It is possible, then, that the MCP determined the reduction and modification of American comics was enough, so long as it was not "Flash Gordon," for which they seemed on the lookout. After all, the continuation of a few modified American stories did not prevent the Minister of Popular Culture, Dino Alfieri, from declaring the successful reclamation of children's literature to the Chamber of Deputies: "We have snatched children's literature away from any foreign influence."[82]

And yet "L'Uomo Mascherato" was not the only American comic to return. "Mandrake" had also disappeared from *L'Avventuroso* at the beginning of 1938. The series briefly continued in its own supplemental magazine of *L'Avventuroso,* but this likewise came to an end in July 1938. In issue 301 on 14 July 1940, Mandrake returned in the story "Il mago 900" but now under the semi-Italianized title of "Mandracke."[83] The lack of the letter "k" in the Italian alphabet prompted another changed to "Mandrache."

80. Guglielmo Emanuel to Mario Nerbini, 14 luglio 1939, quoted in Gadducci et al., *Eccetto Topolino,* 224.

81. Gadducci et al., *Eccetto Topolino,* 222–24; and Meda, *Stelle e strips,* 72.

82. Gadducci et al., *Eccetto Topolino,* 228.

83. *L'Avventuroso,* n. 301 (14 July 1940).

FIGURE 4.4. The original design of "L'Uomo Mascherato" appears on the top in a supplement to *L'Avventuroso* dedicated to the hero. The modified "Il Giustiziere Mascherato," credited as designed by Roberto Lemmi and written by Emilio Fancelli, is on the bottom. *L'Uomo Mascherato,* n. 1 (May 1937); "Il Giustiziere Mascherato," *L'Avventuroso,* n. 249 (17 July 1939).

Nerbini's continued desire for new material appears to have changed the situation with KFS. Nerbini and Emanuel reached an agreement that there would be no charge for sequestered material, reducing the risk taken by Nerbini. Both understood that they were operating in a context in which these publications could "be interrupted at any moment."[84] Despite these changes, *L'Avventuroso*'s circulation remained poor, and it is unclear how many Italians even realized the American comics had returned. Instead, Italian youths turned their attention to *Topolino.*[85] It is likely that the main reason why these efforts to revitalize *L'Avventuroso* proved futile was because "Flash Gordon" was not among the series to return. That Nerbini scrapped proposals for a modified and Italianized "Flash Gordon" suggests he recognized that the MCP was concerned about this series in particular.[86]

Nerbini was not the only Italian publisher to relaunch modified American stories. Mondadori's *Topolino* likewise snuck in a few officially banned American stories in lightly modified formats. For instance, the series "Le isole sotto i ghiacci" (The Island under the Ice), presented in *Topolino* as an Italian original, was an altered Brick Bradford story. Brick Bradford, though, became a brown-haired Italian of the name Guido Ventura. However, Ventura was soon after renamed Giorgio, because Guido was considered too Jewish in light of the anti-Semitic policies in the Racial Laws.[87]

Nerbini's ability to continue publishing American comics with only slight (or no) modifications suggests that the primary problem with American comics was that they were foreign and produced by a country with which Italy no longer had positive relations. Had more officials believed the content to be truly anti-Fascist, a harder stance would likely have been adopted than allowing other heroes to return with slight Italianization. The inability for "Flash Gordon" to return attests to this, as the series had been identified as particularly problematic and would likely have been unable to circulate regardless of any modifications. Interestingly, by specifically targeting American comics, the MCP branded them as anti-Fascist regardless of their messages and, in doing so, *made them* oppositional to the regime.

84. Miniatelli to Guglielmo Emanuel, 11 June 1939. Gadducci et al., *Eccetto Topolino*, 227. This arrangement arose in June 1939 out of negotiations between Emanuel and Miniatelli of the Nerbini Publishing House in regard to the series "Prince Valiant," which was to be published as "Il Principe Valentino" in the Nerbini magazine, *Pisellino*, under the stipulation that the firm was only responsible to pay for that which was printed and circulated.

85. Gadducci et al., *Eccetto Topolino*, 233.

86. According to Francesco De Giacomo around 150 strips were prepared for publication of a reworked Gordon under the name "Astro," now with brown hair. The modified "Flash Gordon" was abandoned in February 1941, without ever appearing in *L'Avventuroso*. Gadducci et al., *Eccetto Topolino*, 236.

87. Laura, "Topolino: Indici."

Conclusion

The persistence of American comics suggests that the MCP was above all concerned with appearances, with what they could *claim* to have achieved. That American comics continued in the periodicals of both Nerbini and Mondadori should not be taken to mean that the regime was hoodwinked by what can only be seen as minor alterations to American comics. This gap between the claims and reality of the regime are not unique to Fascist cultural policies. The regime often made claims of great achievements which were, upon closer reflection, half-truths at best, often covering up deals made behind closed doors. In the case of children's comics, it seems probable that Alfieri and the MCP were content with the reduction of American comics and the Italianization of that which remained, making Italian children's magazines *appear* devoid of foreign influences.

The reasons behind this toleration seem largely financial. As noted above, Nerbini and his competitors made the argument that their publishing firms would lose massive amounts of profits if their periodicals lost their driving series. This would not have been in the interest of the regime, which after all desired the creation of a strong Italian publishing industry. Moreover, many individuals within the regime benefitted heavily from their connections with publishers, which facilitated the publication of their own books and allowed for the request of favors. This continued ability of publishers to negotiate and find ad hoc compromises with the policies of the MCP demonstrates that officials were willing to sacrifice ideology in the name of profits.

This does not mean that the program of cultural *bonifica* was completely futile or mere words. Many American series disappeared, not to return until after World War II, including "Flash Gordon," singled out as the most troubling comic by Italian intellectuals for its cult of technology and sexualized women. The Italianization of heroes, too, was significant for the regime. Even more than that, the reduction of American comics increased space for Italian originals, and the works of artists such as Pedrocchi, Moroni-Celsi, and Albertarelli flourished, contributing to an "Italian approach" to adventure comics.[88] *Topolino* and *Il Vittorioso* certainly achieved the most success in creating a unique Italian approach to comics.[89] On the other hand, the uneven enforcement of these restrictions eliminated certain magazines altogether, such as *Jumbo* and *Audace,* published by Vecchi, and reduced the popularity of the

88. It must be remembered that many other artists of note contributed to the "Italian way" of comics, particularly Walter Molino of Mondadori. Molino and others were not discussed here purely for reasons of space and the selection of stories.

89. Becciu, *Il fumetto in Italia,* 116.

most popular of comics magazines, *L'Avventuroso.* While there is no evidence that *Il Balilla* benefitted from these trends, it certainly did not hurt.

The move to suppress American comics highlights the changing cultural priorities of the regime. The relative openness formerly adopted to attract intellectuals had proven unsuccessful in fostering a sufficiently Fascist culture. Moreover, the desire to gain the support of foreign intellectuals seemed a less profitable avenue as international opinion turned against the regime. At the same time, the regime proved itself willing to sacrifice ideological purity and complete adherence to policies to maintain profits in the publishing sector. While the cultural institutes of the Fascist state made real gains toward cultural *bonifica,* it seems that what was most important was to be able to assert that its totalitarian claim to society extended to culture and to maintain the *appearance* that such goals had been achieved.

CHAPTER 5

Comics at War

Uncertainty and Support in Comics during World War II

As the Second World War approached, Italian comics reflected the hopes, anxieties, and uncertainties felt by many toward the conflict. After an initial phase of uncertainty and ambivalence regarding its outbreak, stories overtly linked to the conflict peaked during the early years as Germany seemed unstoppable. Most publishing activities were suspended in July 1943 in the upheavals produced by the dismissal of Mussolini from power on 25 July. *Balilla* and *L'Avventuroso* never restarted, though *Corriere dei Piccoli, Topolino,* and *Il Vittorioso* (*Vitt*) would return. The two periodicals which relaunched during the war, *Corrierino* and *Vitt,* reflected an Italy divided by civil war and two occupying forces. *Corriere dei Piccoli*—printed in a Milan firmly dominated by the German-backed Repubblica Sociale Italiana (Italian Social Republic, RSI)—followed Fascist propaganda until Italy was fully under Allied control in 1945. *Il Vittorioso,* based in Rome and allowed to restart publication by the Allies after the city's liberation in June 1944, adopted a more neutral orientation.

The war appeared differently in the pages of each of the major periodicals. While *Vitt, Topolino,* and *Corrierino* operated within the parameters set by the Ministry of Popular Culture, creators of these comics focused on different (though often overlapping) aspects of the war. Analyzing the unique elements highlighted by each publishing house in their portrayal of the cause and aims of the conflict to their young readers illustrates that Catholic and conservative circles saw opportunities and benefits in specific aspects of the war. Although the war was never a popular endeavor and fear persisted throughout it, these sources of support demonstrate how the Fascist war resonated with various sociopolitical groups and briefly became an *Italian* one.

The support depicted in comics for the war must be positioned within the heightened censorship of the war years. The parameters within which the producers of these periodicals operated was tightly controlled first by the Ministry of Popular Culture (MCP) and then by the Allied Military Government for Occupied Territories (AMGOT), from which publishers had to receive permission to restart publication. The weight of MCP restrictions is best represented in a memo from the President of Gioventù italiana di Azione Cattolica (GIAC), Luigi Gedda, to GIAC leaders in September 1939 after Germany invaded Poland and Mussolini announced a position of nonbelligerence. In the memo, Gedda noted that directives were already detailing what could and could not be published and asked that writers "cheerfully accept the sacrifices that will be demanded of us."[1] Extra caution was to be exercised by writers for *Vitt,* as numerous GIAC periodicals had already been suspended. The fear that *Il Vittorioso* could follow suit encouraged active support.

On top of these restrictions, publishers operated with limited information. The MCP tightly controlled news on the conflict and the reporting in Italian periodicals.[2] The image of Italian military preparedness and strength that initially appeared in these weeklies was undermined by Allied air raids and defeat. As the reporting remained constant, the gap between propaganda and the lived realities of Italians created a disconnect between the populace and the Fascist regime.[3]

Despite their contribution in creating this misrepresentation, *Corrierino, Vitt,* and *Topolino* remained among the most popular children's periodicals in Italy after the war and still kindle affection today. The role of censorship was significant in fostering an image that any support for the war was a concession to the regime, and control of the press is an essential part of the story of Italian comics during World War II. The very incorporation of the war into children's periodicals was a concession to the regime, as children's periodicals could have remained focused on entertainment and education.

Yet overemphasis on censorship neglects the degree to which publishers made choices in *how* they represented the war. It further ignores the varying sources of support for the war that *did* exist across sectors of Italy's

1. Luigi Gedda, Circolare della GIAC, 14 settembre 1939, ISACEM / Fondo della GIAC / Serie 3, B. 523 / Circolari, 1938–39, 1, 2. Licata, *Storia del Corriere della sera,* 296, 298; and Murialdi, *La stampa del regime fascista,* 226.

2. Licata, *Storia del Corriere della sera,* 301.

3. Petrella, *Staging the Fascist War,* 6; and Willson, *Women in Twentieth-Century Italy,* 99.

sociopolitical circles. After Italy entered the fray in June 1940, Gedda published an article entitled "Quando la Patria Chiama" (When the Patria Calls), in which he asserted that "the duty falls not only on those deployed, but on all Italians and therefore on each of us." He further highlighted the large number of Catholic Action members who "wore the *grigioverde*" of the Italian military, praising God for establishing strong civic bonds in "this beautiful and privileged land."[4] The regime's fellow travelers may not have embraced all aspects of the Fascist war, but that did not mean they lacked a sense of duty or disagreed with Mussolini's rhetoric of an Italy encircled by its enemies. As Nicholas Stargardt argues regarding Nazi Germany, citizens need not be committed to the Fascist war in order to support aspects of it.[5] Although many scholars have discussed how the war appeared in comics, the focus on censorship has resulted in less analysis of how these comics reflected the views of various publishers and sociopolitical groups.[6]

This chapter compares each periodical to *Balilla*—the regime's organ of propaganda—to reveal how producers of comics aligned their stories with the dictates of the regime while also finding unique aspects to highlight. After the first section establishes the anxieties concerning the outbreak of war in Europe and Italy's initial stance of nonbelligerence, the middle section identifies sources of support for the war as depicted in children's periodicals. The final section considers the impact on periodicals of defeat and the Civil War. Although this chapter demonstrates the sources of support for the war in these stories, uncertainty remains an ever-present theme, first over Italy's role in the conflict, then regarding the evolving war and the dictates of the MCP, and finally with the Italian Civil War.

War, Nonbelligerence, and Uncertainty

Gedda, like many Italians, was likely not as enthusiastic about the war as his June 1940 article noted above suggests. In the September 1939 memo circulated by Gedda on the need to follow the directives of the MCP, he expresses

4. Luigi Gedda, "Quando la Patria Chiama," giugno 1940, ISACEM / Fondo Personali / Luigi Gedda, 1934–1978 / Serie 1, B. 1 / F. 6, 1. "Grigioverde" is a reference to the gray-green uniforms of the Italian army.

5. Stargardt argues the German determination to fight on was less out of a commitment to Nazism and more due to a notion of German duty, a belief that the war was to overthrow the unjust Versailles Treaty, and a sense of encirclement by adversaries. Stargardt, *German War*, 15–16.

6. Carabba, *Corrierino, Corrierona*, 104–15; Preziosi, *Il Vittorioso*, 16–17; and Vecchio, *L'Italia del Vittorioso*, 156, 167–70.

relief that Italy was not embroiled in the conflict.[7] After years of fighting in East Africa and Spain, Italian hesitancy to fight is hardly surprising. The alliance between Germany and Italy enshrined in the Pact of Steel troubled many Italians, who often expressed greater admiration for the British and French.[8] Even much of the Fascist and military leadership remained leery, including Mussolini's son-in-law, Galeazzo Ciano, and Chief of Staff Pietro Badoglio, who recognized that Italy was unprepared for a large-scale war.[9]

Children's illustrated periodicals followed the attempts of the Fascist press to combat this perception. In the first issue of *Balilla* after the German invasion of Poland, the characters in "La piccola italiana" (a reference to the female Fascist youth groups) welcomed Caterina from Berlin (figure 5.1). The flags of Fascist Italy and Nazi Germany fly in the background as the children raise the fascist salute. Unprepared to enter the war, Mussolini remained dedicated to the alliance with Germany, and the strip signaled the friendship between the two countries.

The following issues of *Balilla* projected an Italy ready for war, with images of well-equipped soldiers and "The Formidable Military Might of Fascist Italy."[10] Such assertions completely contradicted reports from Mussolini's generals on the severe deficiency of equipment within the navy, air force, and army. The Italian military was outmatched by the French and British navies and air forces, and the Italian military lacked enough fuel for a prolonged war. Moreover, Italy had neither the industrial capability nor the raw materials to redress its deficiencies. Mussolini's awareness of these shortcomings motivated Italy's initial position of nonbelligerence, but the Duce remained dedicated to breaking out of the encirclement that he believed confined Italy to the Mediterranean. Mussolini additionally feared that German dominance of the continent would further marginalize Italy if the nation did not enter the war and make its own territorial gains.[11] The MCP thus tasked the press with crafting the image of a strong Italy military. The effectiveness of this strategy was dubious; reports from police informants reflect that the Italian populace

7. Gedda, Circolare della GIAC, 2 marzo 1939, 1.

8. Bosworth, *Mussolini's Italy*, 452–53; Colarizi, *La seconda guerra mondiale*, 68–69; and Corner, *Fascist Party and Popular Opinion*, 254.

9. De Felice, *Lo Stato totalitario*, 642, 649, 661; Gooch, *Mussolini and His Generals*, 472, 484–85, 495; and Oliva, *La guerra fascista*, 10–18.

10. *Il Balilla*, n. 37 (10 September 1939), 3; *Il Balilla*, n. 39 (24 September 1939), 3; and *Il Balilla*, n. 40 (1 October 1939), 3.

11. Colarizi, *La seconda guerra mondiale*, 23, 76; De Felice, *Lo Stato totalitario*, 637, 642, 649; Gooch, *Mussolini and His Generals*, 472–73, 485–87; and Oliva, *La guerra fascista*, 10–18.

1. Da Berlino stamattina
è arrivata Caterina,
vivamente festeggiata
dalla piccola brigata.

FIGURE 5.1. The caption reads: "Caterina arrived this morning from Berlin, warmly celebrated by the little brigadier." "La piccola italiana," *Il Balilla*, n. 36 (3 September 1939), 9.

remained skeptical, with many blaming Germany and some going so far as to question Mussolini's leadership.[12]

Skepticism, uncertainty, and anxiety created a climate in which the Fascist press was instructed to cautiously report on the war. Aldo Borelli, director of *Corriere della Sera*, seems to have responded by instructing *Corriere dei Piccoli* to avoid commentary during Italy's period of nonbelligerence.[13] The outbreak of hostilities in Europe did appear in the pages of *Il Vittorioso*, though. Even before the invasion of Poland, the periodical's nameplate expressed anxiety about a coming war when a manned heavy machine gun was incorporated on the right side in July. The continued presence of family-friendly characters on the left side of the banner clarified that the periodical would not

12. Licata, *Storia del Corriere della sera*, 298. The Nazi-Soviet Nonaggression Pact further turned Italian public opinion against Germany. Colarizi, *La seconda guerra mondiale*, 23, 73; and Corner, *Fascist Party and Popular Opinion*, 258, 261–62.

13. Carabba, *Corrierino, Corrierona*, 104.

focus exclusively on the war, in contrast to *Balilla.* Nonetheless, a new strip appeared in *Vitt* following the German invasion of Poland, in which a squadron of Italian fighter pilots deployed to intercept enemy aircraft that may be intent on attacking their air base.[14] Italy may not be at war, but, as in the pages of *Balilla,* "Un giorno con una squadriglia da caccia" (A Day with a Fighter Squadron) projected a military capable of defending the Italian people.

Vitt initially expressed discomfort with the war and appeared unwilling to take a side. Such a representation of the war did follow MCP guidelines for a cautious approach to the war that did not cast blame. It was, however, a possible indication of the Vatican's unease with the German invasion of predominantly Catholic Poland (exacerbated by Nazi abuse of the Church in Germany) and the nonaggression pact with the Soviet Union.[15] Ambivalence regarding the German alliance appeared in short stories such as "Il carroccio," in which the cities of Milan and Crema fought "the tyranny of foreign authority" in the form of the Germanic Holy Roman Empire of Federico I in 1158. Most poignant, perhaps, was a short story focused on the brave defenders of Finland against the Soviet advance, suggesting disapproval of the Nazi pact with the USSR, whom the Vatican hierarchy viewed as its chief nemesis.[16] Sympathy for the Finnish defenders extended beyond Catholic circles to many nationalists throughout Italy, including Ciano and other members of the Fascist leadership.[17]

The tension over the alliance with Nazi Germany notwithstanding, articles in *Vitt* emphasized that the link between the Vatican and the Fascist state remained unquestioned. Pius XII distinguished the Nazis, who publicly attacked the Church, from Fascists in Italy, who—at least officially—respected its authority.[18] The eleventh anniversary of the concordat was celebrated in February 1940 in a piece that praised its signing and ended with the prayer: "Our Catholic and Italian heart rejoices: thanks to God for so many favors and we pray every day with the Pope for Italy and for her Emperor King, for her

---

14. "Un giorno con una squadriglia da caccia," *Il Vittorioso,* n. 26 (9 September 1939), 3.

15. Colarizi, *La seconda guerra mondiale,* 23, 71–73; Dagnino, *Faith and Fascism,* 184, 186; and De Felice, *Lo Stato totalitario,* 790–800.

16. "Il carroccio," *Il Vittorioso,* n. 15 (13 April 1940), 3. The term "carroccio" refers to a wagon bearing a city's standards used by Milan and other cities in nothern Italy as a rallying point in battle during the Medieval era.

17. Bosworth, *Mussolini's Italy,* 455; and Colarizi, *La seconda guerra mondiale,* 23, 73. Even *Corriere della Sera,* which typically aligned completely with Fascist rhetoric, cast Finland in a sympathetic light in its reports on the invasion. Licata, *Storia del Corriere della sera,* 297.

18. Kertzer, *Pope at War,* 99, 108, 168.

Duce. May it be great, may it be a beacon of civilization, of peace, of faith to all peoples."[19] Italy's entrance into the war shattered such hopes.

Mussolini declared war on France on 10 June 1940, believing a negotiated peace would follow the fall of Paris. A MCP circular distributed the same day instructed periodicals to harp on the reasons for war expressed by Mussolini, as well as "our irredentist goals."[20] *Balilla* granted the declaration an entire page, featuring a picture of Mussolini speaking from the balcony in Palazzo Venezia accompanied by his speech proclaiming Italy was to go to war against the oppressors of the Italian people.[21] The editors of *Vitt* provided a brief account of the declaration on the second page, borrowing from the Duce's speech and instructing readers of *Il Vittorioso* to do their duty. Beneath the announcement of war was another notice that informed readers that, "in the next issue, Romano, the Italian hero [. . .] will be in action at the service of the Patria in a new *cine-romanzo* [comics with realistic aesthetics] on current events."[22] As Italy went to war, so too did the characters of Italy's comics.

Italy at War: Sources of Support Despite Continued Anxieties

Once Italy entered the war, *Balilla, Corrierino,* and *Il Vittorioso* wasted no time informing Italians of their duties. In an embodiment of Gedda's article "When the Patria Calls," *Vitt*'s popular character Romano and his wife, Isa, immediately interrupt their honeymoon when "they hear the voice of the Duce transmitted over the radio, announcing to the world Italy's declaration of war on France and England. Electrified by the news, Romano, the old legionnaire of Spain, decided to return to the distant homeland [of Italy] and fight for her victory."[23] Their plane is shot down, but they are saved by an Italian submarine, allowing Romano to shoot the planes out of the sky. The visual style adopted by *Il Vittorioso* for the series—fittingly titled "Per l'Italia" (For Italy)—and the placement of Romano as a pilot in the North African campaign cast the comic as a realistic representation of the war, possibly obscuring the embellished nature of the might attributed to the protagonist and the Italian military in which he serves.

---

19. "Undici anni di storia," *Il Vittorioso*, n. 6 (10 February 1940), 7.
20. Velina quoted in Murialdi, *La stampa del regime fascista,* 233.
21. *Il Balilla*, n. 27 (30 June 1940), 3.
22. *Il Vittorioso*, n. 26 (29 June 1940), 2.
23. *Il Vittorioso*, n. 27 (6 July 1940), 1.

Romano's role as a pilot is no casual narrative choice but reflects Fascist propaganda. The Italian air force faced the same challenges as the Italian military at large but, rhetorically, the air force had long been imbued with a Fascist spirit. Fascists such as Italo Balbo and the Futurist intellectual F. T. Marinetti idealized airplanes as the embodiment of the Fascist values of action and dynamism and represented a manifestation of the cult of technology characteristic of Marinetti's faction of Fascism.[24] Editors' focus in *Vitt* on the supposed technological superiority of Italian aircraft exemplified this obsession, and Romano's skills are regularly emphasized: in the fifth episode, Romano's friends are outnumbered by British fighters and yet he effortlessly guns them down.[25] Romano's story conveys the alleged military preparedness of Italy and asserts the duty of all Italian men to join the war effort. If Romano interrupted his blissful honeymoon on the other side of the world to defend the homeland, then you too must do your part.

Everyone had a part to play in the war, including women. Women appeared minimally in the comics throughout the conflict. Where they did, it was in supporting roles. Isa and her friend accompany Romano to North Africa to serve as nurses, but the series upholds the principle that the battlefield is not a place for women, as Romano's heroism is reinforced when he protects and at times rescues Isa from danger.[26]

While the comics in *Il Vittorioso* targeted Italians old enough to serve, those in *Balilla* and *Corriere dei Piccoli* informed the youth of their duties on the home front. Schools and youth groups were tasked with mobilizing young Italians. During the war, children collected material to minimize waste in the *lotta contro gli sprechi* (the battle against waste), and were expected to reduce household consumption, promote savings and war gardens, and inform adults of *their* duties.[27]

Italian boys were *ometti,* or "little men," not old enough to enlist but nonetheless expected to be obedient and make sacrifices for the nation.[28] *Corriere dei Piccoli* went further with the role assigned young boys in defending Italy. "Remoletto e Romolino" told of two young Balilla named after the mythical founders of Rome who set out to support Italy. The first issue shows the boys discussing the natural defenses of Italy, such as the Alps, "which resist any

24. Oliva, *La guerra fascista,* 29–30. Marinetti asserted at the 1938 Bologna Conference that Fascist children's literature must praise "le belle forze micidiali" and "le squisite eleganze" of Italian fighter planes in action. Marinetti, "Accademico d'Italia," 8.

25. *Il Vittorioso,* n. 32 (10 August 1940), 1.

26. *Il Vittorioso,* n. 41 (12 October 1940), 1; and *Il Vittorioso,* n. 48 (30 November 1940), 1.

27. Gibelli, *Il popolo bambino,* 355–59; and Meda, *È arrivata la bufera,* 77–78, 82, 103, 105.

28. Gibelli, *Il popolo bambino,* 319–20; and Meda, *È arrivata la bufera,* 100.

6. « Più gagliarda ancor di tali baluardi naturali
dei soldati è la caterva, coi Balilla di riserva... »

FIGURE 5.2. The caption reads, "Even more vigorous than such natural bulwarks are the multitudes of soldiers with the Balilla in reserve." "Remoletto e Romolino," *Corriere dei Piccoli*, n. 25 (16 June 1940).

assault."[29] Beyond these defenses, there are also the lines of Italian soldiers and behind them, Romolino and Remoletto inform us (figure 5.2), will be the Balilla in reserve. The people of Italy "can work among Italy's mountains and seas with tranquil security, as if inside a fortress."[30]

Girls, too, were enlisted to support the war effort. In the *Balilla* strip "La piccola italiana," the protagonist, Mariella, supervises younger children now that adults are busy with the war. She is tasked with educating the children on the war and their duties. When the children lament that they are too young to serve, Mariella instructs them on the expected role of women and girls: "You are all little soldiers: with a little effort, you can even save soap. And the sugar? It is a bit limited and must be rationed." Indeed, "Every little girl shows that she can do her duty."[31] The strip conveyed the importance of rationing in Italy and of doing so gladly. The story may have been motivated by police reports on the resentment already brewing among the populace over the increased

29. *Corriere dei Piccoli*, n. 25 (16 June 1940).
30. *Corriere dei Piccoli*, n. 25 (16 June 1940).
31. *Il Balilla*, n. 37 (8 September 1940), 1.

regulations on the distribution of goods that were already scarce due to policies of autarky and foreign sanctions.[32]

As comics sought to prepare Italians for the war, they could not hide sources of anxiety. "La piccola italiana," for instance, conveys concern regarding air raids and the potential use of gas against civilians. Nearly a month after Italy's invasion of southern France, Mariella teaches the children how to properly don their gas mask in one disturbing episode when an alarm sounds and the children fear it is an air-raid siren. The strip betrays the reality that Italian cities could be targeted, and that civilians needed to be ready. Preparing Italians for the eventuality of air raids was one of the tasks entrusted to the press, a task which conflicted with its other charge of presenting the Italian air force as superior and capable of defending Italian cities.[33] The comic attempted to reconcile these goals by ending with a reassuring note, as the alarm turns out to be a bill collector ringing the bell at the door; as figure 5.3 shows, the children clearly know how to affix their masks, but the end suggests that all is safe and that they need not worry.

Despite the depiction of anxieties, *Vitt, Corrierino,* and *Balilla* primarily focused on the MCP's directive that they inform young readers of their duties. Everyone had a role. As the war progressed, each periodical continued to focus on different aspects of the war, revealing much about the sources of support for the war in Fascist, Catholic, and conservative circles in Italy. The support depicted in periodicals of the time correlates with sentiments among the broader Italian populace. So long as the Axis armies seemed unstoppable in the early years of the war, Italians were hopeful that Mussolini would prove correct that a quick war would benefit the nation. However, their projection of an Italy prepared to fight was undermined by the fact that Genoa had already been targeted by British bombers and that citizens could find no air-raid shelters during a false alarm in Milan.[34]

For Nation and Empire: Conservative Support for the War

The notion of Italy fighting a *defensive* battle garnered support among Catholic and conservative circles. Mussolini claimed that the corrupt and hypocritical empires of France and Britain had obstructed Italy's interests in the

32. Corner, *Fascist Party and Popular Opinion,* 260, 66; Ferris, "Consumption," 129; and Oliva, *La guerra fascista,* 312.

33. Petrella, *Staging the Fascist War,* 2, 23.

34. Corner, *Fascist Party and Popular Opinion,* 266; and Willson, *Women in Twentieth-Century Italy,* 97.

FIGURE 5.3. Hearing a loud bell, Mariella and the children quickly put on a gas mask. Even the cat has one! The bell turns out not to be the alarm, though, but a man with the gas bill at the door. "La piccola italiana," *Il Balilla,* n. 29 (14 July 1940), 16.

Mediterranean, referred to as *mare nostrum,* "our sea." The hypocrisy of the British was stressed in *Balilla*'s "Teatrino inglese," which presented England's entire history as built on the oppression of others, pointing to the massacres during the Boer War and those of the people of India. The strip identified Italy as England's most recent target: "This history of oppression culminated with the sanctions," referring to those imposed in response to the Italian invasion of Ethiopia.[35] Italy had to claim its imperial destiny.

35. *Il Balilla,* n. 1 (2 November 1941), 12.

The island of Malta became a symbol of the British obstruction of Italy's right to empire. The use of the Italian language and the predominance of Catholicism on the island justified assertions of Malta's *italianità*. The Fascist regime sought throughout the interwar era to advocate its claim and foster support among the population of Malta, which had been under English colonial control since 1815. The island, about fifty miles off the coast of Sicily, had strategic importance in the Mediterranean, symbolized the Mediterranean as *mare nostrum*, and represented an oppressed territory to be reclaimed.[36] Malta became a trope in comics and Italian literature alike to emphasize Italy's imperial destiny in the Mediterranean. Two such novels were published in 1940: *I piccoli cavalieri di Malta* by Gino Chelazzi and *Capinero di Malta* by Olga Visentini. Chelazzi told the story of ethnic Italian children born on Malta who formed a secret society against English rule. Visentini emphasized the *italianità* of Malta, oppressed by a cruel English governor.[37]

Italian comics borrowed both themes. The *Balilla* comic "Meo Mariano" followed the exploits of a young Italian boy born in Malta who pesters English soldiers and promotes Italian rule. In one issue, Meo taught an officer's parrot to say "Evviva l'Italia!," prompting citizens to rush forward waving Italian flags in support of his actions.[38] A similar comic appeared in *Corrierino*, written and illustrated by Antonio Rubino. The series, similarly titled "Marinello," told of a boy, Marinel, and his struggles against the "pompous" (*gonfio*) English governor of Malta, Lord Picnic, who is overweight and lives a life of leisure. The governor proves an easy target, enraged "like a veritable little Churchill" when Marinel has two seagulls fly the Italian tricolor over his head, prompting him to slam his fists on the table and spill tea on his wife.[39]

The liberation of territories claimed to be innately Italian was a common theme across periodicals.[40] Such statements legitimized Fascist irredentist claims on territories that once belonged to an Italian state or the Roman Empire, not through a defense of imperialism but by asserting the *italianità* of the territories and thus validating calls for integration into the Italian state on the basis of national sovereignty.[41] Italy's wars of aggression appeared in *Topolino*, *Corriere dei Piccoli*, and even *Il Vittorioso* as the righteous reclamation of Italian territories, or else as a fight against British oppression, as in

36. Paci, "'Lingua di Dante,'" 551, 558, 561.
37. Colin, *I bambini di Mussolini*, 422.
38. *Il Balilla*, n. 36 (1 September 1940), 1.
39. *Corriere dei Piccoli*, n. 12 (23 March 1941).
40. Even *Il Vittorioso* printed features on the "Italian character" of Nice and the Dalmatian coast. *Il Vittorioso*, n. 34 (24 August 1940), 7; and *Il Vittorioso*, n. 25 (21 June 1941), 7.
41. Pergher, *Mussolini's Nation-Empire*, 9, 18–19.

North Africa. The greed of the British Empire was to blame for the current war, allegedly keeping Italy from her fair share and oppressing people everywhere.[42] Italians, by contrast, fought for humanity.

This rhetoric persisted throughout the war, alleging that the Allied Powers were hypocrites waging war not in defense of democracy, but to preserve their own self-interests. A 1942 report on the progress of the war printed in *Balilla* claimed that the war had begun because France had refused to recognize the *italianità* of various lands in its territory, while England "controlled European commerce and attempted to strangle us, locking us up in *nostro mare.*" England's nefarious dealings were likewise blamed for the Italian campaigns in Yugoslavia and Greece.[43]

The Myth of "Catholic Italy"

Writers for *Vitt* similarly printed stories of Italians fighting against English tyranny. But the stories in *Il Vittorioso* focused predictably on Italy's "Catholic" soldiers and the defense of religion, embracing statements from Bologna's archbishop, Giovanni Nasalli Rocca, that Catholics were soldiers "in the Christian militia."[44]

Rather than discouraging enlistment and collaboration, the notion of a link between Catholicism and Italian-ness *fostered* participation in the war. Mobilizing Catholic support for the conflict was essential given that the population overwhelmingly identified as Catholic at this time. Despite the Vatican's continued desire for peace, the idea that Italy was "naturally" Catholic—that Catholicism was at the core of Italian identity—provided a sense of unity and even nationalism that helped mobilize Catholics into and throughout 1942.[45] Members of the Italian clergy produced sermons, speeches, and articles in favor of Italy's entrance into the war and encouraged active participation.[46] That Evasio Colli, director of GIAC's parent organization Catholic Action, called on the "children of the Church and of Italy" to respond to their duties "without selfish cowardice" attests to Catholic entanglement with the Fascist

42. De Felice, *L'Italia in guerra,* 1, 171.

43. *Il Balilla,* n. 33 (14 June 1942), 2. The use of the Italian "nostro mare" here rather than the Latin "mare nostrum" typical of Fascist propaganda comes from the article. The choice to use the Italian phrase was perhaps meant to mirror Mussolini's 1940 speech declaring war.

44. Kertzer, *Pope at War,* 195.

45. Dagnino, *Faith and Fascism,* 187–88.

46. Kertzer, *Pope at War,* 150, 153, 159.

war effort, and offered legitimation to what in truth represented brutal aggression, not national defense.[47]

Statements such as Colli's directive may have been rooted in a sense of duty to one's country rather than Fascist zeal. It nonetheless amounted to support for the ongoing hostilities and promoted enlistment and sacrifice. Similarly, the war depicted in the pages of *Vitt* amounted to an expression of GIAC's backing for it, and there is little to indicate in the pages of *Il Vittorioso* a critical distance from the war, as maintained by Ernesto Preziosi and Giorgio Vecchio.[48] There is indeed a distinction between the ultranationalism of Fascist Italy and a patriotism that expresses love for one's country but can remain critical of it. Producers of comics have displayed this critical patriotism at times, expressing faith in their country of origin while demanding it adhere to its ideals. It may be true that Luigi Gedda and others of Catholic Action were not committed Fascists despite their patriotic (and often nationalistic) stances. Yet *Il Vittorioso* did not depict a more subdued, liberal, or critical patriotism. The censorship of opposition was likely key here, but that criticism was lacking in *Vitt* means that readers were presented with a noncritical notion of patriotism from GIAC; of devotion to the Patria and its leader and service in the war, embodied best in Romano's instant return to defend Italy at the call of Mussolini.

The stories within *Il Vittorioso* during the war reflect unreserved patriotism. *Vitt*'s reporting on the war expanded beyond these war comics as well, and it should not be assumed that support for the war in *Il Vittorioso* was merely a concession to the increasingly demanding dictates of the MCP. Rather, issues of *Vitt* during the war reveal how the framing of Italian soldiers as "Catholic soldiers" fighting for God and for the Patria was entangled with the Fascist soldier, challenging the view that the war was only supported by radical Fascists.

The idea of Italian soldiers as Christian soldiers comes across most boldly in a section titled "Ragazzi e soldati" (Children and Soldiers), in which *Vitt* printed responses from soldiers to children who had sent letters and donations. One such letter reveals the author's understanding of his role as a soldier.[49] Writing from the Italo-Greco campaign, he identifies his motivations as "the love animated by a sense of duty" which "found me ready for the ultimate sacrifice that the Patria can ask of us true Christian soldiers." The soldier did not see this identity as a Christian soldier as contradictory to his identity as a

---

47. Casella, "L'Azione cattolica dal 1939 al 1946," 71–72.

48. Preziosi, *Il Vittorioso*, 16–17; and Vecchio, *L'Italia del Vittorioso*, 156, 167–70.

49. Letters *from* soldiers were carefully selected due to the gap between the "guerra immaginata" and the "guerra reale" experienced by the soldiers. Meda, *È arrivata la bufera*, 122.

Fascist, since his letter began, "I was also a Balilla as you are now, and at that time I learned to love the Patria."[50] Connecting the Patria to God again at the end of the section, the editor of the feature calls for prayers for the war effort and reminds readers that it is a duty to support the soldiers.

The notion that Italy's soldiers were soldiers of Christ persisted as the war progressed. It even strengthened with the invasion of the USSR, which shifted the Fascist war aims to align with the anti-communism of the Vatican.[51] As a Fascist propaganda poster from 1942 read, "No march on Moscow without the March on Rome."[52] This theme is captured in comics such as "Il medaglione della nonna" (The Grandmother's Locket), which tells of a young Russian boy who embraces the Italian soldiers and tells them he has been awaiting their arrival because, "With your coming, I could freely profess my religion: I believe in Christ; I am a Christian, like you."[53] Italian soldiers are thus cast as liberating true believers from the oppression of the godless communists. This depiction neglects the fact that the cruelties inflicted on Slavic populations by the Nazis and their allies shattered the initial hopes of many people living under Soviet rule that the Axis forces might indeed be liberators.

The sacrifices of Italian soldiers were expected to produce changes within Italy in addition to liberating and transforming Europe. Many in Italy, be they committed Fascists or members of Catholic Action (which were not mutually exclusive), believed a new order would arise out of World War II. Mussolini saw the war as an opportunity to marginalize the authority of the king and increase his own.[54] The strengthened position in the world that Mussolini anticipated for Italy would further the Fascist revolution at home. Similarly, members of Catholic Action had faith in the idea that the noble sacrifice of Italy's Catholic soldiers would revitalize Italian religiosity by displaying the moral integrity of the "new man."

A GIAC report glorifying its members who had fallen in battle claimed that the enlistment of over 60 percent of GIAC affiliates revealed the virtue and high patriotism of the organization and emphasized that their sacrifice would purify and transform Italy: "In this war, GIAC writes a page of history without compare: a purplish page of a blood that fertilizes our Italy for Christ."[55] But while the Fascist new man was to be an aggressive conqueror

50. *Il Vittorioso,* n. 20 (17 May 1941), 2.

51. Colarizi, *La seconda guerra mondiale,* 23, 106.

52. Rhodes, *Propaganda,* 93.

53. *Il Vittorioso,* n. 10 (7 March 1942), 3.

54. De Felice, *Lo Stato totalitario,* 808.

55. Presidenza Centrale della GIAC, Circolare della GIAC, 11 febbraio 1942, ISACEM / Fondo della GIAC / Serie 3, B. 524 / Circolari, 1941–42, 9, 10.

who embraced violence, the Catholic new man was said to be chivalric, humanitarian, and elevated by piety. The new Italy, led by such men, would take its rightful leading role in the world.[56] The goal of the GIAC differed from that of the Fascist state in that it desired a renewed *Catholic* Italy. But this did not prevent understanding the war as furthering its objective.

Comics, short stories, and news bulletins demonstrated the entanglement between the Catholic and Fascist soldier, between Catholic and Fascist Italy at large. The section "Eroi d'Italia" (Heroes of Italy) provided accounts of Italians who earned the *medaglia d'oro* for feats of heroism, with each story invariably praising their virtues as Catholic soldiers motivated by a "love of the Church and the Patria."[57] *Il Vittorioso* depicted the war as one waged against British oppression and the godless Soviet Union in order to create a more just international order. Letters from soldiers revealed faith in this goal.

Pope Pius XII—indeed, many Catholics—harbored concerns about the war, especially as an ally to Nazi Germany. But Pius XII did not vocalize his criticisms of Nazi actions in Poland against Catholics or Jewish people, instead making vague and ambiguous statements buried in speeches or else remaining silent. Fear of reprisals toward Catholics shaped his lack of response, as the Nazis controlled the European continent and appeared likely to win the war. But Pius was also moved by the crusade against Bolshevism and the hope of renewing the Catholic faith in Italy. The piety of Italy's "Catholic soldiers" and the idea that they were primarily mobilized to defend Italy did not prevent them from participating in the Fascist war effort.[58] A rupture in this uneasy alliance with Fascist goals only began to emerge following the disastrous invasion of Greece and losses in North Africa. As defeats became more frequent throughout 1942 and 1943, soldiers turned to traditional forms of faith, and genuine disillusionment with the regime spread.[59]

---

56. Dagnino, *Faith and Fascism*, 189, 198. Dagnino argues that members of the Italian Catholic Federation of University Students (FUCI) and Catholic Action were not innately anti-Fascist and that the majority of members were not seeking alternatives to Fascism prior to or at the beginning of World War II. Support for the war persisted among the *fucini* into the conflict and members only gradually began to plan for a post-Fascist Italy in 1943. Mario Casella argues that there was discussion in the late 1930s within the Vatican and Catholic Action regarding preparation for a "*successione*" to Fascism. However, he suggests that it was not until 1943 that FUCI members began to develop more pluralistic, democratic goals. Casella, "L'Azione cattolica nel Secondo dopoguerra," 78, 79.

57. *Il Vittorioso*, n. 6 (7 February 1942), 3; and *Il Vittorioso*, n. 10 (7 March 1942), 7.

58. Kertzer, *Pope at War*, 133–37 157, 166, 260–62, 269.

59. Duggan, *Fascist Voices*, 355–56, 360. Duggan notes that these letters may have been encouraged by officers who desired to prove the political faith of their unit.

Challenges to Publishers' Support for the War: Restrictions on American Comics

As Italians struggled under the strains of the war, publishers printing comics faced an additional crisis. The MCP heightened its control over Italian comics and the regulation of those from the US in 1941, ending its former toleration. The persistence of American comics in *L'Avventuroso* despite restrictions had been due to the modification of American stories and the US's neutrality. The stance on the war of William Randolph Hearst, owner of King Features Syndicate, likely contributed to this allowance, as Hearst campaigned for the US to remain out of the war in Europe.[60] On 14 February 1941, MCP circular n. 5510 made it obligatory for publishers to obtain "prior ministerial approval" for various types of publications, including "all translations or reproductions of foreign works." In the memo, Pavolini "advises" that "all works intended for children—text and illustrations—be sent to the Ministry (General Direction for Italian Press, Division IV) for examination and approval to avoid harmful repressive measures after publication."[61]

Pavolini and the MCP circulated additional decrees in the fall of 1941, strengthening the preventative censorship around comics. The change in the fall of 1941 may have been due to measures that took the US closer to intervention, including an oil embargo against Japan—the enfeebled "Rusveltaccio" character (discussed in the next section) appeared in *Balilla* immediately following its pronouncement.[62] On 15 October, the MCP declared its intention to crack down on American comics and derided publishers for their failure to follow measures "requested" by the Ministry. *All* periodicals for children were henceforth to receive approval from their regional prefects. The following day, it was announced that all stories with "banditry, espionage, ambushes, aggression, and, in general, dubious locations and violent actions" were to conclude.[63]

60. Frank Gervasi, Frank Gervasi a Alberto Nonis, "Summary of Hearst's speech attacking Churchill's call for intervention against Hitler / Mussolini," 22 ottobre 1938, ACS / MCP, Reports 1926–1944, B. 5, F. 46, William Randolph Hearst. Hearst argued neutrality was the only way to maintain US independence.

61. This memo is discussed in a latter decree from 13 October 1941, in which publishers are reminded of this mandate. Alessandro Pavolini, "Circolare Ministero Cultura Popolare del 13 ottobre 1941-XIX, n. 3041/B," in Gadducci et al., *Eccetto Topolino,* 412.

62. Schmitz, *The Sailor,* 86, 116; and "Rusveltaccio," *Il Balilla,* n. 32 (3 August 1941), 1.

63. Alessandro Pavolini, "Circolare Ministero Cultura Popolare del 15 ottobre 1941-XX, n. 3042/B," in Gadducci et al., *Eccetto Topolino,* 413; and Alessandro Pavolini, "Circolare Ministero Cultura Popolare del 16 ottobre 1941-XIX, n. 3044/B," in Gadducci et al., *Eccetto Topolino,* 413. See also Gadducci et al., *Eccetto Topolino,* 313.

Disney remained exempt, at least until the US naval base at Pearl Harbor was bombed by the Japanese, thrusting the US into the war. Four days later, on 11 December 1941, Mussolini joined his allies by declaring war on the US. Nerbini abandoned all intentions of publishing American comics, even after the war, perhaps at the advice of Pavolini, who was enthusiastically pursuing the reclamation of children's periodicals.[64] In March 1942, Nerbini announced in *L'Avventuroso* that "'L'Uomo Mascherato' [The Phantom] was an American creation and we have torpedoed it, as our courageous Japanese allies have torpedoed Roosevelt's battleships."[65] Nerbini's loss was Mondadori's gain, as he bought the rights to various series previously published by Nerbini.

Meanwhile, Mondadori contemplated his options for *Topolino*. The exemption granted to *Topolino* was null and void after the Italian declaration of war. On 11 December, the same day as that declaration, Mondadori wrote Pavolini that he would print his remaining Disney stockpiles but that *Topolino* would only publish Italian authors after that point. The periodical remained unchanged through the end of 1941, but a new feature entitled "Vincere" (Win) appeared in the first issue of 1942 with the story of an Italian squad retaking a key location in Tobruk, Libya, from the English. The unit suffered heavy losses and displayed what the writers described as heroism that "could be defined as legendary if it did not deal with the hearts of Italians" (who were apparently all uncommonly heroic by nature). The story was fittingly titled "Meglio morire che vivere con gli inglese" (Better to Die than Live with the English).[66]

More significant modifications came throughout January. The name "Disney" disappeared from the periodical in issue 473 (6 January), replaced with Pedrocchi's name as the lead creator.[67] The "Topolino" series was removed from the cover for the first time in the periodical's run, replaced in issue 476 by "Il mozzo del sommergibile" (Cabin Boy of the Submarine) by Pedrocchi, Kurt Caesar, and Edgardo Dell'Acqua.[68] The series focused on the exploits of an Italian naval vessel from the Atlantic to the Pacific. Weeks later, on 10 February, "Topolino" was further altered, as Mickey Mouse was transformed into the human "Tuffolino," and Minnie Mouse ("Minni") became "Mimma."[69] At

---

64. Gadducci et al., *Eccetto Topolino*, 326–37.

65. Meda, *Stelle e strips*, 72.

66. *Topolino*, n. 473 (6 January 1942), 2.

67. Arnoldo Mondadori all'Eccelenza Alessandro Pavolini, 11 dicembre 1941, FAAM / AME, Fasc. Disney, Walt, 1, dal 17.10.1936 al 26.11.1949; and Meda, *Stelle e strips*, 74.

68. *Topolino*, n. 476 (27 January 1942), 2. The series began publication in March 1940 (issue 397) but only moved to the cover page on 27 January.

69. *Topolino*, n. 478 (10 February 1942).

the same time, Mondadori tasked Emanuel with using connections in neutral countries to maintain good relations with Disney for after the conflict.[70]

It should not be assumed that Mondadori anticipated Fascist Italy would lose the war at this point. Rather, his determination to publish Disney material and other American content after the war attests to his confidence that he could adjust to any circumstance. He had, after all, proven he could negotiate with the regime, balancing his firm's own focus on profits with the regime's goal of prioritizing national culture.

Nonetheless, Mondadori's understanding of this nationalist agenda diverged from the broader policy of the MCP to reclaim and reorient children's literature. Stories of violence, brigandry, and crime, which had amounted to 67 percent of comics in 1940 according to the MCP, were said to be completely gone by 1943.[71] The commitment of Pavolini and his successor, Ferdinando Mezzasoma, to the *bonifica* of children's periodicals amid the war attests to the continued importance placed on the next generation by the regime, a problem which Pavolini defined as "essentially political."[72] The gap between Mondadori and Pavolini suggests the limits of the collaboration between the commercial orientation of publishers like Mondadori and the agenda of the Fascist state. While publishers often had objectives entangled with those of Fascist officials, bans on American comics harmed their businesses and fostered resentment.

Enfeebled Enemies and Ambiguous Allies

The belittlement of enemy leaders was a staple in *Balilla* and, to a lesser degree, *Corriere dei Piccoli,* framing them as enfeebled enemies not to be feared. The writers of *Balilla* first targeted the king of England in "Giorgetto e Ciurcillone" (essentially, Little George and Fat Churchill). Starting on 6 October 1940, the recurring comic opened with the same phrase: "Afraid of the war, King Giorgetto of England asked for help and protection from the Minister Ciurcillone." In the first issue, King Giorgetto commands Ciurcillone to defend the coasts. Ciurcillone adopts a curious strategy, depicted in figure 5.4, having men line the coast with banana peels upon which the invaders will slip. But, alas, when the king reviews the defenses, it is Giorgetto who slips and ingloriously falls! The king promptly kicks Ciurcillone. Other episodes follow this formula, with

70. Gadducci et al., *Eccetto Topolino,* 320, 321.

71. Ferdinando Mezzasoma, "Relazione del Direttore Generale della Stampa Italiana del febbraio 1943," in Gadducci et al., Eccetto Topolino, 422.

72. Alessandro Pavolini, "Circolare Ministero Cultura Popolare del 25 marzo 1942-XX, n. 1487/A," in Gadducci et al., Eccetto Topolino, 417.

7. La trovata è alquanto strana:
con le bucce di banana
8. il nemico andrà per terra
sulle coste d'Inghilterra.

FIGURE 5.4. *Il Balilla* mocks a plan that Ciurcillone clearly considers a brilliant protection for the country. "The idea is rather strange: The enemy will land on the English coast covered with banana peels." "Giorgetto e Ciurcillone," *Il Balilla*, n. 41 (6 October 1940), 1.

Ciurcillone engineering creative yet bizarre methods to defend England that always go awry. With a cowardly king and a buffoon for a prime minister, why fear England?

British troops were likewise cast as ill-prepared for war. "Tommy Molly va alla guerra" (Tommy Molly Goes to War) followed a soldier who makes so many stops for tea that the Germans arrive before he's even ready to deploy.[73] A Scotsman goes to war to golf, play tennis, and drink whiskey and is surprised to find he is under attack.[74] *Balilla* mocks Britain as unable to rely on its own people and chides the hypocrisy of the British for opposing the expansion of Italy's empire while the British call upon colonized people to fight its battles. In one episode of "Giorgetto e Ciurcillone," a distraught king calls for "the vassals of the empire" who "are ready like heroes to fight for us!" To his dismay, the imperial troops march off instead, returning to their countries.

Alongside the cowardly King George was Stalin, the "Orco Rosso" (Red Ogre). If *Vitt* primarily focused on the Soviet Union as a nation of godless heathens that suppressed religion, *Balilla* simplified the image to that of a country led by a cruel and incompetent beast. The comic launched about six weeks after the invasion of the USSR and similarly began each time with the same rhyme: "The terrible Stalin, Red Ogre of the Kremlin, yelled like a lunatic to call his palace guard: shoot all the comrades listed here."[75] The Red Ogre

73. *Il Balilla,* n. 42 (13 October 1940), 16.
74. *Il Balilla,* n. 43 (20 October 1940), 1.
75. *Il Balilla,* n. 33 (10 August 1941), 16.

is then infuriated to find that he cannot do something simple—like eat dinner—because he has ordered those responsible to be shot. Interestingly, the comic held some truth, as Stalin's repression was indiscriminate. In fact, the Soviet military faced difficulties due to the large number of officers discharged or executed during the Great Purge.[76] The Stalin of the comic thus places all his hopes on "Generale Inverno" (General Winter—referring to the expectation that the invaders would be stopped by the brutal Russian winter as indeed Napoleon had been), but alas, the general melts in the springtime.[77]

Having ridiculed Stalin for expecting the winter to save the USSR (which it ultimately does help to do), *Balilla* mocks the British anticipation that the US would save them. The Americans could not save anyone, according to *Balilla,* because they are led by the weak "Rusveltaccio Trottapiano," Gimpy Old Roosevelt. The president hobbles around on a cane and is routinely emasculated by his wife whom he continually fails to please. Each "Rusveltaccio Trottapiano" begins with the lines: "'Rusveltaccio Trottapiano,' American president, obeys the *signora,* the terrible 'Eleonora.' 'Today you must make war in support of England!'"[78] Rusveltaccio hurries to find support for the war but discovers Americans are uninterested in fighting in Europe. Even once Roosevelt has gotten "his" war, the Eleonora of "Rusveltaccio" remains unsatisfied, as the mobilization of the American forces progresses too slowly.

The idea that the United States would mobilize too slowly to impact the war appears also in *Corriere dei Piccoli.* In a comic by Bruno Angoletta (creator of strips such as "Marmittone" and "Sor Pampurio") titled "Mister Dollar," a titan of American industry announces his company will create a machine that will win the conflict. His engineers spring to work designing such a contraption. Mister Dollar receives a telegram as he reveals the constructed wonder machine which reads: "Mister Dollar. Stop. We apologize. War lost. Negotiating peace."[79]

These comics presented the image of an Italy embattled by incompetent, weak forces. Fortunately, Italy had strong, competent leaders and strong soldiers, or so readers were regularly assured in comics and features about the war. The emphasis on the strength of Italy was essential because Italy often appeared to be going it alone in the comics. German characters rarely graced the pages of *Balilla,* and even references in short stories and bulletins on the war were infrequent. When the German ally was acknowledged, it was always brief: "In North Africa, the young Fascists battle as carefully selected veteran troops alongside infantry, riflemen, and German comrades,

76. Whitewood, *Red Army,* 2, 257, 263–64.
77. *Il Balilla,* n. 18 (1 March 1942), 1.
78. *Il Balilla,* n. 32 (3 Aug. 1941), 1.
79. *Corriere dei Piccoli,* n. 22 (31 May 1942).

repeating the accomplishments of six months ago at Bir el Gobi."[80] Similarly, an announcement of the military's victorious march into the Yugoslav capital curtly acknowledged the presence of the "allied Germans."[81] Whenever *Balilla* included the Germans, the editors were careful not to present an image of dependence, instead emphasizing any victory as achieved primarily by the Italian military.

Occasional exceptions acknowledged that the fates of the two countries were intertwined, as in the poem "Camerati della vittoria" (Comrades in Victory). The poem tells of two comrades staggering on toward a field hospital as they support one another. It becomes clear that the injuries of the Italian are too severe and that he cannot continue. His German companion recognizes his chances of making it are slim as well, since they remain in enemy territory. As the Italian tells the German to go on without him, the German replies: "This fate will be the same for us, me German and you Italian! [. . .] You go before me; I will follow soon."[82] The story does not inspire hope, especially if it is to be read as an allegory for the fate of the countries themselves. But it does cast the countries as entangled.

Italy's position within the Axis became a question of increasing anxiety throughout the war. After initial hesitancy regarding fighting alongside Germany at the outset of the conflict, enthusiasm for the alliance rose among Italians with the steady stream of German conquests. However, as the conflict progressed and Italian campaigns in both Greece and North Africa stalled and required German interference, a fear emerged that Italy would be relegated to Germany's junior partner. What Mussolini desired to be a *guerra parallela* in which Italy pursued its own war aims became a *guerra subalterna,* in which Italy was subordinate.[83] Comics, short stories, and the press attempted to hide these setbacks and obscure Italy's increasingly marginalized status within the Axis.

The War Progresses: Defeat and Civil War

Continued defeats placed creators of children's periodicals in a difficult position, as the MCP forbade their acknowledgment. These omissions generated a sense of unreality in the pages of these periodicals, and developments in

80. *Il Balilla,* n. 35 (28 June 1942), 1.

81. *Il Balilla,* n. 10 (4 January 1942), 4.

82. *Il Balilla,* n. 33 (14 June 1942), 2.

83. Bosworth, *Mussolini's Italy,* 457, 465–67; Colarizi, *La seconda guerra mondiale,* 23, 103–5; Ben-Ghiat, "Italian Fascists and National Socialists," 268, 271; and Oliva, *La guerra fascista,* ch. 6.

the war forced changes in the progression of stories. The series "Verso A.O.I." (Toward Italian East Africa) in *Il Vittorioso* abruptly ceased after a prolonged effort by the protagonist Romano to bolster the forces in Italian East Africa. A string of defeats throughout 1941 had ended the Italian campaign and likewise concluded any series set there, although no acknowledgment was made of the loss.

The strains of war were felt severely as the Italian war effort entered its third year in 1943. To many, Italy's ultimate defeat appeared imminent.[84] Nonetheless, Pavolini ordered the press to maintain a triumphalist tone, directing them on 27 March:

> 1. To fight until the victory, in the sense that we will not disarm neither materially nor spiritually until victory, and spiritually not even after victory; 2. To hate the enemy; 3. To illustrate with polemical vivacity the enemy's programs to reduce Europe to slavery; 4. To exalt heroes, entrusting the treatment of particular heroes to good writers.[85]

The Allied bombings of Italian cities supported the image of the Allies as barbarians come to impoverish Italy, an image captured well in a 1944 propaganda poster which read, "Here are the 'liberators,'" over the image of a burning Italian city and the looming figure of Lady Liberty removing her mask to show that she is in fact the embodiment of death.[86] But the disjuncture between Fascist propaganda on the superiority of Italian arms and the reality suffered by millions of Italians pushed citizens away from the regime to get their news from Radio London instead.[87] Discontent grew with the entrance into the war of the US, which shattered the illusion that the war could be a short one. Major defeats at Stalingrad and in North Africa further demoralized a people suffering from the deterioration of living conditions.

From 1943, children's periodicals increasingly detached from the fighting in Europe. In *Vitt,* Romano fought in Tibet for the remainder of the series, and the struggle against the English transitioned to Catholic Ireland's struggle for independence. News bulletins continued, but *Vitt* gradually reflected a change in atmosphere, as stories moved away from the war. The tolls of the

84. Colarizi, *La seconda guerra mondiale,* 23, 126–27, 178.

85. Quoted in Murialdi, *La stampa del regime fascista,* 121.

86. Rhodes, *Propaganda,* 1.

87. Murialdi, *La stampa del regime fascista,* 247; and Petrella, *Staging the Fascist War,* 10, 215.

conflict were made clear as the formerly vibrant pages turned to black and white with hues of red or blue as materials became increasingly scarce.[88]

Even *Balilla* reflected the turning tide of the war, minimizing references to it in the spring of 1943. Articles in 1942 had emphasized Italians' martial duties and maintained that they *were* winning. Advances in both Russia and North Africa were proudly proclaimed, as were supposed victories against the British in the Mediterranean. Yet this triumphalist image disintegrated after Axis forces were defeated in North Africa and at Stalingrad, and *Balilla* increasingly printed historical narratives.

This is not to say that *all* reference to the war disappeared from *Balilla.* The periodical maintained the myth of Italian air superiority, and articles mocked the Allied plan to invade Europe as foolish and barbaric. Articles speculated as to the postwar order that the Allies would impose on Europeans should they win. The Italians, according to *Balilla,* were fighting for their imperial destiny, defending their nation and way of life against hypocrites who merely wanted to take credit for what Fascist Italy had already achieved.[89] In other words, do not think life will be better if the Allies win; the Axis was *defending* itself against tyranny. This claim was expressed vividly in an illustrated story in which a British imperialist seeks to swallow the world and keep it all for himself before he is stopped by German soldiers, who carve up the world and share the pieces among the "unfortunate people who were deprived until now."[90]

The Fascist youth periodical continued its mission of spreading Fascist propaganda up until the dismissal of Mussolini. The Party's commitment to maintain the publication of *Balilla* to the end highlights the PNF's dedication to the indoctrination of Italian youth and reflects the state's ambition to preserve a semblance of normalcy. But this came to an abrupt end. The Allies invaded Sicily on 9 July 1943. Weeks later, Mussolini was summoned to a meeting of the Fascist Grand Council on 24 July at which nineteen of the twenty-eight members voted to remove him from power, including his son-in-law, Galeazzo Ciano. The king dismissed the Duce from power the next day and ordered his arrest. *Balilla*'s final issue was published the week following Mussolini's arrest; a comic strip about a boy playing with insects graced the

88. Such changes occurred first in *Topolino* with issue 467 (25 November 1941), and then later in *Il Vittorioso,* beginning with issue 11 on 20 March 1943. Vecchio, *L'Italia del Vittorioso,* 19.

89. "Osservazioni della navicella," *Il Balilla,* n. 28 (9 May 1943), 2.

90. *Il Balilla,* n. 34 (20 June 1943), 5.

cover, and a poem on the second page urged people to fight on. No reference was made to the dismissal of Mussolini or the periodical's imminent demise.[91]

More Uncertainty: Mussolini's Fall

The removal from power of Mussolini by the Fascist Grand Council and the king brought changes for all children's periodicals. *Il Vittorioso* suspended publication that week; *Topolino* ran into December, although war comics such as "Il mozzo del sommergibile" disappeared from the periodical at the end of August.[92]

Corrierino continued uninterrupted and quickly aligned itself with the new government under the king's newly appointed prime minister, Pietro Badoglio. The editors of *Corriere della Sera* in Milan replaced director Aldo Borelli—first with Filippo Sacchi and then with the liberal conservative Ettore Janni—and declared the paper's loyalty to the king. The stage seemed set for the return of "the old *Corriere*" of Luigi Albertini. *Corriere della Sera* and other newspapers were tasked with moderating any criticism of Mussolini's regime and reporting favorably on the royal family, the papacy, and the new government. The vestiges of the Fascist state were also to be reported on positively.[93]

The status of *Corriere della Sera* and its children's supplement reflected the uncertainty of this period of upheaval. When Mussolini fell, millions of Italians took to the streets to celebrate what many believed signified not only the end of the regime but also the end of the fighting. Yet Badoglio's initial continuation of the alliance with Germany created chaos and discontent and left publishers uncertain of the stories to print.

Corriere dei Piccoli and other children's periodicals still in publication pulled away from features and stories on the war. *Corrierino* returned to classics such as "Bonaventura." The popular "Marmittone," though, had ceased publication in 1942, the misadventures of the lovable soldier no longer appropriate as the war effort stalled for Italy (the strip's cancellation probably contributed to the interpretation that it had *always* been anti-Fascist).[94]

Indications that Italians desired an end to the fighting were reflected in *Topolino*. The first signs were subtle, such as the removal of the Axis flags from the title plate of "Il mozzo del sommergibile" on the front cover of the periodical beginning with issue 556 on 10 August 1943. The series ended a few weeks

91. *Il Balilla*, n. 40 (1 August 1943).

92. *Topolino*, n. 559 (31 August 1943).

93. Licata, *Storia del Corriere della sera*, 306–14, 316.

94. Colin, *I bambini di Mussolini*, 427.

longer on 31 August with the safe return of the crew to the shores of Italy. The heartwarming finale of sailors reunited with their families captured the mood in Italy, with most Italians desiring peace.[95]

Italy Divided

More changes followed the announcement of the armistice on 8 September 1943. The German response was swift, and, as the German army descended on Rome, the king and his new prime minister, Pietro Badoglio, fled to the city of Brindisi in Apulia to establish the provisional government of the Kingdom of Italy under the protection of the Allies. During this offensive, German forces occupied the offices of *Corriere della Sera* on 11 September, putting an end to Janni's plans of an Albertinian periodical. Such actions placed publishers in the north, particularly Milan, firmly under the control of the Nazi-backed Repubblica Sociale Italiana (Italian Social Republic, RSI). The RSI reimposed a Fascist orientation on *Corriere dei Piccoli*; while the war was no longer discussed, it appeared in stories, such as when Sor Pampurio abandoned city life due to the Allied bombing of cities.[96]

Mass confusion set in for civilians and the armed forces, as the dual occupations made it unclear where the true seat of Italian sovereignty lay: Was it the RSI in the north, or Badoglio's government under the king in the south? The military was instructed to cease operations against the Allies, but it was unspecified whether they should fight the Axis or disband. Some officers commanded units to disband, but thousands of other soldiers took it upon themselves to desert and head home, embracing the idea of "*tutti a casa*" (everybody go home).[97]

Despite the seriousness of the situation—or perhaps because of it—new, goofy strips emerged in *Corriere dei Piccoli* at this time, such as Carlo Bisi's "Gentile Pastabuona, the man who can't say no." Although they appear unconnected to the war, "Gentile Pastabuona" has been interpreted by some as a commentary on the Civil War raging within Italy; always agreeing to whatever is asked of him, the protagonist is unable to achieve what he sets out to do and often lands in trouble. Claudio Carabba suggests that Pastabuona represents an Italy dragged into both sides of the conflict due to an inability to set its

95. Colarizi, *La seconda guerra mondiale*, 23, 127, 192–94; and Duggan, *Fascist Voices*, 390.
96. Meda, *Stelle e strips*, 74.
97. Forlenza, *On the Edge of Democracy*, 21–22.

own path.[98] Nonetheless, the feature "Corrierino della guerra" continued to give sanitized updates on the war, encouraging Italians to keep fighting despite their exhaustion and lack of supplies.[99]

Corrierino's orientation quickly shifted following the liberation of northern Italy and the end of the RSI. The Germans became the true enemies of the Italian people. A new narrative of an oppressed Italy dragged along by their nefarious Nazi allies began to appear in the periodical which had for so long sympathized with the Fascist regime.

Mondadori's *Topolino* met a different fate, suspending publication in December rather than being controlled by the RSI. This outcome was likely due to Arnoldo Mondadori fleeing with his family to Switzerland on 9 September 1943.[100] Despite his prior relationship to the regime, Mondadori always prioritized the financial success of his company. He had no intention of remaining attached to the losing side now that the regime seemed destined to fail. Tragically, although Mondadori escaped the brutality of the final years of the war and *Topolino* ceased publication, misfortune still befell the firm. In January 1945, as the fighting approached an end in Italy, Federico Pedrocchi was killed in an English bombardment in Lombardy.[101]

GIAC, too, grappled with the chaos of the Civil War, though with a different strategy. The periodical had suspended the week of Mussolini's arrest, and as such *Vitt* offered no commentary on the political upheavals in Italy. The Vatican and its lay social organizations of Catholic Action, however, now broke with the Fascist regime. Although not all Catholics immediately or necessarily became anti-Fascists, Pope Pius XII—who had called for a "new order" upholding human rights in his 1942 Christmas address—publicly came out in support of Mussolini's dismissal and the new government; most Catholic Italians followed suit.

The pope did not cast his support behind the anti-Fascist Resistance, however, fearing that it represented a fifth column of communism in Italy.[102] The Church nonetheless became a source of hope for many, gaining moral author-

98. Carabba, *Corrierino, Corrierona,* 121. The Italian title is "Gentile Pastabuona, l'uomo che non sa dire di no."

99. "Corrierino della guerra," *Corriere dei Piccoli,* n. 20 (16 May 1943).

100. Forgacs and Gundle, *Mass Culture and Italian Society,* 116. Arnoldo Mondadori took with him seventeen million lire worth of shares (85 percent of the company's worth) and attempted to reforge connections severed due to the war, including with Walt Disney.

101. Pedrocchi, "C'era una volta," 21.

102. Despite the public stance of the Vatican, about one-fifth of chaplains remained with the RSI units in the north. Conversely, many Italian Catholics participated in the Resistance, either directly or passively. Casella, "L'Azione cattolica dal 1939 al 1946," 76; Colarizi, *La seconda guerra mondiale,* 23, 273; and Pavone, *Una guerra civile,* 180–84.

ity as the pope remained in Rome. While the royal family and new government absconded to southern Italy, Pius XII suffered the German occupation and the Allied bombing of the cities along with the populace, even being photographed walking amongst the rubble after air raids. The image of the Church was further enhanced by its commitment to taking care of impacted communities, prioritizing the social mission during the Civil War more so than explicit political maneuverings.[103]

Il Vittorioso benefitted from the Church's moves to detach itself from Fascism. Significantly, the GIAC leadership and *Il Vittorioso*'s publishing team existed in a radically different context from that of *Corriere dei Piccoli,* operating in a Rome controlled by the Allies after 4 June 1944. When *Vitt* returned, it did not speak out overtly against the regime or turn toward anti-Fascist stories but adopted instead an apolitical orientation perhaps more typical of a children's periodical. The editors had always retained a mix of stories that did not focus on the war, even in 1942, most popularly those of Benito Jacovitti and Sebastiano Craveri. Jacovitti's Pippo turned away from his original preoccupation with pranking the foolish English. Craveri's funny animal comics set in the world of Zoolandia were even more detached from the fighting. These more child-friendly strips offered wholesome entertainment disconnected from the war.

Jacovitti and Craveri's strips returned with *Vitt* in 1944, offering a degree of continuity that no doubt helped maintain the periodical's popularity. The war comics disappeared, replaced instead with tales of explorers. GIAC's patriotism remained, however, still sending the message to readers that "to die for the Patria is sublime," likely an acknowledgment of the ongoing Civil War over the fate of the Italian nation.[104] At the same time, *Vitt* rejected the notion that the Allies were enemies, as readers were told that love for one another is at the core of Christianity: "It embraces everything and everyone, without evaluations or limits. There is no one who is 'foreign' to the pope's heart."[105]

GIAC managed to publish four issues of *Vitt* before suspending to await approval from AMGOT to continue. The Psychological Warfare Branch (PWB) was responsible for monitoring Italian publications. Though less is known about its dealings with comics and children's magazines, the PWB consciously promoted films that cast Fascism in a negative light and democracy and the Allied forces in a positive one.[106] The wait was not long, and *Vitt* officially relaunched on 27 August, continuing to focus on stories detached

103. Ceci, *Vatican and Mussolini's Italy,* 287, 291, 293.
104. *Il Vittorioso,* n. 1 (4 June 1944), 7.
105. *Il Vittorioso,* n. 3 (18 June 1944), 3.
106. Forgacs and Gundle, *Mass Culture and Italian Society,* 219–20.

from the war. The one exception to *Vitt*'s distance from the war came with the Christmas issue, in which the story "Natale di guerra" acknowledged the suffering caused by the war, sympathizing with the orphaned children and asking, "Will even the baby Jesus be too afraid to come down to earth with his gifts?"[107] Readers are assured that this will be the last Christmas to occur during the war.

Conclusion

During the time when the state wielded its most extensive mechanisms of censorship, the producers of comics who intended to outlast the war had little choice but to cooperate with the MCP's dictates. Yet this chapter has demonstrated that each represented the conflict uniquely, suggesting that each found aspects of the Fascist war which aligned with their own goals. Italians were hesitant to join the fighting, and any support for it did not extend beyond 1942 or 1943. However, it is clear that the war resonated with some in conservative and Catholic circles, who harbored their own aims for the conflict and supported it so long as victory seemed likely.

Balilla, as the regime's official youth periodical, embodied the PNF's ideal representation of the war to children. Many stories sought to educate Italian children about their duties; others demonized enemies as weak and foolish, emphasizing the oppression of the British Empire and the cruelty of Stalin and asserting that the weak, interfering United States would make little impact on the course of the war. Conversely, the might of the Italian military and its seasoned soldiers were routinely praised.

The competitors of *Balilla* all embraced various aspects of this approach. *Il Vittorioso* and *Topolino* both printed veritable war comics, with realistic aesthetics of the fighting and claims that Italian equipment and soldiers were superior. *Corrierino* most enthusiastically followed *Balilla* in demonizing and ridiculing enemies, a trope which appeared little in *Vitt.* Finally, *Topolino* demonstrates that it was possible to limit the extent to which a major children's periodical focused on the conflict, though this was likely a perk of Mondadori's privileged status with the regime. This leeway only went so far, however, as even *Topolino* focused more on the war as it continued.

Each of these periodicals found aspects of the war that became features in their pages. The most frequent trope across all of the periodicals was that of a righteous Italy fighting on behalf of the oppressed against the British Empire.

107. *Il Vittorioso,* n. 21 (24 and 31 December 1944), 3.

The conservative periodicals *Topolino* and *Corrierino* seem to have shared the regime's ambition to unseat the dominance of the British Empire. The editors of GIAC, on the other hand, understood the war as a means to "liberate" oppressed foreigners and spread the influence of the Catholic Church (most notably into the USSR) and represented Italian soldiers as soldiers of Christ. Initially, the emphasis on the war as one to spread the faith did not conflict with the Fascist war of expansion. However, over time the perception of fighting for God and country took precedence over that of fighting for Fascism and ultimately offered an alternative source of meaning and authority.

The periodicals discussed here mirror the course of Italy's Second World War. The careful acknowledgement (or neglect) of the war in 1939 reflected the atmosphere of war and anxiety over what Italy's role would be. The stories printed in 1940, 1941, and even 1942 instead promoted optimism about the course of the war. This optimism was no doubt partly enforced by the MCP but should also be read as a sign that support persisted in some form while the German army appeared unstoppable. As setbacks increased, the war gradually disappeared from the pages. What persisted only spread disillusionment among the Italian people as claims of Italian superiority conflicted with the experiences of bombings and loss. Finally, the periodicals were not immune from the confusion brought on by Mussolini's dismissal from power and the struggle to reorient Italian political life. The coalition of various sociopolitical circles tied to the cultural mission of the regime crumbled, leaving the remnants of the Fascist regime isolated. Yet, as publishers were once again allowed to publish freely, their periodicals foreshadowed an unwillingness to critically engage with the Fascist era, opting instead to assign blame or remain silent about the past.

CHAPTER 6

Sketching a New Society

Comics after Fascism

The end of the Second World War and the fall of the Fascist regime marked a juncture in Italian society. Italy's infrastructure was devastated, food was scarce, and children attended school in shifts, where they were able to attend at all.[1] Surrounded by ruin, Italians found themselves in an existential crisis, during which most had lost faith in their past and their traditions. The narrative of the nation that the regime had imposed for twenty years crumbled.

The era was full of great aspirations as well as anxieties. As many in Italy fell silent about the Fascist past, the political divisions within Italy suppressed by the Fascist state were now points of struggle. Among the myriad competing models for society, three became the most influential and divisive: Catholicism, Americanism, and communism.[2] An ideological struggle for Italy's future opened, expanding beyond the confined political "debates" of the Fascist era.

Publishers of children's periodicals and comics were embroiled in this process. Italians remained concerned with children's education and entertainment amid the destruction. Periodicals that survived the regime—*Topolino, Corriere dei Piccoli,* and *Il Vittorioso*—went to great lengths to demonstrate their anti-Fascist orientation or fell silent about the past. Yet many of the social

1. Ginsborg, *History of Contemporary Italy,* 94; and Ventresca, *From Fascism to Democracy,* 26.

2. Duggan, "Italy in the Cold War Years," 1.

anxieties and values that once aligned conservatives and Catholics with the Fascist regime persisted within this silence, appearing in their children's periodicals. Despite the more critical position taken by Italian intellectuals on the Fascist past identified by Charles Leavitt, Italy was not an "entirely new land."[3] Law and order, the need to defend Italian and European civilization, and a lamentation of the loss of colonies appeared in comics published on the Right. The perseverance of themes that had once been linked to the regime demonstrate that their presence in comics under the regime was not merely a result of Fascist coercion. Many core Fascist ideas resonated with various sociopolitical circles in Italy, and these ideas persisted in new forms in the postwar era, challenging the periodization of a sharp break between Fascism and the Republic.[4]

The comics printed by publishers on the Right from this era reflect the desire to remain silent about the Fascist past and the complications of moving forward. Many of the comics promoted the myth that Fascism had been imposed on Italians, and yet maintained ideas entangled with the Fascist project. As the Left gained more momentum, comics on both sides of the political spectrum were employed to increasingly mobilize children in the political struggles of the era. Editors included features and commentary which cast their opponents as anti-Italian and called on children to get the adults in their lives to vote for the political party with which they aligned.

This more expansive ideological struggle in children's periodicals was enabled by transformations in the structures of Italian politics. Free elections returned to Italy, and the elections for the Constituent Assembly in 1946 entailed universal male and *female* suffrage, allowing Italian women to vote for the first time. The 1946 referendum on the monarchy transformed Italy into a republic. Competing political parties also returned. Foremost among the new parties were the Democrazia Cristiana (DC), the Partito Comunista Italiano (PCI), and the Partito Socialista Italiano (PSI). While the government initially united all the anti-Fascist parties, significant differences existed in the agendas for Italian society advocated by conservatives and the Vatican, on the one hand, and by socialists and communists, on the other.

Most important for cultural production, the policies of the Fascist Ministero della Cultura Popolare (MCP) were dismantled after the liberation of Rome, and the institution itself became the Sottosegretariato di Stato per la Stampa, Turismo e Spettacolo (Undersecretariat of State for the Press, Tourism, and Entertainment), under the Presidenza del Consiglio dei Ministri.

3. Leavitt, "'Entirely New Land'?," 5, 6, 12.
4. Forgacs and Gundle, *Mass Culture and Italian Society*, 4.

Restrictions on "amoral" topics (such as suicide and abortions) remained, and the Allied occupying government suppressed overtly Fascist themes. Freedom of expression largely returned, but the practice of self-censorship persisted as publishers adjusted to the new political climate.[5]

Still, different ideas on Italian society flourished in this new context. The Catholic periodical *Il Vittorioso* campaigned more vigorously for an Italy rooted in Catholicism, while *Topolino* embraced American culture without reserve. Meanwhile, the new periodicals on the Left offered a competing narrative of Italian history and emphasized themes of pacifism, progress, liberty, and international fraternity. The launch in 1950 of the communist youth group's official periodical, *Il Pioniere,* attests to the deepening divisions between the Right and the Left as the anti-Fascist coalition crumbled into a clash of ideologies.

The sections below trace how comics reflected the evolution of Italian political culture after Fascism. The first section discusses the reorientation of the periodicals which survived the regime. The second section examines the Left's position on comics, as well as early experiments in utilizing comics to reach children. Finally, the last section addresses key themes and issues in postwar Italy, identifying lingering themes that had been sources of commonality between Catholics and liberal conservatives within the Fascist regime. This final section identifies shared values across the Italian political spectrum but primarily highlights differences between the Left and the Right in understanding crime, decolonization, and Italy's Catholic traditions—divisions that reached a new height in the heated 1948 election.

Starting Anew

The very persistence of periodicals established during the Fascist era represents a degree of continuity across these pivotal periods. To whatever degree *Topolino, Corriere dei Piccoli,* and *Il Vittorioso* were tainted by their collaboration with Fascist cultural and political agendas, their continued success suggests that Italians wanted to forget the regime and sought refuge in entertainment and familiarity. The continuation of beloved characters such as *Corrierino*'s Bonaventura—which had predated the regime—likely offered comfort in a distressing time.

---

5. Cesari, *La censura in Italia oggi,* 14, 17; and Forgacs and Gundle, *Mass Culture and Italian Society,* 202, 221.

Continuity went deeper than the persistence of characters. Publishing firms were largely family-owned and thus maintained their same personnel and institutional structures.[6] Publishers that had once collaborated in spreading Fascist ideology benefited from a collective narrative that emphasized that the coercive nature of the regime had forced cooperation, which was only part of the story. The rather limited *epurazione* or "purge" of collaborators that occurred in Italy meant that many editors, publishers, and writers remained in the industry.[7] Arnoldo remained at the head of the Casa Editrice Mondadori. The Gioventù Italiana di Azione Cattolica similarly maintained its culture, as Luigi Gedda was promoted to lead Catholic Action and his successor in GIAC was close to him personally and ideologically. The organization's priorities continued to be shaped by a Vatican whose leadership remained in the hands of those who had formed an uneasy alliance with the Fascist state. As for *Corriere dei Piccoli,* although the anti-Fascist Arnaldo Sartori was appointed director in May 1945, the periodical and its mother newspaper, *Corriere della Sera,* remained owned by the Crespi brothers, the Lombard industrialists formerly aligned with the Fascist regime.

As publishers adjusted to the new cultural and political context in Italy, firms confronted the issue of attracting paying readers in an economically devastated Italy beset with inflation. Whereas children's periodicals cost thirty to forty cents before the war, by the fall of 1945 most were priced around ten lire.[8] At this time, the average working-class family spent 93–95 percent of its income on food, leaving between two hundred and four hundred lire for their remaining expenses.[9] Comic readership nonetheless remained high, benefiting from the tendency to share issues among friends.[10]

To maintain and attract new readers, Mondadori sought to fill his periodical, *Topolino,* with American content from both Disney and King Features Syndicate. The continued success of his firm necessitated good relations with American partners. *Topolino* became a vehicle for *americanismo.* For GIAC, however, American culture threatened their mission of evangelizing youth, and *Il Vittorioso* remained an essential vehicle for propaganda against both Americanism and communism. Pius XII and the Church hierarchy diverged from other conservatives' embrace of Americanism in that the Vatican

6. Forgacs and Gundle, *Mass Culture and Italian Society,* 96.

7. Ginsborg, *History of Contemporary Italy,* 40, 53; Duggan, *Force of Destiny,* 544–45; and Avagliano and Palmieri, *Dopoguerra,* 368.

8. *Vitt* reached twelve lire in June 1945, *Giornale dei Piccoli* cost seven lire in September, and *Topolino* sold for eight lire in December. *Il Vittorioso,* n. 22 (17 June 1945); *Giornale dei Piccoli,* n. 15 (2 September 1945); and *Topolino,* n. 565 (5 December 1945).

9. Ventresca, *From Fascism to Democracy,* 25–26.

10. Forgacs and Gundle, *Mass Culture and Italian Society,* 36–37.

remained hostile to the model of modernity seen in the US. Despite the heterogeneity of the Allied occupation, the Vatican singled out the destabilizing impact of American culture, as Americanism again became a dominant influence in Italy.[11]

Even so, Pius XII considered the US a potential ally against communism. Pius did not trust PCI leader Palmiro Togliatti's claim to favor collaboration over confrontation with the Catholic Church.[12] The Soviet suppression of Catholicism in Poland and Ukraine validated the pope's conviction that communism—including the PCI—represented an existential threat to organized religion. A July 1944 article published in *L'Osservatore Romano* argued that Italians could not be both Catholic *and* communist.[13] While the Vatican and its auxiliary organizations such as Catholic Action remained leery of *americanismo,* collaboration with the US was preferred at a time when many political leaders believed they had to choose either the US or the USSR.

Despite papal reluctance, the *mito americano* or "myth of America" grew in Italy. Many Italians embraced Americans as liberators, notwithstanding lingering resentment at the Allied bombardment.[14] The Allied Psychological Warfare Branch selected films sympathetic to the American way of life to promote positive relations.[15] Combined with the *mito americano* established in the first half of the twentieth century by American culture and Italian emigration, these factors positioned the United States as a model of democratic aspirations.[16]

Silence and Subtle Changes in Mondadori's *Topolino*

Arnoldo Mondadori returned to a war-torn Italy in April 1945, having spent the final years of the war in Switzerland. Mondadori relayed to Walt Disney the previous February that,

> For a long period of 15 months, I have been a refugee in Switzerland with my sons and this because I refused to collaborate either with the occupying

11. Forlenza, *On the Edge of Democracy,* 71.

12. Caruso, *Così ricostruimmo l'Italia,* 10–11; Gualtieri, *L'Italia dal 1943 al 1992,* 30, 35; Coppa, *Politics and the Papacy,* 141–54; and Chamedes, *Twentieth-Century Crusade,* 242.

13. *L'Osservatore Romano* (23 July 1944); and Coppa, *Politics and the Papacy,* 154.

14. Foot, *Italy's Divided Memory,* 28–29; and Focardi and Klinkhammer, "Question."

15. Avagliano and Palmieri, *Dopoguerra,* 137–39; Forlenza, *On the Edge of Democracy,* ch. 3; Gennari, *Post-War Italian Cinema,* 11; and Forgacs and Gundle, *Mass Culture and Italian Society,* 219–20.

16. Forlenza, *On the Edge of Democracy,* ch. 3.

> forces or with the Fascists. As my wife and daughters have happily joined me of late, I have no more any fear of reprisals and can send you and Mrs. Disney my heartiest regards in remembrance of the happy days we had the opportunity to spend together in my villa on the Lago Maggiore.[17]

He praised Disney's work of the previous years, reminded Disney of their friendship, and requested a meeting to discuss new material for production.

Mondadori must have been disappointed by the response. The manager of Walt Disney Mickey Mouse LTD—not Disney himself—responded that "we consider that it will be better to wait until the end of hostilities before proceeding further with the matter under discussion," implying that the contract would be revised.[18] In May, after Mondadori had returned to Italy, and just one day after the German surrender, a letter from Walt's brother, Roy, reaffirmed Disney's position: "I hope it will soon be possible for some of us to get over to Europe and see just what the situation is and how it is going to affect our merchandizing activities. Until then, we are making no commitments on the Continent."[19]

As distressing as the letters from Disney likely were for Mondadori, he had bigger problems. At the end of 1944, employees of the Mondadori Publishing Firm established a self-management council. The council invited Arnoldo Mondadori's brother, Bruno, to represent the firm's owners, but accused Arnoldo of collaboration with the Fascist regime and barred him from reclaiming his role.[20]

His son, Alberto, charged him similarly. Alberto had been tasked with representing his father's interests in Milan after the latter fled to Switzerland, and his experiences during the Civil War had pushed his politics to the Left. Writing to his father, Alberto advocated a more decentralized structure in the firm with increased autonomy for authors and editors. He desired the firm to commit to "give the greatest possible mass of readers the ability to educate themselves" and to generate a new ruling class.[21] Arnoldo hesitated to embrace democratic practices and an explicit political orientation. Alberto rejected Arnoldo's claim that he had always been and would remain outside

17. Arnoldo Mondadori to Walt Disney, 22 February 1945, FAAM / AME, Fasc. Disney, Walt, 1, dal 17.10.1936 al 26.11.1949. Letter sent in English.

18. E. J. Davis to Messrs. Helicon, 21 March 1945, FAAM / AME, Fasc. Disney, Walt, 1, dal 17.10.1936 al 26.11.1949.

19. Roy Disney to Arnoldo Mondadori, 8 May 1945, FAAM / AME, Fasc. Disney, Walt, 1, dal 17.10.1936 al 26.11.1949.

20. Forgacs and Gundle, *Mass Culture and Italian Society*, 117.

21. Letter from Alberto to Arnoldo, 9 febbraio 1945, in Mondadori, *Lettere di una vita*, 96.

politics and denounced his father's stance as "a new Fascism camouflaged by apoliticism."[22]

Mondadori embodied the desire of many Italians to simply not discuss the recent past. Benedetto Croce famously referred to the Fascist era as a "parenthesis" in Italian history, which had interrupted the otherwise steady progress and societal development of Liberal Italy. Fascism therefore did not represent a problem with Italian traditions, as the Risorgimento, liberalism, and the Resistance embodied the true national character, and the return to liberal parliamentarism would continue Italy's march toward liberty.[23] Other intellectuals were more critical of the Fascist past. Elio Vittorini and Luigi Russo, for instance, both advocated for a new start for Italy, criticizing Croce's parenthesis theory for not dealing with the Italian traditions that led to Fascism, nor with the legacy of Fascism.[24] Nonetheless, the rhetoric of a new start also worked to dissuade dwelling on the past, a trend exemplified in the general amnesty in 1946 in the name of reconciliation. Talk of an "anti-Fascist consensus" and an "entirely new land" thus at times *obscured* the sources of continuity by fostering a culture of silence.[25]

The Mondadori Publishing Firm is again exemplary, as Mondadori was ultimately allowed to return to his leading position in the firm. Several authors wrote to the self-management council in support of Mondadori's rehabilitation. His return was secured by the arrangement of a 50 percent profit share among workers and the inclusion of an equal number of workers on the board.[26] Once reinstated to his position at the publishing house, David Forgacs and Stephen Gundle argue that Arnoldo Mondadori "threw a democratic cloak over his shoulders and fell silent about his profascist past" and set about restarting operations, including the relaunch of *Topolino.*[27] Mondadori reached out numerous times to Disney over the course of 1945 and early 1946 to request material to fill the pages of *Topolino,* but his requests went unfulfilled.[28] In October 1945, Mondadori wrote to the Italian representative for

22. Letter from Alberto to Arnoldo, 3 marzo 1945, in Mondadori, *Lettere di una vita,* 96.

23. Forlenza and Thomassen, *Italian Modernities,* 39–46.

24. Leavitt, "'Entirely New Land'?," 5, 6, 12.

25. Stone, *Goodbye to All That?,* 45; and Avagliano and Palmieri, *Dopoguerra,* 37. On sources of continuity, see Conti, *Gli uomini di Mussolini,* 12–13; and Mammone, *Transnational Neofascism,* 16–17, 138, 153–54.

26. Forgacs and Gundle, *Mass Culture and Italian Society,* 117.

27. Forgacs and Gundle, *Mass Culture and Italian Society,* 120.

28. Arnoldo Mondadori a Kay Kamen, telegramma, 24 settembre 1945, FAAM / AME, Fasc. Disney, Walt, 1, dal 17.10.1936 al 26.11.1949; and Arnoldo Mondadori to Walt Disney, 23 May 1946, FAAM / AME, Fasc. Disney, Walt, 1, dal 17.10.1936 al 26.11.1949.

Disney to state that, having received permission from the Allied offices, *Topolino* would relaunch that fall.[29]

The first issue of *Topolino* was distributed 15 December 1945, despite the lack of a renewed contract with Disney. Subtle but clear signs indicated change. The name "Disney" returned to the front page, as did the strip "Topolino," with the beloved character once again a mouse. Additionally, *Topolino* now featured many American favorites published by King Features Syndicate, the rights to which Nerbini had relinquished during the war only to be promptly purchased by Mondadori. Speech bubbles likewise returned. Without ever commenting on the fall of Fascism or the abandonment of the MCP decrees, these changes made clear the end of Fascist cultural policies and the suppression of American comics.

Although the MCP's enforcement of *bonifica culturale* was over, the policies had left their mark. *Topolino* contained four American stories and five Italian originals upon relaunch. The Italian stories appear to have been drafted during the war, as they were attributed to the late Federico Pedrocchi and utilized captions over speech bubbles. Mondadori's stockpile of comics created by in-house Italian artists was, to some degree, a by-product of the MCP "guidelines" to generate Italian stories. The periodical, increasingly including American comics, nonetheless maintained elements of a specifically *Italian* approach toward the genre.

The long-sought meeting with Disney finally occurred in mid-1946. By this time, Disney's strategy for distribution had altered. The original 1935 contract between Mondadori and Disney granted the former an exclusive license in Italy to publish Mickey Mouse and use the name "Topolino" for an *unlimited* period.[30] The 1946 contract was limited to eight years, after which Disney could renew the contract or allow it to expire. It also stipulated a minimum weekly printing of 100,000 copies and a minimum payment of 400,000 lire a year, ten times the annual fee established by the 1935 contract (though in the context of a much-inflated currency).[31] The new contract signified the altered

29. Arnoldo Mondadori al avv. Atto Vannucci (Creazioni S.A.I. Walt Disney), 18 ottobre 1945, FAAM / AME, Fasc. Disney, Walt, 1, dal 17.10.1936 al 26.11.1949.

30. Forgacs and Gundle, *Mass Culture and Italian Society*, 114. Contratto tra la Walt Disney Enterprises e la Casa editrice G. Nerbini per la rinuncia da parte di Nerbini dello sfruttamento della figura di "Topolino." Firenze, 25 giugno 1935, FAAM / AME, Archivio storico Arnoldo Mondadori Editore—Ufficio contratti editoriali/Proprieta letteraria (Walt Disney), Cartella 3, F. 1. Contratti 1935. See chapter 2 for more on the 1935 contract.

31. Contratto tra la S.A.I. Creazioni Walt Disney e la Casa Editrice Mondadori inerente alla pubblicazione di Topolino. Milano 1946, FAAM / AME, Archivio storico Arnoldo Mondadori Editore—Ufficio contratti editoriali/Proprieta letteraria (Walt Disney), Cartella 3, F. 7. Contratti 1941–1946.

nature of the relationship between the United States and Italy and demonstrated that Mondadori's negotiating power had greatly decreased.

Despite the increased costs for Mondadori, continued partnership with Disney proved profitable. Mondadori benefitted not just from his partnership with Disney but also from Italy's alliance with the United States. Two years later, with the start of financial aid from the Marshall Plan in 1948, Mondadori received a loan of $9 million with an additional $940,000 the following year, which the firm utilized to purchase state-of-the-art printing presses.[32]

Signs of a New Beginning: Distancing Bourgeois *Corriere dei Piccoli* from Fascism

While Mondadori sought to silently move on from the past, the new director of *Corriere dei Piccoli,* Arnaldo Sartori, set out to establish a break with the Fascist era. The German occupation of Milan and the offices of *Corriere della Sera* had forced the periodical to align with the Fascist Repubblica Sociale Italiana during the Civil War. Sartori needed to demonstrate that this was a fresh start; rebranding of the periodical as *Il Giornale dei Piccoli* from May 1945 until March 1946 was one such signal.[33]

The cover of the first issue of *Giornale dei Piccoli* featured a young boy, Mimmo, who skipped school to welcome the parade of liberators just a month after the end of the war (figure 6.1). A truckload of Italian partisans paraded past first, followed next by the American tanks, projecting the liberation of Milan, Turin, and Genoa as the work of *Italian* partisans.[34] Mimmo waves the Italian tricolor along with the flags of the US and Britain as he cheers, linking the three as allies. The focus on the role of Italians in liberating cities in the north implicitly focuses the war on the occupying Germans. In this way, the editors of *Giornale dei Piccoli* sidestepped the question of Italian responsibility (and thus their own).

The emphasis on the Germans rather than the Fascist regime is all the clearer in the short story, "Fedora e Gianfranco nelle grinfie dei tedeschi" (Fedora and Gianfranco in the Clutch of the Germans). While suffering under

32. Forgacs and Gundle, *Mass Culture and Italian Society,* 121.

33. Carabba, *Corrierino, Corrierona,* 154–55.

34. Responsibility for the liberation of northern Italy is debated. Scholars such as Avagliano and Palmieri maintain that Italian partisans rushed to liberate the northern cities of the peninsula before the Allies rolled in and posit that they pushed the Germans out. Elsewhere it has been suggested that partisans contributed to this liberation but that it was an Allied operation. Avagliano and Palmieri, *Dopoguerra,* 21; and Horn, *Moment of Liberation,* 106–7.

FIGURE 6.1. "'Victory!' Mimmo yelled at the top of his lungs. (Who goes to school?) He vigorously applauds the heroic partisans. On armored vehicles and tanks, now arrive the Allies. Mimmo is so excited that his 'Hurrahs' go up to the stars." *Giornale dei Piccoli*, n. 1 (27 May 1945).

German occupation, one family decides to flee to Switzerland but is separated on their journey, and the children are captured by a German patrol. When Fedora, who is fifteen, confesses that they are fleeing the country, the Germans decide to deport them to a concentration camp in Poland along with a deportation of Jewish Italians. Fortunately, they are rescued by Italian partisans, who escort the family safely across the border.[35] The story touches on the suffering and the difficult choices Italians were forced to endure. Its publication indicates that Italians could not hide from this suffering and suggests the comfort found in assigning responsibility to the Germans.

The emphasis on the Germans as enemies and the Italians as liberators in these stories adopts the "bad German, good Italian" myth prevalent in postwar Italy. The myth emerged in the wartime distinctions made between the brutality of German soldiers and the honorable Italians. It developed further with the notion that World War II was the product of Nazi Germany and Mussolini, and that Italians' fight against the German occupiers demonstrated their "true" sentiments.[36] This perspective fueled an "image of acquittal" that facilitated overlooking war crimes and collaboration in favor of reconciliation and rebuilding.[37]

And Italy had much rebuilding to do, as demonstrated in Mimmo's story. The young Italian attempts to aid in the reconstruction of his city after the parade, but his efforts prove disastrous: he spills a wheelbarrow of bricks on someone's head; he cannot control a hose and sprays someone in the face instead of watering newly planted crops; and he drops a lightbulb on

35. "Fedora e Gianfranco nelle grinfie dei tedeschi," *Giornale dei Piccoli*, n. 2 (3 June 1945).

36. Forlenza and Thomassen, *Italian Modernities*, 194–95.

37. Focardi and Klinkhammer, "Question," 335–36.

someone's head.[38] The comedic piece conveys that rebuilding Italy would not be that simple.

GIAC and the Renewed Conquest of Italy

The leaders of GIAC continued to understand *Il Vittorioso* as "our journal of [ideological] penetration" to further the goal of the "conquest" of society, of continuing the long-sought re-Christianization of Italy.[39] GIAC adopted new campaigns to drive circulation through groups called Stormovitt (sometimes printed as Stormo-Vitt in early publications and memos). These groups were intended to discuss and sell *Il Vittorioso.* Groups were led by a *pilota* (guide), consisted of no more than fifteen members, and met to examine the periodical and respond to questions from the Pilota Maggiore, the leader of the initiative.[40] More than a discussion group, membership was dependent on selling copies of *Il Vittorioso.* GIAC considered the two functions of Stormovitt to be "a new experience through which *Il Vittorioso* can become the organ of penetration among the mass of Italian children."[41]

GIAC made this position clear to readers. In a 20 January 1946 announcement, the Pilota Maggiore informed members: "You must conquer! Speak of these ideals to all your friends. The '*vittoriosi*' must multiply: form a large, energetic, wonderful family that gathers under the banner of *Vitt* all youth who wish to love God, the Church, family, and the Patria at any cost!"[42] For GIAC, it was not enough that Italian boys read *Vitt*; the periodical was to be a tool of propaganda and conversion, as members of Stormovitt were expected to ultimately join the Catholic Youth group and become Aspiranti. As GIAC announced in *Il Vittorioso,* "Every GREST [Gruppo estivo, or 'summer groups'] equals a StormoVitt," displaying images of Aspiranti reading, promoting, and selling the periodical.[43] The ad, which solely features boys, conveyed that Stormovitt was an endeavor for Italians *boys.* While GIAC leaders

38. *Giornale dei Piccoli,* n. 1 (27 May 1945).

39. Aldo and Albino Galletto Notario, Circolare dell'Ufficio Centrale Aspiranti della GIAC, 21 ottobre 1945, ISACEM / Fondo della GIAC / Serie 3, B. 525 / Ciclostilati Aspiranti, 1945–46, 2.

40. Aldo and Albino Galletto Notario, Circolare della GIAC ai Delegati Diocesani Aspiranti, 6 giugno 1946, ISACEM / Fondo della GIAC / Serie 3, B. 525 / Ciclostilati Aspiranti, 1945–46.

41. Notario, Circolare della GIAC ai Delegati Diocesani Aspiranti, 6 giugno 1946.

42. *Il Vittorioso,* n. 3 (20 January 1946), 8.

43. *Il Vittorioso,* n. 26 (14 July 1946), 3.

hoped that *Vitt* would reach *all* Italian children, it seems that only boys were to be active participants in distributing the periodical.

The 1946 campaign to mobilize voters heightened the need to distribute *Vitt* to an ever-wider audience. On 2 July 1946, Italian men and women twenty-one and older were called to vote for the Constituent Assembly, set to establish the Italian constitution. Although the major Italian parties were collaborating in a coalition government, the Vatican considered Italian politics a battleground pitting conservative forces aligned with the vision of the Church against parties on the Left. The Vatican threw its support behind the Democrazia Cristiana. While not ideologically committed to democracy (Pius XII continued to praise Franco's dictatorship in Spain into the 1950s due to its "protection" of Catholicism), the pope considered democracy and political rights in Italy essential to countering the appeal of communism.[44]

On election day, *Vitt* editors encouraged readers to mobilize voters and ensure that the chosen deputies were Christian, because Italy is Christian, and "if the Deputies are 'so-so' or 'against' our religion, we will have a state lacking a Christian soul."[45] Although the parties of the Left combined received more votes, the DC received the most votes for a single party, totaling 31.5 percent of the votes.[46] Italy's first deliberative assembly would be chaired by Alcide De Gasperi and the DC.

The Italian Right's Tentative Embrace of the US

Even as *Il Vittorioso* mobilized readers against the political Left, GIAC remained concerned with the spread of American-style entertainment and consumerism. And American-style entertainment *was* spreading. The image of America in *Topolino* was one of abundance, technology, modernity, and justice. The first story of "Mandrake" embraced the launch of the atomic era by sending the protagonists into the X-dimension. "Flash Gordon," too, maintained its cult of technology. The image of the US as modern, technologically advanced, and wealthy contrasted clearly with war-torn Italy and promoted the *mito americano*.[47]

Sci-fi comics also portrayed Americans as liberators committed to justice. Flash Gordon's fight against the dictatorial emperor Ming now appeared

44. Chamedes, *Twentieth-Century Crusade*, 236, 38; Gualtieri, *L'Italia dal 1943 al 1992*, 72; and Hebblethwaite, "Pope Pius XII," 75.

45. *Il Vittorioso*, n. 20 (2 June 1946), 2.

46. Avagliano and Palmieri, *Dopoguerra*, 256.

47. Forlenza, *On the Edge of Democracy*, ch. 3.

FIGURE 6.2. The guard shouts, "Surrender! In the name of Emperor Ming." Flash Gordon responds, "At your disposal! Go ahead, Lita, I'll hold them off." *Topolino*, n. 587 (18 May 1946), 5.

to target Nazism more directly. The postwar context made it difficult not to associate Gordon's fight against tyranny with the recent war against the Axis. Moreover, as figure 6.2 shows, the helmets, armbands, and weaponry of Gordon's foes recall those of Nazi Germany.

The incorporation into *Topolino* of American comics which were once condemned also reflected more freedom for publishers, who could now pursue profitable series without concern for Fascist cultural autarky. This is clear, as *Topolino* began to print *fewer* Italian stories over time. *Topolino* was balanced in its division between Italian and American comics at its relaunch in 1945. In fact, it printed *one more* Italian story. But the balance evolved until *Topolino* was *entirely* comprised of comics from the US for a brief period in the spring of 1947. Issue 629 on 5 March 1947, for instance, featured "Topolino" on page one; "Agente segreto X-9" spanned pages two and three; "Flash Gordon," pages four and five; "Paperino" (Donald Duck) was granted pages six and seven; and the final page was again graced with "Topolino."[48] This arrangement did not last long but demonstrates how Mondadori benefitted from the new political climate and access to more American stories.

Not everyone welcomed the renewed influx of American culture into Italy. The concern that American culture had a disintegrative impact on Italian

48. *Topolino*, n. 629 (5 March 1947).

society persisted. American culture depicted alternative social norms, styles of dress, gender roles, and notions of acceptable sexual behavior. It also brought with it a particular style of consumerism. Both developed further in the postwar period and provoked concern from, among others, the Catholic Church.[49] Arguably, the formation of *Il Vittorioso* had been a product of this clash, an effort to combat the popularity of noneducational or even amoral comics. In 1946, the GIAC leadership contrasted its educational *Vitt* with the questionable nature of its competition. The "amoral characters" in American comics were denounced, with "L'Uomo Mascherato" declared "a form of Satanic idolatry." Even "Topolino" was disparaged for its "careless morals" (*faciloneria morale*).[50]

Il Vittorioso aligned with the Vatican's ambiguous position on American culture. Jacovitti's 1945 page for Christmas (figure 6.3) illustrates how the periodical offered subtle critiques. Italians attempt to go about their business, but their daily lives were clearly dictated by the destruction. At the top under "Natale," for instance, a bourgeois family living in a destroyed house pretends everything is normal as the father tells others, "Close the window, it's cold." Elsewhere, parishioners line up for service in a bombed-out church, and a man sells tickets outside a nearly collapsed cinema. The statue of Dante Alighieri in the center of the courtyard suggests that Italian traditions persist.

The American GIs seem unconcerned with the destruction. An Italian man tips his hat in respect to a pair strolling leisurely at the top, while another pair riding in their Jeep is hit with a snowball thrown by a boy, either in jest or resentment. The inclusion of the Jeep captures the ambiguity felt toward the Allied occupiers, which, again, targeted Americans despite the heterogenous occupying force. Initially, the Jeep embodied the technological superiority, dynamism, and freedom Italians associated with the US. But it became a muddled symbol as soldiers driving Jeeps caused accidents, resulting in the deaths of 3,548 Italians by December 1946, which Jacovitti comments on by showing an Italian woman attempting to get out of the way of the Jeep.[51] The problem was so prevalent that a 1946 article denounced "The Jeep of Death."[52] The Jeep embodied the promise of America and the burden of occupation.

Writers for *Vitt* made GIAC's ambiguous stance on the US felt in other ways as well. In 1946, Jacovitti created "Mandrago," "a satire of the celebrated

49. Forgacs and Gundle, *Mass Culture and Italian Society*, 2.

50. GIAC, "Apri l'occhio," 1946, ISACEM / Fondo della GIAC / Serie 3, B. 525 / Ciclostilati Aspiranti, 1945–46, 3.

51. Williams, *Allies and Italians under Occupation*, 43.

52. Avagliano and Palmieri, *Dopoguerra*, 137–39; and "La Jeep della morte," *l'Avanti* (1 October 1946).

FIGURE 6.3. Jacovitti's "Merry Christmas" page depicts a war-ravaged Italy. *Il Vittorioso,* n. 49 (23 December 1945), 8.

American magician" and comics hero, Mandrake.[53] In the series, Mandrago gains magical powers, and, after initially using his powers for selfish gain, he attempts to help people. Flying around the globe, Mandrago spots a destroyed Italian town, torn between the DC and the PCI. Mandrago wants to help and

53. *Il Vittorioso,* n. 27 (21 July 1946), 8.

decides to "return the cities of the destroyed countries to as they were before [the war]."[54] In an instant, Mandrago reverses the destruction around the world. Cities are rebuilt. Missing limbs are regained. But the Fascist regime is resurrected as well. Soon, Fascist blackshirts are chasing communists who, unaware of what has happened, are advocating for rights.

The Allied powers are stumped by this change, which overturns their leadership in the postwar order. They resolve to fight *each other* to establish leadership in this new world. Mandrago again uses his magic to establish peace by turning them into the babies they are behaving like. As Mandrago attempts to leave earth to aid other planets, the being possessing him—the source of his mysterious powers—breaks free, and Mandrago tumbles back to earth to find all his hard work undone. Italy is in ruins, and he is powerless to change it. The country will have to fix its own problems.

The strip conveys the idea that there is no easy fix. The Americans cannot simply wave a magic wand as do the heroes in American stories, nor can a check from the US government repair Italy. A *moral* restoration is required. Furthermore, the strip raises questions regarding the US agenda in Italy, framing the destruction as benefiting the US by legitimizing the extension of their power. Finally, the mockery of Mandrago in the series is a clear critique of the American culture that was becoming so prevalent throughout the peninsula. If the Vatican welcomed the US as an ally in its fight against communism, it remained hostile toward its cultural influence.

This rift in the two conservative periodicals' approaches to American comics is demonstrated by their rival adaptations of the Italian classic *Pinocchio*. The publication of Disney's 1940 adaptation was unthinkable in the Fascist era, during which the author's nephew filed a lawsuit against Disney for removing *Pinocchio*'s "national nature" and corrupting the author's message.[55] Mondadori attempted to defend the adaptation but found little support in the context of the MCP's agenda of *bonifica culturale*.

No longer constrained by the MCP in 1946, Mondadori printed Disney's "Pinocchio" on the cover of *Topolino* from 24 August to 14 December. Exactly one week later, *Il Vittorioso* printed its *own* adaptation. Whereas *Topolino* listed its version as "Disney's Pinocchio" with no reference to the author Carlo Collodi, *Vitt* printed "Collodi: Pinocchio. Illustrated by Jacovitti."

---

54. *Il Vittorioso*, n. 35 (15 September 1946), 8.

55. Atto di controdiffida della Società Anonima Periodici Italiani nei confronti del diffidatario Paolo Lorenzini. Firenze, data sconosciuta, FAAM / AME, Archivio storico Arnoldo Mondadori Editore—Ufficio contratti editoriali/Proprieta letteraria (Walt Disney), Cartella 3, F. 12. Contratto (Albi Topolino) 1938–1946, 2.

The story's immediate appearance in *Il Vittorioso* after its conclusion in *Topolino* demonstrates how the editors envisioned it as a response to the American version. The "Pinocchio" in *Vitt* followed the original story closely and aligned with the style of early Italian comics, relying on captions, not speech bubbles. It positioned an Italian style against that of Disney, as Jacovitti arranged the images uniquely in his construction of the visual narrative rather than relying on panels arranged in a grid. Jacovitti's adaptation defended Italian culture by preserving a classic and demonstrating the creativity of Italian *fumettisti.*

The different priorities of Mondadori and GIAC attest to their distinct concerns in the postwar era. Mondadori's desire to rebuild his firm's profits incentivized embracing the free market and cultural exchange. GIAC, on the other hand, pursued the Vatican's political and social goals for a Christian Italy and the defense of Italian (Christian) culture. The divergent approaches toward American culture adopted by Mondadori and GIAC demonstrate that the cultural elites in postwar Italy were not a unified, coherent bloc, even on the political Right.

The Left on Comics and the Left in Comics

The Italian youth organizations of the Left trailed their Catholic rivals. Although the Federazione Giovanile Socialista Italiana (Italian Socialist Youth Federation) dated back to 1903, it had to rebuild after twenty years of suppression, during which GIAC had been allowed to coexist alongside the Fascist youth groups and therefore grow its base.

A foundation for new youth groups emerged during World War II with the Fronte di Gioventù (FdG), which assembled democratic youths associated with the Resistance. After World War II, many local youth groups associated with democratic parties emerged that were loosely organized under the FdG, some already adopting the name Associazione Pionieri d'Italia (API).[56] In time, the various regional socialist and communist youth groups were unified in 1949 under the Federazione Giovanile Comunista Italiana. Children aged eight to thirteen were formed into the API.

The centralization of these organizations was in part a response to the clerical offensive against youth organizations on the Left. The Vatican's crusade against communism, waged since 1946, escalated into formalized GIAC campaigns against Left-wing youth groups around the 1948 election. Actions

56. Magnanini, "L'Associazione Pionieri d'Italia," 177 n. 36; and Marchioro, "Esperienze."

taken by youth groups on the Right and Left fueled the other; the formation of the API was in part to better combat the offensive of the Church, while GIAC's campaigns accelerated following the establishment of the API.[57]

In addition to the mounting pressure from Catholic Action, intellectuals on the Left grappled with the challenge of American culture. Many Italian intellectuals of the Left viewed American culture as crude and insidious. Togliatti criticized American cultural products as using entertainment to lure Italians into the American way of life and away from their own traditions. Ironically, these critiques shared much with those voiced by Catholic intellectuals. Their agendas diverged, however, and the PCI considered Catholic attempts to forge a hybrid between provincialist and American culture insufficient. Communists advocated a nationalist front oriented toward Soviet values and rooted in Italian cultural independence.[58]

This rejection of American culture and commitment to Italian cultural traditions informed the PCI's response to comics. Enrico Berlinguer, the secretary of the Federazione Giovanile Comunista Italiana, believed comics were naturally bad and capitalistic, intended to "narcoticize" the youth. Echoing concerns raised in the 1930s, Togliatti deemed comics a mode of capitalist escapism, distracting people from class struggle.[59]

The discussion on the Left regarding comics was most explicit in the 1950s, when a debate unfolded regarding whether it was possible to distinguish form from content.[60] Marisa Musu launched the dispute with the article "Let's Discuss Comics," arguing that the popularity of comics made them dangerous to ignore. She asserted American comics were "truly a weapon against the youth" that needed countering.[61] Giovannella Autuori seconded Musu's point by stating that 90 percent of Italian youth organizations reported that their members were passionate about comics.[62] G. B. Giudiceandrea even went so far as to suggest that comics' detachment from reality might be beneficial. Arguing that comics "offer young people the opportunity to distance themselves from the confines of a monotonous and hopeless life" and provide the "opportunity to dream," Giudiceandrea asserted, "Our error is having left the monopoly on comic books to reactionaries."[63]

57. Fincardi, "Ragazzi tra il fuoco," 102; Magnanini, "L'Associazione Pionieri d'Italia," 166.

58. Brogi, *Confronting America*, 16, 19, 140–41, 145; and Meda, *Stelle e strips*, 237–38, 242.

59. Goretti, "Pattuglia," 272.

60. Repetti, "L'universo comunista," 251.

61. Marisa Musu, "Discutiamo sui fumetti," *Gioventù Nuova*, n. 4 (April 1950), 25, 29–30.

62. Giovannella Autuori, "I personaggi dei giornali a fumetti," *Gioventù Nuova*, n. 5 (May 1950), 24.

63. G. B. Giudiceandrea, "Perchè i giovani leggono i fumetti," *Gioventù Nuova*, n. 10 (October 1950), 31, 32.

Not everyone agreed. Giuliano Pajetta, in an article presumptuously titled "Conclusion of the Debate on Comics," responded that the style of comics could not be separated from the content. Pajetta distinguished comics from illustrated stories by defining them as "an abbreviated story, impoverished, comprised only of stupid and insensitive dialogue, the form of which corresponds to the miserable content of today's decadent bourgeois literature."[64]

Gianni Rodari, a journalist and writer who served as editor of *Il Pioniere,* rejected Pajetta's thinking. The Left must and should *want* to spread educational stories in comics. Like Musu, Autuori, and Giudiceandrea, Rodari recognized the simple fact that the youth *liked* comics, and that pedagogists had to acknowledge that Italian youth had *agency* in shaping the entertainment and stories aimed at them: "Whoever wants to talk to children and youth must take into account the language they are used to and what has become the most important method of communicating with them."[65]

Perhaps most importantly, Rodari pointed out that periodicals aimed at communist youth *already* published comics. *Il Pioniere* was in circulation and had been predated by the comics magazine *Il Moschettiere,* printed in Rome by Edizioni Astrea. In June 1947, the periodical became the official journal of a regional Pionieri organization and was rebranded *Il Pioniere dei Ragazzi.*[66] It changed again shortly after to become *Noi Ragazzi* upon gaining the sponsorship by the Unione Donne Italiane (Union of Italian Women), whose periodical was similarly titled *Noi Donne.* The UDI had ties to the PCI and had many members concerned with what Italian children were reading. Rather than creating a new magazine, they decided to sponsor one that already portrayed values they promoted. The new *Noi Ragazzi* became the periodical of the Leftist youth group in Reggio Emilia as well.[67] *Noi Ragazzi* restarted many series from the journal's previous iterations and added more.

The editors of *Noi Ragazzi* were intentional with the values they promoted, and they were cognizant of the concerns among Left-wing intellectuals regarding comics. To complaints that the periodical printed too many

64. Giuliano Pajetta, "Conclusione del dibattito sui fumetti," *Gioventù Nuova,* n. 11–12 (November–December 1950), 34. This article has been attributed to Giuliano's brother, Giancarlo, but *Gioventù Nuova* credits Giuliano. Giancarlo Pajetta was an editor for *Gioventù Nuova.* Repetti, "L'universo comunista," 274.

65. Gianni Rodari, "La questione dei fumetti: Lettera al direttore," *Rinascita,* n. 1 (1952), quoted in Repetti, "L'universo comunista," 252.

66. *I Pionieri dei Ragazzi,* n. 25 (22 June 1947). It is unclear to what API group the editor is referring, as the Pionieri did not form as a national body in Italy until 1949. The periodical continued the issue numeration from *Il Moschettiere.*

67. The group at the time was known as the *Associazione Giovani Esploratori.* Mori, "Prima del *Pioniere,*" 230–32.

comics, one editor, Ceralacca, responded, "We also think *Noi Ragazzi* has too many comics, but the problem is that many children find instead that there are too few."[68] Ceralacca believed comics could be good if they contained the right values: "*Noi Ragazzi* published comics that highlighted justice, liberty, and equality."[69]

After a nearly two-year run, the Federazione Giovanile Comunista Italiana determined it needed an official periodical for the API, *Il Pioniere*. Lorenzo Repetti identifies several defining themes of the magazine. The comics in the Leftist periodical often adhered to a sense of reality, with postwar Italy a common setting. Collective action was stressed in opposition to the hyperindividualism of American comics. Peace, tolerance, and pacifism were promoted, and stories emphasized a culture of social and scientific progress. In short, young readers were to learn how to love their families; to be studious, work hard, and respect workers; to love their country but also to love the people of *all* countries; to help the old, young, and weak; and to face challenges with courage, joy, and serenity.[70] The periodicals discussed above had incorporated these values into their stories since 1946.

Scientific and Social Progress

Among the most notable stories printed in *Il Moschettiere* is "I pionieri della speranza," (Pioneers of Hope), a French science-fiction comic originally published in 1945 in *Valliant*. Influenced by "Flash Gordon" and perhaps also "Saturno contro la Terra," the story focuses on humanity's investigation of an approaching planet. The spaceship design of an Italian engineer, Roberto, is selected for the mission, and an international team is assembled which includes a Russian physicist. Complications arise when "i capitalisti" want to invest in the project to exploit whatever resources are found on the new planet. Captions provided the commentary that these men were "capitalists without conscience," provoking Roberto's disgust as he laments, "You can only think of money when humanity is in danger!"[71] Roberto's refusal is met with violence when gangsters arrive to threaten the workers into compliance. Although the strip never identifies them as Americans, the emblem of a white

68. *Noi Ragazzi*, n. 7 (12 February 1950).

69. *Noi Ragazzi*, n. 22 (28 May 1950). For comparison, Mori, "Prima del *Pioniere*," 232.

70. Repetti, "L'universo comunista," 254–56, 259, 262, 264. Michela Marchioro has discussed similar themes in *Pioniere*. Marchioro, "*Il Pioniere*," 74.

71. *Il Moschettiere*, n. 22 (1 June 1947).

star on the plane in which they arrived marks them as such, as do the tommy guns in the hands of the gangsters.

"I pionieri della speranza" continued with the exploratory team finding a scientifically advanced civilization of pacifists on the new planet. However, the team is followed by the capitalists, who created their own ship and land in the untamed wilds of the planet. The series develops into an adventure not unlike "Flash Gordon," as the team searches for survivors and encounters massive animals and blue humanoid aliens.

The series was exemplary of the Left's complicated stance on gender, which was more progressive but nonetheless maintained traditional tropes. On the one hand, the scientific team included two accomplished and capable women: a Chinese chemist and an American doctor. However, as the team heads into the jungles of the planet, Roberto is forced to rescue the American doctor after she is captured by blue men serving a capitalist explorer who installed himself as warlord, reverting to formulas familiar to readers of adventure comics discussed in previous chapters.

Liberty and International Fraternity

Il Moschettiere, Il Pioniere dei Ragazzi, and *Noi Ragazzi* all championed the fight for liberty and international fraternity. While *Balilla* had praised Napoleon's exploits and claimed him as ethnically Italian, "Le vendicatore dell'Atlantico" (The Avenger of the Atlantic) villainized him and extolled the efforts of the Portuguese to fight tyranny.[72] The protagonists included an officer, a soldier, and a priest rescued from the French. It was not important that the heroes were Portuguese. What mattered was their commitment to independence and liberty everywhere.

This emphasis on national determination, liberty, and international fraternity is most apparent in "Il cavaliere della libertà" (The Knight of Liberty) in *Noi Ragazzi.* The series focused on the adventures of Giuseppe Garibaldi, claiming him as a hero for democracy and the Left, combating rival claims to his legacy, including those of Fascists during the Civil War.[73] Rather than centering solely on his struggle for Italian unification, the series told of his fight against tyranny in Latin America. To highlight Garibaldi as a *democratic* hero, the series portrayed him meeting Giuseppe Mazzini and defending

72. *Il Moschettiere,* n. 1 (15 September 1946).

73. Forlenza and Thomassen, *Italian Modernities,* 166; Pavone, *Una guerra civile,* 217, 224.

the short-lived Republic of Rome. His great personal sacrifices only further attested that this was a man willing to give up all for liberty.

As the strip continues, the authors include his campaigns in the Italian Wars of Liberation, first in the north and then as "The Thousand" famously launched an invasion of Sicily. His liberating quality is stressed here, with no mention of his brief time as dictator of Sicily.[74] After helping to unify Italy, the strip depicts Garibaldi's defense of French liberty in the Franco-Prussian War and his advocacy of democracy as member of the Chamber of Deputies.

Garibaldi's discontent regarding the lack of democracy in Italy is hardly discussed, and no mention is made of his dismay when his home of Nice was ceded to France in exchange for Napoleon III's assistance against the Austrians. This decision was likely a means to frame Garibaldi's commitment to international fraternity and liberty and to avoid turning the story into an irredentist tale promoting the need to regain Nice. Readers were to love their country and defend it, but nationalism was rejected in favor of internationalism and peace.

A Fractured Italy: Between Left and Right

The parties of the Right and Left offered competing visions for how to rebuild Italy. But, while the causes of problems and the solutions they proposed may have differed, intellectuals across the political spectrum were responding to the same issues, including the loss of Italy's colonies, a rise in crime, and the place of religion in Italian society.

The divisions over these issues deepened with the approach of the 1948 election. Increasingly, children's periodicals presented the image of a civilizational conflict, exacerbated by the onset of the Cold War. Young readers were tasked with mobilizing voters. The various points of commonality between the Italian Left and Right were eclipsed by the rising tensions.

Colonial Fantasies and the Reality of Decolonization

The Italian Empire—so proudly championed by Mussolini as symbolizing the nation's return to glory—crumbled during the Second World War. Yet conservative children's periodicals continued to print colonial adventures. While many of these stories would likely have been considered acceptable

74. *Noi Ragazzi*, n. 42 (24 October 1948).

to the MCP under Fascism, none explicitly aligned with the dictates of the MCP. These stories were often not "Italian stories" in "Italian settings," but drew instead on the Italian adventure tradition established by authors such as Emilio Salgari by setting stories in British colonies in Africa or India. For instance, "Sunda e Upasunda" in *Topolino* is set in "uncivilized" India, as European explorers stumble across a community that worships a sapient telepathic statue.[75] These comics share more with the adventure stories of Liberal Italy. Nonetheless, these colonial adventures upheld Orientalist themes by casting foreign lands as exotic and relying on racial stereotypes in the depiction of non-Western peoples.

The foundational belief in European superiority validated past colonial actions, legitimizing the relationship as beneficial. This myth of Italians as benevolent colonizers is portrayed clearly in "Bagonghi il pagliaccio," in which an Italian engineer works to develop infrastructure in an Italian colony. Meanwhile, his wife, Anna, is shown interacting with the Indigenous population, referred to as "Padrona Anna" by the young African girl who accompanies her.[76]

Such imagery of Italians in Africa supported the notion that Italians uplifted their colonial territories by treating colonized people well and developing modern infrastructure. Positive allusions to colonialism remained in the precursors to *Pioniere* as well. The short story "Oro, Oro" (Gold, Gold) discussed the contribution of Italian explorers in the Americas. Their fight against local rulers was framed as a struggle against tyranny, as when they "liberated" a city from the hands of the oppressive Maganataz: "Thus it was that Antonio Barin, a forgotten Italian, added a new gem to the crown of His Most Catholic Majesty Philip V of Aragon."[77]

The idea of Italians as benevolent colonizers fueled resentment at the loss of Italy's colonies. The Paris Peace Treaty in 1947 ratified these losses and required Italy to pay reparations to Ethiopia. That countries colonized by Italy before Fascism obtained their independence further provoked controversy in Italy. Desires to regain pre-Fascist colonies led members of the DC, including De Gasperi, to dismiss reports of wrongdoing in the Italian colonies. The Ministry of Foreign Affairs distinguished "gentle" Italian colonial rule from its oppressive counterparts, a myth which persists to this day and continues to shape discourse on immigration.[78]

---

75. *Topolino*, n. 594 (6 July 1946), 2.

76. *Topolino*, n. 565 (15 December 1945), 3.

77. *Il Moschettiere*, n. 7 (27 October 1946).

78. Del Boca, "Myths, Suppressions, Denials, and Defaults," 18, 20, 22. The use of chemical warfare in Ethiopia was denied by the Italian government until 1996.

Grappling with Crime, Social Unrest, and the Partito Comunista Italiano

Stories of Italy's glorious colonial past no doubt offered an escape from the devastated state of Italy and assuaged the loss of national prestige. Over 1.2 million urban dwellings had been destroyed during the war. The black market was widespread, families were separated, criminals and banditry were rampant, and many Italian women turned to prostitution.[79] The Italian comics of *Giornale dei Piccoli* reflected this new reality in a story (figure 6.4) in which Mimmo encounters not one, but *five* instances of theft throughout his day. The day begins with optimism, with his father proclaiming, "Now we are finally living among good people: here are the fruits of peace!" But the "fruits of peace" are either rotten or not yet ripe, as the two encounter first a pickpocket on the train, then a bicycle theft, a stolen car, and two robberies. Mimmo is forced to ask his father, "Are you certain that respectable people have finally returned?"[80]

The strip pictured in figure 6.4 recalls the 1948 neorealist film, *Ladri di biciclette* (which has been known in English as both as *The Bicycle Thief* and *Bicycle Thieves*), directed by Vittorio De Sica and written by Cesare Zavattini. Neorealist cinema aimed to depict everyday life to highlight "the burdensome conditions of wartime and early postwar Italy."[81] In many ways, comics such as "Mimmo" in *Giornale dei Piccoli* likewise portrayed Italy as it really was, representing a break with the comics produced under Fascism, which were either set in foreign locales or depicted a crime-free Italy. However, whereas neorealism in film was framed in a manner that would foster sympathy for the characters, *Giornale dei Piccoli* presented thieves not as desperate individuals but as criminals holding back the return to normalcy in Italy. It furthermore deepened an image that the republic was failing ordinary people and was associated with disorder.[82]

Leaders of GIAC were likewise concerned with high crime rates, particularly among Italian youths. Rationing continued after World War II, and studies have estimated that Italians received about 900 of the 2500 calories needed per day.[83] The black market flourished as a result, and many young Italians were involved in this trade. Juvenile delinquency became associated with the

79. Avagliano and Palmieri, *Dopoguerra*, 152, 173.

80. *Giornale dei Piccoli*, n. 15 (2 September 1945).

81. Pirro, "Cinematic Traces," 408.

82. Forlenza, *On the Edge of Democracy*, 42; and Ginsborg, *History of Contemporary Italy*, 99–100.

83. Avagliano and Palmieri, *Dopoguerra*, 112–13; and Caruso, *Così ricostruimmo l'Italia*, 44.

Anno I - N. 15
2 Settembre 1945
Lire 7.— la copia
1. « Or si vive finalmente - fa il papà - tra brava gente:
ecco i frutti della pace! » Mimmo ascolta e si compiace.
2. Ma ad un tratto nel tranvai s'ode un urlo: « Dalli, dai!
Dai, al ladro! Sono stato d'un milione borseggiato! »
3. Un milion?! Via tutti in corsa giù dal tram, alla rincorsa
dell'audace borsaiuolo. Ma scomparso è già il mariuolo.
4. Ora, in mezzo a quel vocio, grida un altro: « Anch'io, anch'io!
M'han rubato - oh, che disdetta! - la mia bella bicicletta. »
GIOIELLIERE
5. Via di nuovo a gran galoppo! Ma che c'è? C'è un terzo intoppo.
Un signore urla: « La mia auto m'han soffiato via! »
6. Cosa accade stamattina? Accidenti! Una vetrina
che va in pezzi... Un bel piacere stan facendo al gioielliere!
BANCA
7. Di rubar non ci si stanca. Qui svaligiano una banca:
portan via biglietti a pacchi, a valigie colme, a sacchi.
8. « Ma, papà, sei proprio certo - chiede Mimmo alquanto incerto -
che perbene finalmente ritornata sia la gente? »

FIGURE 6.4. Mimmo and his father are on the tram when another passenger is pickpocketed. The crowd chases the thief before encountering another theft, this time of a bicycle. Then another theft occurs, followed by the robbery of a jewelry store and then of a bank. "'But papa, are you certain,' asks Mimmo, not so certain himself, 'that respectable people have finally returned?'" *Giornale dei Piccoli,* n. 15 (2 September 1945).

term *sciuscià*, an Italianization of the American "shoeshine" in reference to the young shoe shiners who operated as black-market vendors.[84]

The rampancy of the black market and fears of juvenile delinquency were captured in *Il Vittorioso*'s "I ragazzi di Piazza Cinquecento" (The Boys of Piazza Cinquecento), referring to the square in front of the Rome train station. Beginning in August 1945, the story was framed around the German occupation and then Allied liberation of Rome. Life remains hard after liberation, and yet Danilo discovers that his friend is flush with cash because he has been selling goods on the black market. Danilo begins to sell in the piazza until his mother finds out. He renounces his ways after reflecting on the courage and moral fortitude of his brother, who fights with Italian partisan forces. Danilo finds his friend cleaning the shoes of an African American GI.[85] The scene captures the connection of *sciuscià* to juvenile delinquency, but also reflects the tendency of Italians to target Black Americans specifically as responsible for social unrest, violence, and the black market.[86] The image of an Italian youth serving a Black soldier presents a reversal of the racial hierarchy preached under Fascism and suggests unease with this change, framed as it is around the corruption of Italian youth. Danilo's desire to quit is met with resistance from his old gang until his older brother shows up to help him, and Danilo's tale ends with him working an honest job and inspiring his friends to fight *against* the black market.

The story mirrors remarks made by the clergy regarding the problem of juvenile delinquency. Commenting in a 1947 pastoral letter, Bishop Giuseppe Gagnor expressed concern for the suffering and harm done to children, who numbered among the bands of criminals plaguing Italy. These boys, he argued, "shun honest work to live on robbery and banditry," not out of desperation, but because they lacked proper morals. Gagnor concluded that they represented a "serious threat to society."[87]

The discussion of crime is much different from that depicted in the periodicals of the Left. "I ragazzi di Amina" (Amina's Boys), printed in *Noi Ragazzi* throughout 1948, told of a group of youths orphaned by the war who stole and operated within the black market to survive. The story is unique in that the group is led by Amina, a young girl searching for her mother.[88] The comic depicted the extent of devastation in Italy after the war and emphasized the

84. Avagliano and Palmieri, *Dopoguerra*, 145.

85. *Il Vittorioso*, n. 36 (23 September 1945), 1.

86. Avagliano and Palmieri, *Dopoguerra*, 168; and Forlenza, *On the Edge of Democracy*, 70.

87. Giuseppe P. Gabnor, "Salviamo la gioventù" (11 February 1947), quoted in Avagliano and Palmieri, *Dopoguerra*, 148.

88. The story began in *Il Pioniere dei Ragazzi* as "I Ragazzi della Grotta."

desperation of the children, who had to find food somehow. Like the Catholic Church, the comic framed American GIs as exacerbating these issues. In one episode, Amina's request for a ride to a distant town is met with a salacious response from a soldier. She refuses the offer, and they fling small candies at the orphan boys as they drive off laughing.[89] In a latter episode, when two US military police catch one of the boys attempting to steal goods, the sergeant must give the order not to use excessive force. His subordinate protests, "That's not a boy: it's a ferocious wolf!"[90]

The story frames the issue of crime as an act born of desperation and emphasizes the harsh response of American soldiers and administrators. To a degree, there was a shared view across the Left and Right of the American occupation as harmful and corrupting. However, periodicals on the Left go further by presenting the US as a nation with a crime problem. "I pionieri della speranza," discussed above, presented American capitalists as thugs, willing to kill and put humanity at risk to chase profits.

Despite the common concern regarding crime and what both saw as the corrupting influence of the US, the depiction of crime differed greatly between the Left and Right. According to the Left, criminal activity is not driven by greed, but by desperation for work, goods, and shelter. As with neorealist films, these comics tend to be interpreted as calling for social programs to support the sympathetic, impoverished characters of its stories. By contrast, in *Corriere dei Piccoli*'s "Mimmo," crime is an issue of a lack of order. Meanwhile in "I ragazzi della Piazza Cinquecento," *Il Vittorioso* treats crime as a *moral* failing, and thus the solution is not social programs, but Christian teachings. What Italy needs, then, is Catholic leadership.

Defending Christian Europe: From Crusades to the 1948 Election

The importance of Catholic leadership and traditions was unsurprisingly a frequent theme of *Il Vittorioso*. Historical tales of the defense of Christian kingdoms provided rich material for adventure comics that aligned with the values of Catholic Action. Comics such as "Il cavaliere di Castiglia" (The Knights of Castile), for instance, told of efforts to liberate Spain from the Moors, spreading Christianity and liberty alike.

"L'ultima pattuglia" (The Last Patrol) likewise told of the defense of a Catholic territory. The story focuses on three young sons of merchants—one Italian, one French, and one Spanish—who join to help in whatever way they can

89. *Pioniere dei Ragazzi*, n. 34–35 (1947).

90. *Noi Ragazzi*, n. 16 (18 April 1948).

when Cyprus, a Venetian colony, is under attack from the Ottoman Empire. They are praised by their commander, who says, "You, boys, have achieved what men have not yet been able to: the union of Christian forces!"[91]

The defenders put up a brave fight on Cyprus, but all seems lost until Pope Pius V launches a new crusade. The crusade is answered by the Holy League formed at the behest of Pius V, including various Spanish and Italian territories. The defense of Cyprus was but one part of a larger crusade to push back Ottoman forces, which had appeared in *Il Vittorioso* in 1937 as the short story "Ottobre 1571: Lepanto." Both stories stressed the Christian foundations of European unity and Pius V's leading role in forging that unity which aimed at liberating Christian Europe and the Mediterranean from the Turks.[92]

Moving beyond the explicit emphasis on Muslims, it seems that the core of the story is the Christian basis of European unity. Considered further, the threat highlighted is both imperial *and* spiritual, as it is a foreign religion coming to enslave or convert Christians. GIAC calls on Christian readers to defend that foundation.

When considered in the context of 1948, it seems plausible that readers connected this story to the perceived civilizational threat posed by communism. Statements from the Church underlined this connection. For instance, in 1946, the Vatican held its first postwar World Congress of Catholic social organizations in Spain. In his keynote address, the archbishop of Cardiff, Michael McGrath, declared "that Spain saved Europe during her Civil War, as she did at Lepanto," connecting Pius V's crusade against Islam with the modern struggle against communism.[93] Franco was even dubbed the "modern El Cid," hero of the peninsula.[94] Readers were asked to participate in this modern crusade.

GIAC once again utilized *Vitt* as a tool to fight communism during the 1948 elections. The 1948 elections were the first to be held since the ratification of a constitution and were understood by all political parties as decisive in establishing the course of Italian politics. It was even more significant because De Gasperi and the Democratic Christians had split with the parties on the Left in May 1947, dismissing Leftist cabinet members.[95] The 1948 election would thus decide which of these forces would govern without the other.

91. *Il Vittorioso*, n. 29 (18 July 1948), 1.

92. *Il Vittorioso*, n. 44 (6 November 1937), 7. "Ottobre 1571: Lepanto" is discussed in further detail in chapter 3.

93. Chamedes, *Twentieth-Century Crusade*, 266–67.

94. Corrin, *Catholic Intellectuals*, 5.

95. Gualtieri, *L'Italia dal 1943 al 1992*, 7; and White, *Modern Italy's Founding Fathers*, 148–51.

Once again, GIAC leaders used *Il Vittorioso* to encourage readers to mobilize their family and acquaintances to vote in this election, "one of the most important acts in the life of our Italy." This election, the announcement continued, would decide the destiny of the nation and, if it went well, "assure order and liberty for all citizens." The editors warned, however, that "some groups of Italians use the words, peace, liberty, independence, and work to hide their desire to cut from the heart of Italians the only thing that made them great in the world: love of God and of Italy." How can readers defend Italy? By getting everyone to vote and assert that "they want a Christian Italy."[96]

The periodical of the youth groups on the Left countered with their own attacks. The election did not appear in the magazines devoted to comics. Instead, features on the election appeared in *Pattuglia,* the newsletter for youth groups on the Left. A full page was devoted to inspiring young readers to canvas for votes, depicting a skull in a soldier's helmet beside a denunciation of De Gasperi, "who opens the door to American warmongering." To calls for war, the editors called on young readers "to respond no! The youth want to live."[97] The ad insisted that the only way to resolve international issues peacefully was to vote for the Fronte Democratic Popolare (FDP), which included the PCI and the Italian Socialist Party.

The PCI and PSI had performed well the year before in Sicilian elections. The Vatican, their DC allies, and American officials feared that the FDP would again win a majority. Soviet actions in Eastern Europe prompted fears that a communist insurrection might accompany the election.[98] Contrary to such worries, the DC won 48.5 percent of the votes in comparison to the 30.98 percent obtained by the FDP. The transition to power was peaceful, and De Gasperi formed a centrist coalition. The DC remained the leading party in all coalitions until 1994.

Conclusion

The postwar era created a new political landscape to which publishers had to orient themselves. For some, such as Mondadori and the publishers of *Topolino,* this process entailed falling silent about the past and embracing the return of *americanismo.* Others were required to demonstrate that they had split with the Fascist past, as in the case of *Corriere dei Piccoli.* With *Il Vittorioso,* GIAC forged ahead with the objective it had pursued under Fascism,

96. *Il Vittorioso,* n. 13 (28 March 1948), 7.

97. *Pattuglia,* n. 6 (15 April 1948).

98. Caruso, *Così ricostruimmo l'Italia,* 98; and White, *Modern Italy's Founding Fathers,* 149.

pursuing the conquest of society for Christian values. Each of these periodicals reflected the reality that Italy had entered a new political climate, as evidenced by the return of American comics, the use of speech bubbles, and the stories situated in Italy's current condition.

However, these periodicals additionally reflected the persistence of ideas once associated with Fascism, ideas which had smoothed the transition to the regime and fostered support from fellow travelers. Crime was presented as an issue of moral failing and a lack of order. The loss of Italy's colonies was lamented. The Catholic Church remained concerned about the impact of American culture, despite the embrace of Americanism by conservative publishers. Catholicism and bourgeois values were touted as the basis of Italian unity and the answer to Italy's problems. Finally, communism was to be countered at all costs, as it threatened Italy's national identity and traditions. While these values do not represent uniquely Fascist ideas, they had once helped to bridge these various sociopolitical positions and encouraged collaboration with Fascism.

The threat of communism, as perceived by conservative and Catholic forces, grew with the increasing appeal of the PCI and youth groups of the Left. Socialist and communist youth groups started to rebuild after the fall of Fascism, and publishers associated with the Left began to experiment with the use of comics to disperse socialist ideas of internationalism, pacificism, and social progress. Just as children's preference for comics and the growing appeal of American culture had motivated GIAC leaders to adopt comics, communist and socialist youth groups determined to reach children in the format of their choosing, in this case, comics.

Although comics on the Left suggested *some* commonality between the Left and Right, the rift between these ideological positions grew deeper and increasingly apparent, especially in *Il Vittorioso* and its communist counterparts. Explicit anti-communism did not appear in the pages of *Il Vittorioso* in the immediate postwar years. However, as the sections above have demonstrated, GIAC found ways to comment on political and social issues in a manner which challenged communism. *Il Vittorioso* and the precursors to *Il Pioniere* increasingly denounced the other.

The official embrace of comics by the Left in 1950 with the launch of *Il Pioniere* reflects the rising tensions in this ideological struggle. While, in 1946, many on the Left expressed the belief that collaboration was both desirable and possible, distrust was too engrained. Fears within the Vatican—stoked by Soviet actions—and the DC's split with the Left in 1947 proved that cooperation between the PCI and the DC would be impossible. The 1948 election further escalated these tensions, reflecting the start of the Cold War in Italy.

Although the ideological struggle was only beginning and the legacy of Fascism was hardly settled, the election indicated the start of a new era by establishing Italy's new constitution and signifying a peaceful transition of power. Questions over the future of Italian society endured, as did the battle for Italy's youth. Comics remained a crucial site in this conflict, expanding the contestation in children's periodicals that had begun under Fascism from the narrow political parameters approved by the regime into an ideological struggle spanning the political spectrum.

CONCLUSION

Fascism, Italy, Culture, and Comics

With the transition into the postwar era, Italy entered another comics craze, as dozens of new comics magazines hit newsstands. In addition to the relaunch of long-standing comics, the second half of the 1940s saw the return of American comics and the start of new comics series, including the Italian classic *TEX*. Although many were no doubt ostensibly oriented toward entertainment, the use of comics as transmitters of political and social ideas persisted, particularly in *Il Vittorioso* and their new rival, the official comics magazine of the communist youth group, *Il Pioniere*. Far from ending the contestation over society in comics, the collapse of the Fascist dictatorship *expanded* the use of comics to bring ideology to children in the postwar era and renewed concerns over what children read.

As this study ends with the 1948 election, marking Italy's transition to a new constitution and democracy, a new phase of the comics debate was beginning in Italy. The devastation of Italy had not distracted intellectuals from the youth question. Rather, as the coalition of anti-Fascist forces splintered and tensions rose between the political Left and Right, the task of educating children toward a particular ideological viewpoint only escalated in importance. In the 1950s, Gioventù Italiana di Azione Cattolica (GIAC) was increasingly concerned with the activities of the "satanic" communist youth organizations, devoting great attention to the Associazione Pionieri d'Italia. Once again, conferences and exhibits were organized on youth literature. Newsreels of these exhibits highlighted children's love of comics and displayed their content. One newsreel from 1951 asked, "Cosa leggono i nostri ragazzi?" (What Are Our Children Reading?), displaying the sexuality and violence depicted in comics.[1]

The comics debate was hardly confined to Italy. An international convention on publications aimed at children was held in 1951 in Milan. Similar debates occurred in the United States. Concerns regarding comics had been raised in the US as early as 1909 and resurfaced during the 1930s but reached new heights in the 1950s as Fredric Wertham published *Seduction of the Innocent* in 1954 and comics gained the attention of J. Edgar Hoover. Wertham's study argued that reading comics negatively impacted the development of children due to the corrupting influence of the depiction of violence, horror, and crime. His study was so impactful that the Senate Subcommittee on Juvenile Delinquency called Wertham to testify.

No legislation was passed in the United States regulating comics as had happened under the Ministry of Popular Culture in Italy, but only because the comics industry formed the Comics Magazine Association of America. The CMAA established the Comics Code in 1954, signaling the self-regulation of the publication of comics, much as the film industry had done in 1934 with the Motion Picture Production Code.[2] Although steps were taken outside the state to address the production of comics in the US, the result was strikingly similar to that in Italy in the late 1930s; content deemed undesirable was removed from mainstream comics because retailers would not sell comic books without the Comics Code seal into the 1970s. Morality became a simple question of good versus evil, and readers were prevented from seeing sex, violence, or crime. Even unflattering depictions of authority were not permitted.

Other countries *did* establish legislation restricting comics. In Canada, the 1949 passage of Bill 10 outlawed the publication, sale, or distribution of publications that visually depicted crime, effectively banning detective comics.[3] West Germany similarly established the Federal Act on the Distribution of Writings That Endanger Juveniles (1953), which broadly prohibited the sale of "immoral" publications to children. A committee was formed to interpret this act regarding comics, and in 1956 the Federal Auditing Board ended numerous comics deemed dangerous to the development of children.[4] Britain like-

1. La Settimana Incom, "Cosa leggono i nostri ragazzi?," *Archivio Luce,* 20 April 1951, https://patrimonio.archivioluce.com/luce-web/detail/IL5000019395/2/cosa-leggono-i-nostri-ragazzi.html.

2. Lent, "Introduction: The Comics Debates Internationally," 10; and Nyberg, "Comic Book Censorship," 54–55.

3. Gleason, "'They Have a Bad Effect,'" 129.

4. Jovanovic and Koch, "Comics Debate in Germany," 100–102.

wise passed The Harmful Publications Act (Children and Young Persons) in 1955, which disproportionately targeted American comics as corrupting.[5]

The similarities in debates about comics around the world prompt the query of what is unique about the case of Fascist Italy. This question is twofold: what is *Fascist* about the story of comics in Italy during the 1930s and '40s, and what is *Italian* about this same story?

In the realm of culture and the question of comics, one aspect that sets Fascist Italy apart is the regime's totalitarian claims. As demonstrated by this study and others, there were clear limits to the state's totalitarian ambition. The Fascist state never fully developed its authoritarian control over all aspects of society, and its appropriation of children's literature can only ever be deemed imperfect.[6] However, this does not change the fact that the regime claimed the *right* to interfere in all aspects of society, including the cultural production of publications aimed at Italian youth; the looming threat of further intervention or the suspension of periodicals impacted the production of comics.[7] To the extent that other countries adopted similar debates and policies, they were often limited, or politicians went to great lengths to justify infringements on the freedom of expression. In the US, for instance, debates about comics grappled with the First Amendment's protection of free speech, and self-regulation of the industry was adopted instead. While the result paralleled that of Fascist Italy, the difference in the means is significant.

Fascist Italy's totalitarian claim makes it even more interesting that the regime permitted publishers from numerous sociopolitical currents to print comics magazines. The conservative and bourgeois *Corriere dei Piccoli* was allowed to continue publication, and the Catholic youth organization launched their own as well. Editors and artists were expected to situate their stories within the parameters of the Fascist worldview, but there was room to negotiate, and producers of comics were left to form their own interpretations of Fascism to be depicted in their comics. Rather than suppressing these periodicals as rivals to the Fascist Party's own youth magazine, *Il Balilla*, Fascist cultural policies preferred to appropriate and mediate, even comics from the US. This was a markedly different approach to comics from that in Nazi Germany, where comics were suppressed.[8]

Fascism's cultural policy was based on the goal of attracting intellectuals and artists to its cause, be they Italian or international. Banning comics—whether conservative, Catholic, or American—would have detracted from

5. Barker, "Getting a Conviction," 70, 73.
6. Scotto di Luzio, *L'appropriazione imperfetta*, 10.
7. Gentile, forward to *The Enemy of the New Man*, xvi–xvii.
8. Gadducci et al., *Eccetto Topolino*, 166.

this goal. Whether or not this was an effective policy in the context of Fascist goals, it reveals much about the tools of governance available to dictators. When confronted with the challenge of American comics, Fascist Italy initially tried mediation and appropriation before following the example of Nazi Germany in banning them.

The evolution of Fascist policy toward comics represents another unique feature of the regime. Its changing policies reflect the phases of the regime. The regime's approach to *Corriere dei Piccoli* in the 1920s aligns with the consolidation of the regime, as it tried to attract allies and gradually fascistize existing industries. The initial boom of the comics craze and the state's tolerance of American comics reflect the positive nature of Italo-American relations at this time, as well as the state's relationship to publishers, who desired to maximize profits. This period was marked by experimentation and negotiation as the regime sought to define Fascist principles.[9] Comics in the mid-1930s reveal the height of the regime's popularity as well as its ability to make its agenda manifest in cultural production despite relatively relaxed formal mechanisms of censorship. This is best demonstrated in the prevalence of adventure comics with colonial settings surrounding the Italian invasion of Ethiopia. And yet, it was this same campaign that led to the deterioration of relations with the US, pushed the regime toward its most radical phase, and motivated the centralization of cultural policies and increased censorship.

The regime's approach to comics demonstrates the advantages and limits of its cultural policies. By initially adopting a more open policy that encouraged publications to align with the values of the regime, the state was able to fascistize existing periodicals such as the bourgeois *Corriere dei Piccoli* and entice *Il Vittorioso* to adhere to a "Catholicized" Fascism in its pages. Despite differences in the ways in which traditional values, imperialism, sacrifice, and national glory were depicted, these magazines nonetheless spread values advocated by Fascism and legitimized its worldview for readers.

The regime set the parameters of political debate toward which all others had to orient themselves, but these parameters were sufficiently wide that fellow travelers could display their unique interpretations and priorities. The ideology and values supported by authoritarian-minded conservatives and Catholics may not have been as radical as those of Fascists, and Catholics often prioritized religion over the nation. However, these sociopolitical circles shared a model of society rooted in hierarchy and traditional values, and the sense that parliamentary democracy had failed Italy and that socialism represented an existential threat to be resisted at all costs created bedfellows.

9. Stone, *Patron State*, 7.

Enough overlap existed between these sociopolitical positions that they could contest the structures and norms of society in Fascist Italy, while nonetheless remaining within the parameters of the Fascist worldview and thus offering support for the regime.

These benefits initially extended to American comics. This study has demonstrated that there were values in American comics that challenged Fascist and Italian traditions, including the emancipation or sexualization of women, a cult of technology and wealth, and the depiction of violence. However, the ban on American comics was not inevitable, nor was American culture innately anti-Fascist. While American culture and history is characterized by values oppositional to Fascism, American history is also stamped by imperialism, racism, and elitism. Many Americans sympathized with the political and social model of Fascist Italy, including the two American publishers of comics most printed in Italy, Walt Disney and William Randolph Hearst. Likewise, many Fascist intellectuals—including Mussolini—were fascinated with the model of modernity offered by the US and believed that America might be an ally as the Fascist state sought to create its own, alternative model of modernity. It was only due to the changing international context and the deterioration of Italo-American relations after the invasion of Ethiopia that American comics *became* anti-Fascist. The regime swapped the carrot for the stick, abandoning the mediation of American comics in favor of suppression.

Despite these benefits for the state, the regime's approach to cultural production and comics in particular had many disadvantages. It did not, for instance, help develop a uniquely *Fascist* culture, as it drew heavily on Catholic, bourgeois, and even American culture. While this proved sufficient during the height of the regime when no alternatives existed, it crumbled as first American culture was marked anti-Fascist and then the war turned Catholics and conservatives against the regime. Finally, the insistence on *overt* Fascist propaganda, according to which publishers had to establish beyond a doubt their adherence to Fascist principles, limited writers' ability to create entertaining stories that incorporated Fascist values, instead often creating series such as "Lio e Dado" or those of *Il Balilla,* which failed to attract and retain devoted readers. Such stories could hardly compete with American rivals, and conservative and Catholic stories similarly outsold their Fascist counterparts.

The regime's policies toward comics—indeed, the history of comics in Italy in general—was further shaped by and reflective of trends specific to Italy. The plethora of sociopolitical positions adopting comics to spread their worldview highlights a uniquely Italian aspect of this history. From their inception in Italy, comics aimed at children and adolescents were imbued with a pedagogical and moralizing agenda. *Corriere dei Piccoli* was originally conceived as furthering the reform of Italian youths by spreading bourgeois values. The Italo-Turkish War of 1911 and the Great War showed the potential of utilizing comics to spread nationalistic values in support of the war.[10] Far from the regime pioneering the use of comics to spread ideology to children, a model was provided in the form of *Corriere dei Piccoli.* Eventually, the Fascists' periodical, *Il Giornale dei Balilla,* and the popularity of American comics encouraged the Catholic Church to likewise adopt comics to spread its values, motivating the formation of *Il Vittorioso.* In light of these magazines, it is no surprise that the communist youth group ultimately launched its own periodical as well, especially because communists had experimented with youth periodicals in the past.[11]

Italy's long tradition of visual narratives further shaped the debate about comics. Upon its launch in 1908, *Corriere dei Piccoli* primarily utilized captions rather than speech bubbles. Speech bubbles were considered a crude American invention. In addition, then, to the more universal concern regarding comics detraction from literacy skills, there was concern in Italy that American comics were supplanting Italy's own tradition of sequential art.

Finally, in Italy, the question of the influence of American culture and values was shaped by Italy's ambiguous relation to the US. Long-standing connections between the two countries due to immigration fostered a myth of America as a land of prosperity and opportunity, and this *mito americano* was enhanced by movies, magazines, and music. This heightened sense of *americanismo,* though, at times sparked equally intense *anti-americanismo.*

But even as Fascist Italy had its particularities in responding to comics, it shared much with other cases around the globe. The use of comics by a variety of sociopolitical circles in Italy highlights the importance of popular culture as a transmitter of political and social ideas. Not everyone engages with political speeches and treatises, but most watch TV shows and movies, read books and comics, or partake in other forms of popular culture. The stories we engage with shape our worldviews by providing models for interaction, norms of behavior, and social values. They comment on the structures of our society and what we want our society to be. It is for this reason that many intellectuals became preoccupied with what children were reading or, today, with the video games children play.

Intellectuals' concerns with comics were stimulated by several issues that transcended national boundaries and were shared across the political spectrum. First among these is the challenge posed by any form of new media.

10. Loparco, *I bambini e la guerra,* 29–31, 61, 194.

11. Meda, "When Italy's Communists Made Comics."

New media threaten traditional ones and established professions, as seen in the defensiveness and anger provoked among Italian authors by the fact that comics were granted more space over traditional serialized novels. Comics were seen as unsophisticated narratives, adopting sensational and poorly written plots that caught the attention but were hardly serious writing. Many intellectuals considered comics innately violent and detached from reality, corrupting children and distracting them from the real issues of the world. Comics were thus seen by many around the world as inhibiting education, even more so because many argued that it was not the content of comics alone that was problematic, but their very form. The popularity of a new, hybrid media that was highly visual despite its incorporation of text further led to fears that comics detracted from literacy skills.

These concerns were exacerbated by the increasing attention given to youth around the world. The twentieth century saw an explosion of youth groups. As laws were increasingly passed restricting child labor, young people had leisure time, and political and social groups were concerned with how best to mediate this time. With the rise of new forms of popular culture, such as comics, these same sociopolitical groups saw the need to adapt the media to their own needs. In one sense, this adaptation represents adults intervening to define what is appropriate for children to read, attempting to shape children by investing popular comics with the values advocated by adults. But, even so, such efforts attest to the agency of young people, who established the terms upon which adults had to interact with them. The popularity of comics led many Catholic and communist intellectuals to consider the incorporation of comics in their magazines as necessary, despite continued criticism of the medium.

Numerous factors contributed to the unfolding of comics debates across the globe in a relatively short period of time. It seems that a sense of social or national crisis is key here. Rates of juvenile delinquency and the disruption of the family increased during and after World War II in all Western states, including Italy and the United States. Concerns over crime and threats to traditional styles of living motivated attacks on comics as intellectuals sought to identify destabilizing influences. Comics were targeted as educators, parents, and politicians became concerned with these trends, and the immense popularity among the youth made comics a likely focus, as did their nature as a relatively new, unregulated form of media.[12]

Additionally, the interwar and postwar eras were times of crisis regarding national and political identity, and concerns over excessive violence in

12. Nyberg, "Comic Book Censorship," 43.

media are often connected to fears about the representation of authority.[13] As in the case of Fascist Italy, crime comics were perceived in various countries as depicting officials as corrupt or inept, prompting their suppression. It is not coincidental that comics debates reached their apexes in moments of heightened political tensions, be it in Fascist Italy's most radical phase in the late 1930s, World War II, or the Cold War era when many countries were experiencing political struggles *and* concerns over national identity.

Since intellectuals across the globe were motivated by similar concerns about comics, it should be no surprise that the groups involved in the comics debate were often similar across national cases. In the US, Canada, Australia, Italy, Britain, West Germany, and France, the groups mobilized against comics regularly consisted of conservatives and nationalists, women's organizations, educators, the clergy, and communists.[14] As in Italy, the Catholic Church was regularly at the forefront. Interestingly, although many conservatives targeted comics as vehicles of communist ideology (as was the concern in the US), communists aligned with their Right-wing rivals in denouncing comics, drawing on all the same concerns about comics as being distracting, detracting from education, and corrupting.

Even communists' rejection of comics as a vehicle of American cultural imperialism shared commonalities with the medium's opponents on the Right. During the Fascist era, many intellectuals were particularly concerned with the influence of *foreign,* that is *American* comics. The Catholic Church, as stated above, was in part motivated by the popularity of American comics to create its own comics magazine, attempting to push back against the prevalence of Americanism and the Americanization of Italian society. In the postwar era, Catholic youth organizations balanced a political alliance with the US against communism with continued unease about the influence of American culture.

The focus on resistance to Americanism is a broader trend as well. Bans on comics in Britain, Australia, and Canada disproportionately targeted American comics. In each case, legislation was connected to concerns about the Americanization of culture and the protection of jobs for local artists.[15] In France, too, the proposal to expand the Law on Publications Aimed at Youth to include a clause limiting the amount of imported material published in

13. Barker, *Comics,* 35.

14. Gleason, "'They Have a Bad Effect,'" 142; Lent, "Introduction: The Comics Debates Internationally," 19; and Osborne, "Comics Discourse in Australia," 167.

15. On protectionism for national artists in the French and Canadian cases, see Grove, *Comics in French,* 134; and Osborne, "Comics Discourse in Australia," 167.

a given periodical was founded upon concerns about American comics and marked American strips as specifically "un-French."[16]

Debates about comics, especially in Europe, were thus heavily linked to the rise of American culture and its challenge to Europe's perception of the cultural capital of the West. In a more generalized sense, it could be said that it is not Americanism itself, but the increasing influence of *any* foreign culture that was considered problematic. Whenever a foreign culture threatens to dominate, nationalists are provoked to defend a country's traditions, especially at a time when national identity is being reshaped, as in Italy in the interwar and postwar eras. In East Asia, this often resulted in the denouncement of Japanese manga rather than US comics.[17]

More often than not, however, Americanization is at the heart of these debates. As American films and comics spread in Europe, they brought with them new modes of style, behavior, and slang, all of which contributed to the growing divide between generations. Officials from the US identified free markets and consumer choice as democratic in nature and supported a notion of culture which emphasized entertainment preferences in determining sales, a model averse to the understanding of educational entertainment oriented toward political socialization at the foundation of children's literature in Italy. The public space of other nations was considered *open* by American publishers, not a space which governments could regulate.[18] Even worse from the standpoint of those concerned about their national cultures, this market empire attracted locals to its side in the name of best practices. Italian publishers who printed American comics, such as Mondadori and Nerbini, did so out of a pursuit of profits.

As the topic of American culture in Italy suggests, there were many trends, concerns, and values that transcended the break between the Fascist and Republican eras. Italians' partial embrace of American culture continued and accelerated, at the same time as many remained concerned about protecting Italian traditions.

The Catholic Church embodied this ambiguous position in the postwar era. The lay social organizations of the Catholic Church reflected additional continuities, however. The Vatican and its youth groups remained fixated on the "conquest" of Italian youth, intent on re-Christianizing Italy. The Church thus demonstrated great continuity while it was also flexible, adapting to a new democratic framework. During this era, the Vatican began to reorient itself toward democracy. Pius XII remained more comfortable with authoritarian

16. Vessels, *Drawing France*, 16.

17. Lent, "Comics Controversies and Codes," 201.

18. De Grazia, *Irresistible Empire*, 7–9.

states, but World War II and the Civil War turned him against totalitarian regimes and fostered an uneasy embrace of democratic politics, which he understood as necessary to keep communism at bay. Nonetheless, the priorities of the Church and its periodical, *Il Vittorioso,* reveal a continued emphasis on many traits which were shared with but not unique to Fascism. Such commonalities had facilitated the Vatican's uneasy alliance with the regime and, moreover, justified the persistence of Fascist policies and the suppression of communists in the 1950s in the name of order.[19]

The more bourgeois periodicals of *Corriere dei Piccoli* and *Topolino* likewise continued to incorporate values indicative of their past collaboration. Although editors of *Corrierino* did much to detach the periodical from its Fascist past, many of its stories reflected an ambivalence with the new social transformations gripping Italy. The regime might be gone, but the fall of Fascism could not eliminate all the ideas that once attracted individuals to support it. Rather, these ideas remained a part of political discourse.

But the periodicals still reflected the reality that a change had occurred. *Topolino*'s increasing reliance on American comics represented a sharp contrast to their suppression by the regime. Politics no longer appeared in the overt manner it had in *Corriere dei Piccoli*'s "Lio e Dado," and while that publication continued to print strips on reconstruction and elections, it often sent the message that citizens should participate. Finally, the very existence of openly distributed periodicals on the Left signified the return of the freedom of expression. The publishing industry in the postwar era thus reflected the start of a contestation of politics in Italian comics that for the first time truly spanned the political spectrum.

19. Conti, *Gli uomini di Mussolini,* 12–13, 18.

ACKNOWLEDGMENTS

My work on this project has been aided along the way by numerous people. This endeavor would not have been possible without the support and guidance of Carl Ipsen, Roberta Pergher, Cara Caddoo, and Jeffrey Isaac. Their encouragement and feedback were monumental in clarifying and organizing my thoughts, shaping my research, and maintaining steady progress. Nor could I imagine having had the time and focus to complete this book had it not been for the support granted me by my department at Marian University. I am indebted to Melissa Buehler, Evan Casey, and my chair, Adrianna Ernstberger. Additionally, I am extremely grateful to the Institute for European Studies and the Office of International Partnerships at Indiana University Bloomington for their generous support in financing my research.

I am also thankful to my friends and colleagues who supported me along the way. Special thanks to George Andrei, Hallie Chu, Samuel Fajerstein, Tommy Stephens, and Leah Valtin-Erwin for providing feedback on specific chapters. A special thanks to Travis Wright, who read countless drafts, talked through ideas with me, and generally kept me in good spirits throughout the project. His insightful and constructive feedback helped clarify my ideas.

I would also like to thank the archivists at the Archivio Centrale dello Stato in Rome for their assistance, as well as those at the Billy Ireland Cartoon Library & Museum at Ohio State, where I accessed copies of *Topolino.* Simona Ferrantin and Tiziano Chiesa went above and beyond in assisting my research at the Istituto per la Storia dell'Azione Cattolica e del Movimento Cattolico in Italia and the Fondazione Arnoldo e Alberto Mondadori, respectively. I must also thank Lucia Casiraghi for scanning images of *Il Balilla* at the Biblioteca Comunale Centrale in Milan and Dr. Giorgio Vecchio for sharing his photographs of *Il Vittorioso* so that I could continue my research when I could not travel during the pandemic.

Lastly, I'd like to thank my family for their continued support throughout my studies. In particular, I am grateful to my wife, Lauren, who has always encouraged me to pursue my goals, reminded me to be patient, and helped me to stay motivated throughout this process. Her support and patience through years of research, writing, and editing made this project possible.

BIBLIOGRAPHY

Adamson, Walter L. *Avant-Garde Florence: From Modernism to Fascism.* Harvard University Press, 1993.

Adamson, Walter L. "The Culture of Italian Fascism and the Fascist Crisis of Modernity: The Case of *Il Selvaggio.*" *Journal of Contemporary History* 30, no. 4 (October 1995): 555–75. https://doi.org/10.1177/002200949503000401.

Adamson, Walter L. "Fascism and Political Religion in Italy: A Reassessment." *Contemporary European History* 23, no. 1 (2014): 43–73. https://doi.org/10.1017/S0960777313000519.

Allen, Holly. *Forgotten Men and Fallen Women: The Cultural Politics of New Deal Narratives.* Cornell University Press, 2015.

Arnaudo, Marco. *The Myth of the Superhero.* Translated by Jamie Richards. John Hopkins University Press, 2013.

Avagliano, Mario, and Marco Palmieri. *Dopoguerra: Gli italiani fra speranze e disillusioni (1945–1947).* Mulino, 2019.

Baily, Samuel L. *Immigrants in the Lands of Promise: Italians in Buenos Aires and New York City, 1870–1914.* Cornell University Press, 1999.

Barker, Martin. *Comics: Ideology, Power, and the Critics.* Manchester University Press, 1989.

Barker, Martin. "Getting a Conviction: Or, How the British Horror Comics Campaign Only *Just* Succeeded." In Lent, *Pulp Demons,* 69–92.

Bates, Thomas R. "Gramsci and the Theory of Hegemony." *Journal of the History of Ideas* 36, no. 2 (1975): 351–66. https://doi.org/10.2307/2708933.

Becciu, Leonardo. *Il fumetto in Italia.* G. C. Sansoni, 1971.

Ben-Ghiat, Ruth. *Fascist Modernities: Italy, 1922–1945.* University of California Press, 2001.

Ben-Ghiat, Ruth. *Italian Fascism's Empire Cinema.* Indiana University Press, 2015.

Ben-Ghiat, Ruth. "Italian Fascists and National Socialists: The Dynamics of an Uneasy Relationship." In *Art, Culture, and Media under the Third Reich,* edited by Richard A. Etlin, 257–84. University of Chicago Press, 2002.

Ben-Ghiat, Ruth, and Mia Fuller, eds. *Italian Colonialism.* New York: Palgrave Macmillan, 2005.

Benjamin, Walter. *The Work of Art in the Age of Its Technological Reproducibility, and Other Writings on Media.* Translated by Edmund Jephcott. Edited by Michael W. Jennings and Brigid Doherty. Belknap Press of Harvard University Press, 2008.

Berezin, Mabel. *Making the Fascist Self: The Political Culture of Interwar Italy.* Harvard University Press, 1997.

Beynet, Michel. "L'image fasciste de l'Amérique." *Aspects de la culture italienne sous le fascisme: Actes du Colloque de Florence, 14–15 décembre 1979,* 45–70. Université des langues et lettres de Grenoble, 1982.

Bonsaver, Guido. *America in Italian Culture: The Rise of a New Model of Modernity, 1861–1943.* Oxford University Press, 2023.

Bonsaver, Guido. *Censorship and Literature in Fascist Italy.* University of Toronto Press, 2007.

Bossaglia, Rossana. "The Iconography of the Italian Novecento in the European Context / L'iconografia del Novecento italiano nel contesto europeo." *Journal of Decorative and Propaganda Arts* 3, Italian Theme Issue (Winter 1987): 52–65.

Bosworth, R. J. B. *Mussolini's Italy: Life under the Dictatorship, 1915–1945.* Penguin Books, 2006.

Bramlett, Frank. "The Role of Culture in Comics of the Quotidian." *Journal of Graphic Novels and Comics* 6, no. 4 (2015): 246–59. https://digitalcommons.unomaha.edu/englishfacpub/38/.

Bricchetto, Enrica. "Aldo Borelli e la fascistizzazione del 'Corriere della sera' (1929–1933)." *Studi storici* 43, no. 2 (April–June 2002): 545–71.

Brogi, Alessandro. *Confronting America: The Cold War between the United States and the Communists in France and Italy.* University of North Carolina Press, 2011.

Burleigh, Michael. *The Racial State: Germany, 1933–1945.* Cambridge University Press, 1991.

Cannistraro, Philip V. *La fabbrica del consenso: Fascismo e mass media.* Laterza, 1975.

Cannistraro, Philip V. *Historical Dictionary of Fascist Italy.* Greenwood Press, 1982.

Cannistraro, Philip V., and Brian R. Sullivan. *Margherita Sarfatti: L'altra donna del Duce.* Arnoldo Mondadori Editore, 1993.

Carabba, Claudio. *Corrierino, Corrierona: La politica illustrata del Corriere della Sera.* Guaraldi, 1976.

Carabba, Claudio. *Il fascismo a fumetti.* Guaraldi, 1973.

Carli, Alberto. "Paola Marzòla Lombroso fra psicologia, pubblicistica e letteratura per l'infanzia." In *Il 'Corriere dei Piccoli' in un secolo di riviste per ragazzi, Università Cattolica del Sacro Cuore di Milano, 28 March 2008,* edited by Renata Lollo, 20–43. Vita e pensiero, 2009.

Carpi, Michela. *Cesare Zavattini direttore editoriale.* Aliberti Editore, 2002.

Caruso, Alfio. *Così ricostruimmo l'Italia. 1945–1959.* Neri Pozza Editore, 2020.

Casanova, Juliàn. *The Spanish Civil War: A Short History.* Bloomsbury, 2019.

Casella, Mario. "L'Azione cattolica dal 1939 al 1946." In Preziosi, *Storia dell'Azione cattolica,* 63–128.

Casella, Mario. "L'Azione cattolica nel Secondo dopoguerra: Aspetti del decennio geddiano (1949–1959)." In *Luigi Gedda nella storia della Chiesa e del Paese,* edited by Ernesto Preziosi, 59–90. Rubbettino, 2013.

Cavallo, Luigi. *Soffici e Malaparte: Vento d'Europea a strapaese.* Comune di Poggio a Caiano, Assessorato alla Cultura, 1999.

Cavazza, Stefano, ed. *Consumi e politica nell'Italia repubblicana.* Mulino, 2013.

Cavazza, Stefano. "Formazione dei giovani e fascismo." *I quaderni del 'Cardello'* 6 (1996): 87–108.

Cavazza, Stefano. *Piccole Patrie: Feste popolari tra regione e nazione durante il fascismo.* Mulino, 1997.

Cavazza, Stefano. "La politica di fronte al consumo di massa negli anni '60 e '70." In *Consumi e politica nell'Italia repubblicana,* edited by Stefano Cavazza, 13–48. Mulino, 2013.

Ceci, Lucia. *The Vatican and Mussolini's Italy.* Translated by Peter Spring. Brill, 2017.

Cesari, Maurizio. *La censura in Italia oggi (1944–1980).* Liguori Editore, 1982.

Chamedes, Giuliana. *A Twentieth-Century Crusade: The Vatican's Battle to Remake Christian Europe.* Harvard University Press, 2019.

Chang, Natasha V. "Forgetting Fascism: Memory, History, and the Literary Text in Umberto Eco's *La misteriosa fiamma della regina Loana.*" *Italian Culture* 26 (2008): 105–32. https://doi.org/10.1179/itc.2008.26.1.105.

Chapman, Jane, Anna Hoyles, Andrew Kerr, and Adam Sherif. *Comics and the World Wars: A Cultural Record.* Palgrave Studies in the History of the Media. Palgrave Macmillan, 2015.

Clarke, Joseph Calvitt. *Alliance of the Colored Peoples: Ethiopia and Japan before World War II.* James Currey, 2011.

Colarizi, Simona. *La seconda guerra mondiale e la Repubblica.* Edited by Galasso Giuseppe. Vol. 23. Unione Tipografico-Editrice Torinese, 1984.

Colin, Mariella. *I bambini di Mussolini: Letteratura, libri, letture per l'infanzia sotto il fascismo.* La scuola, 2012.

Conti, Davide. *Gli uomini di Mussolini: Prefetti, questori e criminali di guerra dal fascismo alla Repubblica italiana.* Einaudi, 2017.

Convegno Nazionale per la letteratura infantile e giovanile: Bologna, 1938. Ente Nazionale per le Biblioteche popolari e scolastiche and Sindicato Nazionale Fascista autori e scrittori, 1939.

Coppa, Frank J. *Politics and the Papacy in the Modern World.* Praeger Publishers, 2008.

Coradeschi, Sergio. "The Novecento Style in Italy: Commercial and Graphic Design / Lo stile novecento italiano: Grafica di massa e design esclusivo." *Journal of Decorative and Propaganda Arts* 3, Italian Theme Issue (Winter 1987): 66–83.

Corner, Paul. *The Fascist Party and Popular Opinion in Mussolini's Italy.* Oxford University Press, 2012.

Corrin, Jay P. *Catholic Intellectuals and the Challenge of Democracy.* University of Notre Dame Press, 2002.

Cuccolini, Giulio C. "Carlo Bisi, sociologo a quadretti, e il borghessimo Pampurio." In *Un maestro dell'ironia borghese: Carlo Bisi, fumettista e illustratore nella cultura del suo tempo,* edited by Paolo Gallinari. ANAFI, 2011.

Dagnino, Jorge. "Catholic Modernities in Fascist Italy: The Intellectuals of Azione Cattolica." *Totalitarian Movements and Political Religions* 8, no. 2 (June 2007): 329–41. https://doi.org/10.1080/14690760701321304.

Dagnino, Jorge. "Catholic Students at War: The Federazione Universitaria Cattolica Italiana, 1940–43." *Journal of Modern Italian Studies* 14, no. 3 (2009): 285–304. https://doi.org/10.1080/13545710903031747.

Dagnino, Jorge. *Faith and Fascism: Catholic Intellectuals in Italy, 1925–1943.* Palgrave Macmillan, 2017.

Dalla Torre, Giuseppe. "Azione Cattolica e fascismo (Roma, 1945)." In *I catttolici e la vita pubblica italiana: Articoli, saggi e discorsi,* edited by Gabriele De Rosa, 297–334. Vol. 2. Edizioni cinque lune, 1962.

De Cesaris, Valerio. "The Catholic Church and Italian Fascism at the Breaking Point: A Cultural Perspective." *Telos,* no. 164 (January 2013): 151–70. https://doi.org/10.3817/0913164151.

De Felice, Renzo. *Mussolini, il duce: Gli anni del consenso, 1929–1936.* Einaudi, 1974.

De Felice, Renzo. *Mussolini, il duce: Lo Stato totalitario, 1936–1940.* Einaudi, 1981.

De Felice, Renzo. *Mussolini, l'alleato: L'Italia in guerra, 1940–1943. Dalla guerra 'breve' alla guerra lunga.* Vol. 1. Einaudi, 1990.

De Giorgi, Fulvio. "La Chiesa totalitaria di Pio XI." In *Luigi Gedda nella storia della Chiesa e del Paese,* edited by Ernesto Preziosi, 39–58. Rubbettino, 2013.

De Grand, Alexander J. *Italian Fascism: Its Origins and Development.* 3rd ed. University of Nebraska Press, 2000.

De Grand, Alexander. "Mussolini's Follies: Fascism in Its Imperial and Racist Phase, 1935–1940." *Contemporary European History* 13, no. 2 (2004): 127–47. https://doi.org/10.1017/S0960777304001602.

De Grazia, Victoria. *How Fascism Ruled Women: Italy, 1922–1945.* University of California Press, 1993.

De Grazia, Victoria. *Irresistible Empire: America's Advance through Twentieth-Century Europe.* Belknap Press of Harvard University Press, 2005.

Decleva, Enrico. *Arnoldo Mondadori.* Mondadori, 2007.

Del Boca, Angelo. "The Myths, Suppressions, Denials, and Defaults of Italian Colonialism." In *A Place in the Sun: Africa in Italian Colonial Culture from Post-Unification to the Present,* edited by Patrizia Palumbo, 17–36. University of California Press, 2003.

Di Tizio, Franco. *D'Annunzio e Mondadori: Carteggio inedito, 1921–1938.* Ianieri, 2006.

Diggins, John P. *Mussolini and Fascism: The View from America.* Princeton University Press, 1972.

Dini, Antonio. "Saturno contro la Terra: Fantascienza, surrealismo e autarchia." *Fumetto logica,* 15 December 2016, https://fumettologica.it/2016/12/saturno-contro-la-terra-fumetto-pedrocchi-zavattini/.

Dogliani, Patrizia. *Storia dei giovani.* Bruno Mondadori, 2003.

Duggan, Christopher. *Fascist Voices: An Intimate History of Mussolini's Italy.* Oxford University Press, 2013.

Duggan, Christopher. *The Force of Destiny: A History of Italy since 1796.* Houghton Mifflin Company, 2008.

Duggan, Christopher. "Italy in the Cold War Years and the Legacy of Fascism." In *Italy in the Cold War: Politics, Culture & Society, 1948–58,* edited by Christopher Duggan and Christopher Wagstaff, 1–25. Berg, 1995.

Dunnett, Jane. "Anti-Fascism and Literary Criticism in Postwar Italy: Revisiting the *mito americano.*" In *Culture, Censorship and the State in Twentieth-Century Italy,* edited by Guido Bonsaver and S. C. Gordon, 98–120. Legenda, 2005.

Eco, Umberto. *La misteriosa fiamma della regina Loana: Romanzo illustrato.* Bompiani, 2004.

Evangelista, Rhiannon. "The Particular Kindness of Friends: Ex-Fascists, Clientage and the Transition to Democracy in Italy, 1945–1960." *Modern Italy* 20, no. 4 (October 2015): 411–25. https://doi.org/10.1080/13532944.2015.1094734.

Fabre, Giorgio. *Il censore e l'editore: Mussolini, i libri, Mondadori.* Fondazione Arnoldo e Alberto Mondadori, 2018.

Fabre, Giorgio. *L'elenco: Censura fascista, editoria e autori ebrei.* Zamorani, 1998.

Falasca-Zamponi, Simonetta. *Fascist Spectacle: The Aesthetics of Power in Mussolini's Italy.* University of California Press, 1997.

Fanciullui, Giuseppe. "Il giornalismo per i ragazzi: Quello che è stato, quello che è, quello che potrebbe e dovrebbe essere." In *Convegno Nazionale*, 155–70.

Fava, Sabrina. "Il progetto culturale del 'Corriere dei Piccoli' avviato da Silvio Spaventa Filippi." *Il 'Corriere dei Piccoli' in un secolo di riviste per ragazzi, Università Cattolica del Sacro Cuore di Milano, 28 March 2008,* edited by Renata Lollo, 45–71. Vita e pensiero, 2009.

Fava, Sabrina. "'Il Vittorioso': A Magazine for Youth Education beyond Italian Fascist Propaganda." *History of Education & Children's Literature* 9, no. 1 (2014): 649–66.

Ferris, Kate. "Consumption." In *The Politics of Everyday Life in Fascist Italy: Outside the State?,* edited by Joshua Arthurs, Michael Ebner, and Kate Ferris, 123–50. Palgrave Macmillan, 2017.

Ferris, Kate. "Parents, Children and the Fascist State: The Production and Reception of Children's Magazines in 1930s Italy." In *Parenting and the State in Britain and Europe c. 1870–1950,* edited by Hester Barron and Claudia Siebrecht, 183–206. Palgrave Macmillan, 2017.

Fincardi, Marco. "Ragazzi tra il fuoco: Una crociata per la riconquista cattolica della gioventù." *L'Almanacco: Rassegna di studi storici e di richerche sulla società contemporanea* 17, no. 29/30 (December–February 1997–98): 97–151.

Fiore, Massimiliano. *Anglo-Italian Relations in the Middle East, 1922–1940.* Ashgate, 2010.

Focardi, Filippo, and Lutz Klinkhammer. "The Question of Fascist Italy's War Crimes: The Construction of a Self-Acquitting Myth (1943–1948)." *Journal of Modern Italian Studies* 9, no. 3 (2004): 330–48. https://doi.org/10.1080/1354571042000254755.

Foot, John. *Italy's Divided Memory.* Palgrave Macmillan, 2009.

Forgacs, David. *Italian Culture in the Industrial Era, 1880–1980: Cultural Industries, Politics, and the Public.* Manchester University Press; Martin's Press, 1990.

Forgacs, David, and Stephen Gundle. *Mass Culture and Italian Society from Fascism to the Cold War.* Indiana University Press, 2007.

Forlenza, Rosario, and Bjørn Thomassen. *Italian Modernities: Competing Narratives of Nationhood.* Palgrave Macmillan, 2016.

Forlenza, Rosario. *On the Edge of Democracy: Italy, 1943–1948.* Oxford University Press, 2019.

Forno, Mauro. *La stampa del Ventennio: Strutture e trasformazioni nello stato totalitario.* Rubbettino, 2005.

Foster, Elizabeth A. *Faith in Empire: Religion, Politics, and Colonial Rule in French Senegal, 1880–1940.* Stanford University Press, 2013.

Franchini, Silvia. *Diventare grandi con il Pioniere (1950–1962). Politica, progetti di vita e identità di genere nella piccola posta di un giornalino di sinistra.* Università degli Studi di Firenze, 2006.

Fromm, Erich. *Escape from Freedom.* Henry Holt and Company, 1994.

Gadducci, Fabio, Leonardo Gori, and Sergio Lama. *Eccetto Topolino: Lo scontro culturale tra fascismo e fumetti.* NPE, 2011.

Galfré, Monica. *Il regime degli editori: Libri, scuola, e fascismo.* Laterza, 2005.

Gennari, Daniela Treveri. *Post-War Italian Cinema: American Intervention, Vatican Interests.* Routledge, 2009.

Gentile, Emilio. Forward to *The Enemy of the New Man: Homosexuality in Fascist Italy,* by Lorenzo Benadusi, ix–xvii. University of Wisconsin Press, 2012.

Gentile, Emilio. "Impending Modernity: Fascism and the Ambivalent Image of the United States." *Journal of Contemporary History* 28, no. 1 (January 1993): 7–29. https://doi.org/10.1177/002200949302800102.

Gentile, Emilio. "New Idols: Catholicism in the Face of Fascist Totalitarianism." *Journal of Modern Italian Studies* 11, no. 2 (2006): 143–70. https://doi.org/10.1080/13545710600658479.

Gentile, Emilio. *The Origins of Fascist Ideology.* Enigma, 2005.

Gentile, Emilio. *The Sacralization of Politics in Fascist Italy.* Translated by Keith Botsford. Harvard University Press, 1996.

Gentile, Giovanni. *Genesis and Structure of Society.* Translated by H. S. Harris. University of Illinois Press, 1960.

Gibelli, Antoio. *Il popolo bambino: Infanzia e nazione dalla Grande Guerra a Salò.* Einaudi, 2005.

Giesen, Rolf, and J. P. Storm. *Animation under the Swastika: A History of Trickfilm in Nazi Germany, 1933–1945.* McFarland, 2012.

Gillette, Aaron. *Racial Theories in Fascist Italy.* Routledge, 2002.

Ginsborg, Paul. *A History of Contemporary Italy: Society and Politics, 1943–1988.* Palgrave Macmillan, 2003.

Giovanazzi, Giuseppe. "Gusti letterari dei ragazzi." In *Convegno Nazionale,* 13–26.

Gleason, Mona. "'They Have a Bad Effect': Crime Comics, Parliament, and the Hegemony of the Middle Class in Postwar Canada." In Lent, *Pulp Demons,* 129–54.

Goggi, Cinzia. "Arnoldo Mondadori Editore di Walt Disney." Corso di Laurea, Università degli Studi di Milano, 2002–3.

Gooch, John. *Mussolini and His Generals: The Armed Forces and Fascist Foreign Policy, 1922–1940.* Cambridge University Press, 2007.

Gordon, Ian. *Comic Strips and Consumer Culture, 1890–1945.* Smithsonian, 1998.

Goretti, Leo. "*Pattuglia*: La rivista dei giovani comunisti tra zhdanovismo e americanismo (1947–1953)." In *Falce e fumetto: Storia della stampa periodica socialista e comunista per l'infanzia in Italia*, 1893–1965, edited by Juri Meda, 267–82. Nerbini, 2013.

Gori, Leonardo. "Con *L'Avventuroso* arriva il vero fumetto." *Giornale Pop,* 14 February 2019. https://www.giornalepop.com/avventuroso-il-vero-fumetto/.

Gori, Leonardo. "L'editore Mondadori si appropria di *Topolino.*" *Giornale Pop,* 9 May 2019. https://www.giornalepop.com/topolino-scippato-dalla-mondadori/.

Gori, Leonardo. "Lucio, fascista per caso su *Jumbo.*" *Giornale Pop,* 13 June 2019. https://www.giornalepop.it/lucio-di-jumbo/.

Gori, Leonardo. "Mandrake il Mago arriva nell'Italia fascista." *Giornale Pop,* 25 February 2019. https://www.giornalepop.com/mandrake-il-mago/.

Gori, Leonardo. "La nascita della scuola del fumetto avventuroso in Italia." *Giornale Pop,* 21 May 2019. https://www.giornalepop.com/nascita-fumetto-avventuroso/.

Gramsci, Antonio. *The Gramsci Reader. Selected Writings 1916–1935.* Edited by David Forgacs. New York University Press, 2000.

Griffin, Roger. "The 'Holy Storm': 'Clerical Fascism' through the Lens of Modernism." *Totalitarian Movements and Political Religions* 8, no. 2 (June 2007): 213–27. http://dx.doi.org/10.1080/14690760701321130.

Griffin, Roger. *The Nature of Fascism.* Routledge, 1993.

Griffin, Roger. "The Sacred Synthesis: The Ideological Cohesion of Fascist Cultural Policy." *Modern Italy* 3, no. 1 (1998): 5–23. https://doi.org/10.1080/13532949808454789.

Groensteen, Thierry. *System of Comics.* University Press of Mississippi, 2007.

Grove, Laurence. *Comics in French: The European Bande Dessinée in Context.* Berghahn Books, 2010.

Gualtieri, Roberto. *L'Italia dal 1943 al 1992: DC e PCI nella storia della Repubblica.* Carocci, 2006.

Hall, Stuart. *Cultural Studies 1983: A Theoretical History.* Edited by Jennifer Daryl Slack and Lawrence Grossberg. Duke University Press, 2016.

Hall, Stuart, and Paddy Whannel. *The Popular Arts.* Pantheon Books, 1964.

Harvey, Elizabeth. "The Cult of Youth." In *A Companion to Europe, 1900–1945,* edited by Gordon Martel, 66–81. Blackwell, 2006.

Hearst, William Randolph. "The Democratic Party" (29 August 1934). In *Selections from the Writings and Speeches of William Randolph Hearst,* edited by Elon F. Tomkins, 459–61. Private Publisher, 1948.

Hearst, William Randolph. "Exclusion of Asiatics" (September 1933). In *Selections from the Writings and Speeches of William Randolph Hearst,* edited by Elon F. Tompkins, 257–58. Private Publisher, 1948.

Hebblethwaite, Peter. "Pope Pius XII: Chaplain of the Atlantic Alliance?" In *Italy in the Cold War: Politics, Culture & Society, 1948–58,* edited by Christopher Duggan and Christopher Wagstaff, 67–76. Berg, 1995.

Helstosky, Carol. *Garlic and Oil: Politics and Food in Italy.* Berg, 2004.

Hofmann, Reto. *The Fascist Effect: Japan and Italy, 1915–1952.* Cornell University, 2015.

Horn, Gerd-Rainer. *The Moment of Liberation in Western Europe: Power Struggles and Rebellions, 1943–1948.* Oxford University Press, 2020.

Iannuzzi, Giulia. "The Cruel Imagination: Oriental Tortures from a Future Past in Albert Robida's Illustrations for *La Guerre Infernale* (1908)." In *Law, Justice and Codification in Qing China: European and Chinese Perspectives; Essays in History and Comparative Law,* edited by Guido Abbattista, 193–212. Edizioni Università di Trieste, 2017.

Ipsen, Carl. *Dictating Demography: The Problem of Population in Fascist Italy.* Cambridge University Press, 1996.

Jovanovic, Goran, and Ulrich Koch. "The Comics Debate in Germany: Against Dirt and Rubbish, Pictorial Idiotism, and Cultural Analphabetism." In Lent, *Pulp Demons,* 93–128.

Kertzer, David. *The Pope and Mussolini: The Secret History of Pius XI and the Rise of Fascism in Europe.* Random House, 2014.

Kertzer, David. *The Pope at War: The Secret History of Pius XII, Mussolini, and Hitler.* Random House, 2022.

Koon, Tracy. *Believe, Obey, Fight: Political Socialization of Youth in Fascist Italy, 1922–43.* University of North Carolina Press, 1985.

Kukkonen, Karin. *Studying Comics and Graphic Novels.* Wiley-Blackwell, 2014.

Labanca, Nicola. "Italian Colonial Internment." In Ben-Ghiat and Fuller, *Italian Colonialism,* 27–36.

Landau, Paul. "An Amazing Distance: Pictures and People in Africa." In *Images and Empires: Visuality in Colonial and Postcolonial Africa,* edited by Paul Landau and Deborah D. Kaspin, 1–40. University of California Press, 2002.

Larebo, Haile. "Empire Building and Its Limitations: Ethiopia (1935–1941)." In Ben-Ghiat and Fuller, *Italian Colonialism,* 83–94.

Laura, Ernesto G. "*Topolino*: Indici generali, 1935–1943/nn. 137–564." In *Topolino, 1943–2,* edited by Ernesto G. Laura. Editrice Comic Art, 1992.

Leavitt, Charles L. "'An Entirely New Land'? Italy's Post-War Culture and Its Fascist Past." *Journal of Modern Italian Studies* 21, no. 1 (April 2016): 4–18. https://doi.org/10.1080/1354571X.2016.1112060.

Lent, John A. "Comics Controversies and Codes: Reverberations in Asia." In Lent, *Pulp Demons,* 179–214.

Lent, John A. "Introduction: The Comics Debates Internationally; Their Genesis, Issues, and Commonalities." In Lent, *Pulp Demons,* 9–41.

Lent, John A., ed. *Pulp Demons: International Dimensions of the Postwar Anti-Comics Campaign.* Farleigh Dickinson University Press, 1999.

Licata, Glauco. *Storia del Corriere della sera.* Rizzoli, 1976.

Listri, Pier Francesco. *Il mondo di Nerbini: Un editore nell'Italia unita.* Nerbini, 1993.

Liu, Xin. "Italian Literary and Cinematic Representations of China and the Chinese (1949–2011)." PhD diss., University of North Carolina at Chapel Hill, 2015.

Livingston, Michael A. *The Fascists and the Jews of Italy: Mussolini's Race Laws, 1938–1943.* Cambridge University Press, 2013.

Lombardi-Diop, Cristina. "Pioneering Female Modernity: Fascist Women in Colonial Africa." In Ben-Ghiat and Fuller, *Italian Colonialism,* 145–54.

Loparco, Fabiana. *I bambini e la guerra: Il Corriere dei Piccoli e il primo conflitto mondiale (1915–1918).* Nerbini, 2011.

Lutz, Raphael. "Pluralities of National Socialist Ideology." In *Visions of Community in Nazi Germany: Social Engineering and Private Lives,* edited by Martina Steber and Bernhard Gotto, 73–86. Oxford University Press, 2014.

Magnanini, Giannetto. "L'Associazione Pionieri d'Italia (A.P.I.): Il caso reggiano." *L'Almanacco: Rassegna di studi storici e di richerche sulla società contemporanea* 17, no. 29/30 (December–February 1997–98): 153–80.

Malgeri, Francesco. "La riforma di Pio X." In Preziosi, *Storia dell'Azione cattolica,* 23–38.

Malgeri, Francesco. *Stato e Chiesa in Italia dal fascismo alla Repubblica: Aspetti, problemi, documenti.* La goliardica, 1976.

Mammone, Andrea. *Transnational Neofascism in France and Italy.* Cambridge University Press, 2015.

Marchioro, Michela. "Esperienze dei pionieri a Bologna." *L'Almanacco: Rassegna di studi storici e di richerche sulla società contemporanea* 17, no. 29/30 (December–February 1997–98): 235–39.

Marchioro, Michela. "*Il Pioniere,* settimanale di tutti i ragazzi d'Italia." *L'Almanacco: Rassegna di studi storici e di richerche sulla società contemporanea* 17, no. 29/30 (December–February 1997–98): 71–95.

Marinetti, Tomasso. "Accademico d'Italia: Prefazione-manifesto della letteratura giovanile." In *Convegno Nazionale,* 7–12.

Mayer, Ruth. *Serial Fu Manchu: The Chinese Supervillain and the Spread of Yellow Peril Ideology.* Temple University Press, 2014.

McCulloch, Tony. "FDR as Founding Father of the Transatlantic Alliance: The 'Roosevelt Doctrine' of January 1936." *Journal of Transatlantic Studies* 8, no. 3 (2010): 224–35. https://doi.org/10.1080/14794012.2010.498122.

McLean, Eden K. *Mussolini's Children: Race and Elementary Education in Fascist Italy.* University of Nebraska Press, 2018.

Meda, Juri. *È arrivata la bufera: L'infanzia italiana e l'esperienza della guerra totale (1940–1950).* EUM, 2007.

Meda, Juri. *Stelle e strips: La stampa a fumetti italiana tra americanismo e antiamericanismo (1935–1955)*. EUM, 2007.

Meda, Juri. "When Italy's Communists Made Comics for Children." *Jacobin*, 14 October 2021. https://jacobin.com/2021/10/italy-communist-party-comics-illustrated-children-press.

Melograni, Paul, ed. *Corriere della Sera (1919–1943)*. Cappelli, 1965.

Melosh, Babara. *Engendering Culture: Manhood and Womanhood in New Deal Public Art and Theater.* Smithsonian Institution Press, 1991.

Mitchell, W. J. T. *Picture Theory: Essays on Verbal and Visual Representation.* University of Chicago Press, 1994.

Mondadori, Alberto. *Lettere di una vita: 1922–1975*. Edited by Gian Carlo Ferretti. Fondazione Arnoldo e Alberto Mondadori, 1996.

Mori, Sara. "Prima del *Pioniere*: Il settimanale *Noi Ragazzi*." In *Falce e fumetto: Storia della stampa periodica socialista e comunista per l'infanzia in Italia*, edited by Juri Meda, 229–47. Nerbini, 2013.

Moro, Renato. "Pio XI: Il papa dell'Azione cattolica; Dagli statuti del 1922 al difficile rapporto con il fascismo." In Preziosi, *Storia dell'Azione cattolica*, 39–62.

Moro, Renato. *Il mito dell'Italia cattolica: Nazione, religione e cattolicesimo negli anni del fascismo.* Studium edizioni, 2020.

Moyd, Michelle. *Violent Intermediaries: African Soldiers, Conquest, and Everyday Colonialism in German East Africa*. Ohio University Press, 2014.

Mugridge, Ian. *The View from Xanadu: William Randolph Hearst and United States Foreign Policy.* McGill-Queen's University Press, 1995.

Murialdi, Paolo. *La stampa del regime fascista*. Laterza, 1986.

Musella, Luigi. "Il fascismo dei moderati." *Ventunesimo Secolo* 12, no. 30 (2013): 31–52.

Mussolini, Benito. "Ai combattenti della battaglia del grano" (11 October 1925). In *Opera Omnia di Bennito Mussolini*, edited by Edoardo Susmel and Duilio Susmel, Vol. 21, 407–8. La Fenice, 1956.

Mussolini, Benito. "Ai veliti del grano" (10 October 1926). In *Opera Omnia di Bennito Mussolini*, edited by Edoardo Susmel and Duilio Susmel, Vol. 22, 234–37. La Fenice, 1957.

Mussolini, Benito. "La forza e la saggezza governano l'Italia" (21 November 1922). In *Opera Omnia di Bennito Mussolini*, edited by Edoardo Susmel and Duilio Susmel, Vol. 19, 35–36. La Fenice, 1956.

Mussolini, Benito. "Libertà e civilità" (17 August 1925). In *Opera Omnia di Bennito Mussolini*, edited by Edoardo Susmel and Duilio Susmel, Vol. 21, 381–82. La Fenice, 1956.

Mussolini, Benito. "Per essere liberi" (8 January 1921). In *Opera Omnia di Bennito Mussolini*, edited by Edoardo Susmel and Duilio Susmel, Vol. 16, 104–6. La Fenice, 1955.

Mussolini, Benito. "Il primo discorso presidenziale al Senato" (16 November 1922). In *Opera Omnia di Bennito Mussolini*, edited by Edoardo Susmel and Duilio Susmel, Vol. 19, 24–25. La Fenice, 1956.

Mussolini, Benito. "Il programa fascista" (8 November 1921). In *Opera Omnia di Bennito Mussolini*, edited by Edoardo Susmel and Duilio Susmel, Vol. 17, 216–23. La Fenice, 1955.

Mussolini, Benito. "Siamo tutti servitori della nazione" (1 January 1924). In *Opera Omnia di Bennito Mussolini*, edited by Edoardo Susmel and Duilio Susmel, Vol. 20, 147–48. La Fenice, 1956.

Nasi, Franco. *Il peso della carta: Giornali, sindaci e qualche altra cosa di Milano dall'unità al fascismo.* Edizioulì ALFA, 1966.

Negash, Tekeste. *Italian Colonialism in Eritrea, 1882–1941: Policies, Praxis and Impact.* Uppsala Universitet, 1987.

Negash, Tekeste. "The Ideology of Colonialism: Educational Policy and Praxis in Eritrea." In Ben-Ghiat and Fuller, *Italian Colonialism,* 109–19.

Neocleous, Mark. *Fascism.* University of Minnesota Press, 1997.

Nyberg, Amy Kiste. "Comic Book Censorship in the United States." In Lent, *Pulp Demons,* 42–68.

O'Brien, Albert C. "Italian Youth in Conflict: Catholic Action and Fascist Italy, 1929–1931." *Catholic Historical Review* 68, no. 4 (October 1982): 625–35.

Oliva, Gianni. *La guerra fascista.* Arnoldo Mondadori Editore, 2020.

Osborne, Graeme. "Comics Discourse in Australia and Fredric Wertham's *Seduction of the Innocent.*" In Lent, *Pulp Demons,* 155–78.

Paci, Deborah. "'Lingua di Dante, fede di Roma.' La battaglia per l'italianità a Malta tra le due guerre." *Contemporanea* 17, no. 4 (October–December 2014): 551–75.

Padellaro, Nazareno. "Traduzioni e riduzioni di libri per fanciulli." In *Convegno Nazionale,* 35–42.

Palumbo, Patrizia. "Orphans for the Empire: Colonial Propaganda and Children's Literature during the Imperial Era." In *A Place in the Sun: Africa in Italian Colonial Culture from Post-Unification to the Present,* edited by Patrizia Palumbo, 225–51. University of California Press, 2003.

Parrott, Cecil. Introduction to *The Good Soldier Švejk and His Fortunes in the World War,* by Jaroslav Hašek, vii–xxiii. Penguin Books, 2000.

Pasquero, Maurizio. "Federico Pedrocchi nella Milano degli anni Trenta, fucina dei fumetti." *Terra Insubre: Cultura del territorio e identità* 16, no. 57 (2011): 74–83.

Patriarca, Silvana. *Italian Vices: Nation and Character from the Risorgimento to the Republic.* Cambridge University Press, 2010.

Pavone, Claudio. *Una guerra civile: Saggio storico sulla moralità nella Resistenza.* Bollati Boringhieri, 1991.

Pedrocchi, Carlo. "C'era una volta." In *Federico Pedrocchi,* 19–22. Grandi firme, 1971.

Pergher, Roberta. "The Ethics of Consent—Regime and People in the Historiography of Fascist Italy and Nazi Germany." *Contemporary European History* 24, no. 2 (May 2015): 309–15. https://doi.org/10.1017/S0960777315000119.

Pergher, Roberta. *Mussolini's Nation-Empire: Sovereignty and Settlement in Italy's Borderlands, 1922–1943.* Cambridge University Press, 2018.

Peterson, Richard A. "Five Constraints on the Production of Culture: Law, Technology, Market, Organizational Structure and Occupational Careers." *Journal of Popular Culture* 16, no. 2 (1982): 143–53. https://doi.org/10.1111/j.0022-3840.1982.1451443.x.

Petrella, Luigi. *Staging the Fascist War: The Ministry of Popular Culture and Italian Propaganda on the Home Front.* Peter Lang, 2016.

Pinto, António Costa. *The Nature of Fascism Revisited.* Columbia University Press, 2012.

Pirro, Robert. "Cinematic Traces of Participatory Democracy in Early Postwar Italy: Italian Neorealism in the Light of Greek Tragedy." *Italica* 86, no. 3 (Autumn 2009): 408–29.

Pizzi, Katia. "'L'Intuizione del fantastico': Antonio Rubino, Futurist Manqué." *Modern Language Review* 94, no. 2 (1999): 395–408.

Pollard, John. "'Clerical Fascism': Context, Overview, and Conclusion." *Totalitarian Movements and Political Religions* 8, no. 2 (June 2007): 433–46. https://doi.org/10.1080/14690760701321528.

Ponzio, Alessio. *Shaping the New Man: Youth Training Regimes in Fascist Italy and Nazi Germany.* University of Wisconsin Press, 2015.

Preziosi, Ernesto. "Luigi Gedda e la stampa: Un settimanale illustrato per ragazzi." In *Luigi Gedda nella storia della Chiesa e del Paese,* edited by Ernesto Preziosi, 247–75. Rubbettino, 2013.

Preziosi, Ernesto, ed. *Storia dell'Azione cattolica: La presenza nella Chiesa e nella società italiana.* Rubbettino, 2008.

Preziosi, Ernesto. *Il Vittorioso: Storia di un settimanale per ragazzi, 1937–1966.* Mulino, 2012.

Procter, Ben H. *William Randolph Hearst: Final Edition, 1911–1951.* Oxford University Press, 2007.

Re, Lucia. "Women and Censorship in Fascist Italy: From Mura to Paola Masino." In *Culture, Censorship and the State in Twentieth-Century Italy,* edited by Guido Bonsaver and S. C. Gordon, 64–76. Legenda, 2005.

Repetti, Lorenzo. "L'universo comunista e i suoi valori attraverso i fumetti del Pioniere." In *Falce e fumetto: Storia della stampa periodica socialista e comunista per l'infanzia in Italia, 1893–1965,* edited by Juri Meda, 249–66. Nerbini, 2013.

Rhodes, Anthony. *Propaganda. The Art of Persuasion: World War II.* Edited by Victor Margolin. Vol. 1. Chelsea House Publishers, 1976.

Rhomber, Sax. *Insidious Dr. Fu Manchu.* The Floating Press, 1913.

Ricci, Steven. *Cinema and Fascism: Italian Film and Society, 1922–1943.* University of California Press, 2008.

Roberts, David D. *Fascist Interactions: Proposals for a New Approach to Fascism and Its Era, 1919–1945.* Berghahn Books, 2016.

Roberts, David D. "'Political Religion' and the Totalitarian Departures of Inter-War Europe: On the Uses and Disadvantages of an Analytical Category." *Contemporary European History* 18, no. 4 (2009): 381–414. https://doi.org/10.1017/S0960777309990051.

Ross, Corey. *Media and the Making of Modern Germany: Mass Communications, Society, and Politics from the Empire to the Third Reich.* Oxford University Press, 2008.

Rossi, Ernesto. *Il manganello e l'aspersorio: L'uomo della provvidenza e Pio XI.* Parenti, 1958.

Rumi, Giorgio. "Un'occasione di riconoscimento per la gioventù credente." *L'Osservatore Romano,* 25 February 1987.

Said, Edward W. *Culture and Imperialism.* Knopf, 1993.

Said, Edward W. *Orientalism.* Vintage, 2003.

Sbacchi, Alberto. "Poison Gas and Atrocities in the Italo–Ethiopian War (1935–1936)." In Ben-Ghiat and Fuller, *Italian Colonialism,* 47–56.

Scalvedi, Caterina. "*Cruce et Aratro*: Fascism, Missionary Schools, and Labor in 1920s Italian Somalia." In *Education and Development in Colonial and Postcolonial Africa,* edited by Damiano Matasci, Miguel Bandeira Jerónimo, and Hugo Gonçalves Dores, 143–72. Palgrave Macmillan, 2020.

Scarpellini, Emanuela. *Material Nation: A Consumer's History of Modern Italy.* Oxford University Press, 2011.

Schmitz, David F. *The Sailor: Franklin D. Roosevelt and the Transformation of American Foreign Policy.* University Press of Kentucky, 2021.

Scotto di Luzio, Adolfo. *L'appropriazione imperfetta: Editori, biblioteche e libri per ragazzi durante il fascismo.* Mulino, 1996.

Seroni, Adriano. "Fascismo e riviste letterarie italiane negli anni Trenta." *Studi storici* 23, no. 3 (1982): 541–54.

Shavit, Zohar. *Poetics of Children's Literature.* University of Georgia Press, 1986.

Sinibaldi, Caterina. "Between Censorship and Propaganda: The Translation and Rewriting of Children's Literature during Fascism." PhD diss., University of Warwick, 2012.

Sinibaldi, Caterina. "Dangerous Children and Children in Danger: Reading American Comics under the Italian Fascist Regime." In *The Nation in Children's Literature: Nations of Childhood,* edited by Christopher (Kit) Kelen and Björn Sundmark, 53–68. Routledge, 2013.

Spagnolli, Nicola. "Bambini in guerra: Infanzia ed eventi bellici nelle pagine del *Corriere dei Piccoli.*" *Altrestorie,* no. 55 (2019): 10–13.

Spaventa Filippi, Silvia. *Silvio Spaventa Filippi e il Corriere dei Piccoli.* Osanna Venosa, 1987.

Sperber, Jonathan. *The European Revolutions, 1848–1851.* Cambridge University Press, 2005.

Stargardt, Nicholas. *The German War: A Nation under Arms, 1939–45.* The Bodley Head, 2015.

Stellavato, Ornella. "La nascità dell'Opera nazionale balilla." *Mondo contemporaneo,* no. 2 (2009): 5–81.

Stoler, Ann, and Frederick Cooper. *Tensions of Empire: Colonial Cultures in a Bourgeois World.* University of California Press, 1997.

Stone, Dan. *Goodbye to All That?: The Story of Europe since 1945.* Oxford University Press, 2014.

Stone, Marla. *The Patron State: Culture & Politics in Fascist Italy.* Princeton University Press, 1998.

Talbot, George. *Censorship in Fascist Italy, 1922–43.* Palgrave Macmillan, 2007.

Tarquinio, Marco. Forward to *L'Italia del Vittorioso* by Giorgio Vecchio, 3–4.

Turi, Gabriele. *Casa Einaudi: Libri, uomini, idee oltre il fascismo.* Mulino, 1990.

Vallecchi, Enrico. "Aspetti commerciali del libro da ragazzi." In *Convegno Nazionale,* 43–52.

Vecchio, Giorgio. *L'Italia del Vittorioso.* Editrice AVE, 2011.

Ventresca, Robert A. *From Fascism to Democracy: Culture and Politics in the Italian Election of 1948.* University of Toronto Press, 2004.

Ventresca, Robert A. "The Vatican and Mussolini's Italy." *Journal of Modern Italian Studies* 21, no. 1 (2016): 146–53. https://doi.org/10.1080/1354571X.2016.1112071.

Vessels, Joel E. *Drawing France: French Comics and the Republic.* University Press of Mississippi, 2010.

Von Henneberg, Krystyna Clara. "Monuments, Public Space, and the Memory of Empire in Modern Italy." *History & Memory* 16, no. 1 (Spring–Summer 2004): 37–85. https://doi.org/10.1353/ham.2004.0003.

Webster, Richard A. *The Cross and the Fasces: Christian Democracy and Fascism in Italy.* Stanford University Press, 1960.

White, Steven F. *Modern Italy's Founding Fathers: The Making of a Postwar Republic.* Bloomsbury, 2020.

Whitewood, Peter. *The Red Army and the Great Terror: Stalin's Purge of the Soviet Military.* University Press of Kansas, 2015.

Williams, Isobel. *Allies and Italians under Occupation: Sicily and Southern Italy 1943–45.* Palgrave Macmillan, 2013.

Willson, Perry. *Women in Twentieth-Century Italy.* Palgrave Macmillan, 2010.

Wright, Bradford W. *Comic Book Nation: The Transformation of Youth Culture in America.* John Hopkins University Press, 2001.

Wright, John L. "Mussolini, Libya, and the Sword of Islam." In Ben-Ghiat and Fuller, *Italian Colonialism,* 121–30.

Zapponi, Niccolò. "Il partito della gioventù: Le organizzazioni giovanili del fascismo 1926–1943." *Storia contemporanea* 13, no. 4–5 (1982): 569–634.

Zavattini, Cesare, Federico Pedrocchi, and Giovanni Scolari. *Saturno contro la Terra: Almanacco di Linus 1969*. Milano Libri, 1969.

Zavattini, Cesare, Federico Pedrocchi, and Pier Lorenzo de Vita. *La primula rossa del Risorgimento*. Ennio Ciscato Editore, 1974.

INDEX

STUDIES IN COMICS AND CARTOONS

CHARLES HATFIELD AND REBECCA WANZO, SERIES EDITORS
LUCY SHELTON CASWELL AND JARED GARDNER, FOUNDING EDITORS EMERITI

Books published in Studies in Comics and Cartoons focus exclusively on comics and graphic literature, highlighting their relation to literary studies. The series includes monographs and edited collections that cover the history of comics and cartoons from the editorial cartoon and early sequential comics of the nineteenth century through webcomics of the twenty-first. Studies that focus on international comics are also considered.

Comic Fascism: Ideology, Catholicism, and Americanism in Italian Children's Periodicals
Zane Elward

On Black Bandes Dessinées and Transcolonial Power
Michelle Bumatay

Petrochemical Fantasies: The Art and Energy of American Comics
Daniel Worden

Drawing (in) the Feminine: Bande Dessinée and Women
Edited by Margaret C. Flinn

Lost Literacies: Experiments in the Nineteenth-Century US Comic Strip
Alex Beringer

Growing Up Graphic: The Comics of Children in Crisis
Alison Halsall

Muslim Comics and Warscape Witnessing
Esra Mirze Santesso

Beyond the Icon: Asian American Graphic Narratives
Edited by Eleanor Ty

Comics and Nation: Power, Pop Culture, and Political Transformation in Poland
Ewa Stańczyk

How Comics Travel: Publication, Translation, Radical Literacies
Katherine Kelp-Stebbins

Resurrection: Comics in Post-Soviet Russia
José Alaniz

Authorizing Superhero Comics: On the Evolution of a Popular Serial Genre
Daniel Stein

Typical Girls: The Rhetoric of Womanhood in Comic Strips
Susan E. Kirtley

Comics and the Body: Drawing, Reading, and Vulnerability
Eszter Szép

Producing Mass Entertainment: The Serial Life of the Yellow Kid
Christina Meyer

The Goat-Getters: Jack Johnson, the Fight of the Century, and How a Bunch of Raucous Cartoonists Reinvented Comics
Eddie Campbell

Between Pen and Pixel: Comics, Materiality, and the Book of the Future
Aaron Kashtan

Ethics in the Gutter: Empathy and Historical Fiction in Comics
Kate Polak

Drawing the Line: Comics Studies and "INKS," 1994–1997
Edited by Lucy Shelton Caswell and Jared Gardner

The Humours of Parliament: Harry Furniss's View of Late-Victorian Political Culture
Edited and with an Introduction by Gareth Cordery and Joseph S. Meisel

Redrawing French Empire in Comics
Mark McKinney

www.ingramcontent.com/pod-product-compliance
Lightning Source LLC
Chambersburg PA
CBHW030648270326
41929CB00007B/259
9780814259528